MW01194200

Essential Python

Dr. Sridevi Pudipeddi
Dr. Ravi Chityala

Published by

Essential Python

First Edition

by Sridevi Pudipeddi and Ravi Chityala

Copyright © 2018 Ravi Chityala, Sridevi Pudipeddi, and Essential Education

Visit us at http://essentialeducation.co

All rights reserved. This book may not be reproduced in any form without the written permission of the authors.

The information provided "as-is" without any warranty, either expressed or implied. The authors will not be liable for any damages caused either directly or indirectly by the contents of this book.

The Python logo on the cover is a trademark of the Python Software Foundation.

This book is dedicated to Guido van Rossum and other Python contributors.

Page left intentionally left blank

Contents

8

Preface

Python is a widely popular programming language. It is fun, easy yet versatile. It is taught at many schools and colleges. Even young kids are learning it.

We have taught hundreds of students (close to a thousand) advanced Python programming at the University of California Santa Cruz, Silicon Valley Extension, Santa Clara, CA and also conducted corporate training for Fortune 500 companies. In the process, we understood how students can learn Python in a better way. This book is a result of all these years of teaching and answering students' questions. The book contains enough examples, so that you can get started with programing in Python. The advanced concepts are clearly marked, so that readers can make a choice of learning them at that time or later.

Audience

Python is a fun and easy language both syntactically and logically. It is easy enough for people at any age group. Hence, this book is accessible to people of all skill levels. You do not need to be a full-time programmer in order to use the book. If you are interested in programming and if you have written code in some programming language, then you should be able to pick up the book and learn from it.

This book covers most of the functionalities in Python with simple examples. However, this book is not an exhaustive book that covers all the possible options for these functionalities. At appropriate places, we have provided references to books and links for readers to continue their learning via web pages and videos. The topics were picked based on our extensive experience in teaching and programming desktop, web and scientific applications. Our aim in picking these topics is to make the reader productive as quickly as possible without compromising on quality. The readers who complete all the chapters in the book will be able to read and write Python programs ranging from scripts to large applications.

We designed the book to read like a training session, as we believe it is a better suited format for the current generation of learners.

The advanced sections in many chapters are identified with 'Python**' in their title. You do not have to master those topics in the first round of learning. You can first learn the rest and come back to learn the advanced sections later.

Learning strategy

To obtain the full benefit, we recommend that you read the chapters in order of its presentation. If you are already a programmer, we believe that most of the chapters should not take more than 2 hours to complete including the learning activities. However, some chapters such as data structures, functions and few chapters on object-oriented programming may take longer. A total of 50 hours will be needed to cover all the chapters in the book.

We recommend spending significant time learning and practicing data structure and object-oriented programming. The former is needed for writing concise code that runs efficiently. The latter is needed for writing complex code or for using many of the popular Python libraries like Django.

Once you have completed all the chapters, we recommend that you work on projects that will use many of the concepts from the book. We learnt to become a Python programmer by doing projects and we recommend our readers do the same. The scale or coolness of the project is irrelevant but applying the concepts is important.

Acknowledgments

We would like to thank Andy Hou, the former director at University of California Santa Cruz Extension in Silicon Valley for giving us the opportunity to teach Python programming. The experience of teaching the students over many terms was the seed for writing this book.

We would like to thank all the questions that our students asked over the years. In the advanced sections of this book, we tried to answer those questions.

We would like to thank all the commenters (listed below and not presented in any specific order) who helped identify improvements to the book. We would also like to thank Glen Jarvis for writing a review for the book.

Book commenter's bio

Carl Eckhardt is the software HMI lead for a 3D printer startup. He has many years of experience writing software automation tools for the semiconductor industry as well as systems companies. He is fluent in about 9 programming languages including Python.

Flávio Juvenal is a software engineer from Brazil and partner at Vinta Software (http://vinta.software). At Vinta, Flávio builds high-quality products for US companies with Django and React. When not coding, he's trying to find the perfect coffee beans to use at his company's Gaggia espresso machine."

Atma Mani is the lead product engineer for ArcGIS API for Python at Esri. He has over 11 years of experience in different facets of the geospatial

14

industry ranging from advanced satellite imaging to GIS modeling and software development. Attracted by the number crunching abilities of Numpy, he quickly fell in love with the simplicity of Python and its rich and expansive ecosystem. He likes to connect with the Python and open source community to understand latest trends and apply them to his work at Esri. He holds a master's degree in Geography from University of Northern Iowa.

Nasa Quba is Security Engineer at Oath for over 4 years. As a Paranoid, she brings the experience of digital forensics and investigations to the Security Visibility team at Oath. Before joining Oath in 2014 (Yahoo at the time) she worked as a VoIP Engineer for two years. Her educational background includes MS in Digital Forensics from University of Central Florida and a BE in Telecommunications Engineering from NEDUET in Pakistan.

Kausar Khizra is professionally paranoid. Over the years, she has experienced different roles - forensics, incident response, operations and software development. Besides computer security, she has worked in the telecom industry. She holds M.S. in Digital Forensics and B.E in Telecommunications.

Isaac Steinberg is a Senior Consultant and Application Developer at Capgemini and has a BA in Philosophy. He works primarily on FinTech web applications encouraging open source tools and interdisciplinary thinking to create products that business enjoy using and add value. When not working for clients he enjoys spending time with family and friends, traveling, photography, yoga, and creating machine learning models.

Filipe Ximenes (@xima) is co-founder of Vinta (https://vinta.software), a consultancy were developers and designers join forces to build well engineered products that customers love. He loves riding his bike to work and tries to apply 'simple is better than complex' to most things in life.

Simeon Franklin is a long-time software developer and Pythonista. He works as a Technical Instructor at Twitter and helps organize SF Python Meetup and PyBay.

Dan Callahan is the Developer Advocate at Mozilla and a key note speaker at PyCon 2018.

Avy Faingezicht is a Senior Software Engineer at Apple, photographer, and writer based in San Francisco. He has worked on data problems at small startups and big companies alike. He is interested in complexity, emerging behavior, and the systems that humans build to tame the two.

When Ravi asked me to review this book, I was honored. I received an early copy that still had errors in it. However, even with that early version, I could tell that there were some interesting approaches in writing this book.

I really like that this book has focused almost completely upon Python 3 syntax and uses Jupyter Notebook for its examples. I also like the authors' approach of being succinct without compromising on details while giving compact examples of Python implementation details.

In this way, this book reminds me of Douglas Crockford's "JavaScript: The Good Parts" or even the "K&R C Programming Language Book."

The features of this book that I particular liked are:

- for-else
- list internals
- tuple internals
- dictionary internals
- design patterns

This book would be useful for programmers who are proficient in other languages and want to learn the details of Python quickly.

Glen Jarvis is the owner of Glen Jarvis Training & Consulting, organizer of the Silicon Valley Python Users Group, and co-organizer of the Bay Area Python Users Group. He has worked for such companies as IBM, Informix, UC-Berkeley, Sprint and many Silicon Valley Start-ups. He works as a

DevOps engineer with Python, Ansible and Amazon Web Services. He also does online training in these technologies.

Dr. Sridevi Pudipeddi is a CEO of Reed With Us. She has more than 9 years of experience in image processing and Python. She taught advanced Python course at the University of California Santa Cruz, Silicon Valley Extension, Santa Clara, CA.

Dr. Ravi Chityala is a Senior Engineer at Elekta Inc. He has more than 12 years of experience in image processing and scientific computing. He is also a part time instructor at University of California Santa Cruz, Silicon Valley Extension, Santa Clara, CA, where he teaches two courses: Advanced Python programming and Deep learning using Tensorflow. He uses Python for web development, scientific prototyping and computing and as a glue to automate process.

Introduction

In 1989, Guido van Rossum

[https://en.wikipedia.org/wiki/Guido_van_Rossum] created Python.

It is a widely used popular programming language. There are many reasons for its popularity. Some of these are:

1. It works on almost all operating systems such as Windows. Mac, Linux and can work on devices of varying capacity from servers with large memory and CPU to small devices like raspberry PI and even micro devices. In most cases, the same code can be run on any OS without any change.

2. It is a dynamically typed high-level language. Dynamically typed means, you don't have to declare the variable type before using the variables. For example, the statement A = 10.0 defines a variable A that will contain the value 10.0 of type float. The data type is inferred by the interpreter.

3. It is an interpreted language. Hence it follows Read–Eval–Print Loop (REPL) philosophy where each statement is read, evaluated and the output if available is printed. Since it is an interpreted language, there is no extra step of compilation needed to execute the code.

4. It is designed with readability in mind. So, we do not have to use curly braces to represent begin and end of a loop. Indentation is used to represent block of code.

5. It is versatile. It can be used to write scientific programs, web applications, desktop applications etc.

    a. Modules like Django, Flask or Pyramid can be used for web development.

    b. Modules like Pygame, WxPython, etc. can be used to develop desktop applications.

    c. Modules like Numpy and Scipy are used for numerical and scientific programming.

    d. Modules like Pandas, Scikit-learn, PyTorch, and Tensorflow are used for data science and machine learning.

6. It has a supportive community. You can find answers to Python related questions on stackoverflow.com. Many people have written

blogs on programming in Python. There are excellent books written including this one.

7. It is highly extensible using its ecosystem of modules and packages. There are more than 150, 000 packages in https://pypi.org/ which is the official package repository as of October 2018. Python modules are also easy to install and maintain.

8. It has automatic memory management using reference counter and garbage collection that we will discuss later. Unlike in C or C++, the user does not have to delete objects. The objects are automatically cleared when they are no longer in use.

9. It supports the most popular programming paradigms such as procedural, functional, object-oriented and declarative style allowing creation of small scripts and even large-scale enterprise applications.

10. And many more.

Python is fun to learn and use and the best description of its simplicity and power, is in the XKCD comic strip [https://xkcd.com/353/].

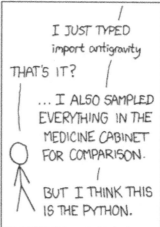

Types of Python

Even though Python is described as a programming language in reality, it is a definition of the language. Python defines the behavior that is expected for a given syntax. The interpreter of this definition can be written in any language. The first version was written by Guido van Rossum in C. This version is generally referred as CPython [https://en.wikipedia.org/wiki/CPython] and is used the reference implementation that other versions.

The other popular Python implementation are:

1. IronPython [https://en.wikipedia.org/wiki/IronPython] written in .NET and Mono.

2. Jython [https://en.wikipedia.org/wiki/Jython] written in Java.

3. Pypy [https://en.wikipedia.org/wiki/PyPy] written in RPython, a subset of Python.

In this book, we will concern ourselves with CPython. Since all the other implementations are based on CPython, they follow the same syntactical and execution rules as CPython. Hence, if you learn to program CPython, you should be able to use other implementations as well. It is possible that other implementation may not implement all the functionalities of CPython. You need to refer to the documentation for more details.

CPython versions

CPython version 3 was released in 2008. It had several breaking changes. Since the language is so old and has been used for a long time, there is significant number of codes written in CPython 2. Hence today, there are two versions of CPython in use. The latest version as of November 2018 for CPython 2 is version 2.7.15 while the latest version for CPython 3 is version 3.7.1.

Which version should I use?

1. Python community no longer adds new features to CPython 2. If you need the latest and coolest feature, then you need to use CPython 3.

2. If you do have some code that needs CPython 2 and you cannot change the code, then running that code on CPython 3 might give error. In such cases, you might have to use CPython 2.

3. There might be scenarios where a new code you write might have to be run in both CPython 2 and CPython 3.

4. Although most of the popular packages have been migrated to CPython 3, it is possible that a specific module you need may not be available in CPython 3. In such a case, you might have to use CPython 2.

NOTE: In this book, the code examples you will learn are in CPython 3. If there are specific examples that use CPython 2, it will be clearly identified. As this book concerns only with CPython, so for the rest of the book, we will use the term Python when referring to CPython.

Python installation

You can download the latest version of Python from https://www.python.org/downloads/. This might not provide Jupyter notebook functionality that you need to run the code examples supplied with this book. It might also not have all the modules you need for this book.

Alternately, you can download one of the distributions listed at https://www.python.org/download/alternatives/. These distributions also install some of the popular modules and also Jupyter notebook. We have run the example code in this book on Enthought Canopy Express and Anaconda. Your code should work fine on other Python distributions as well.

Jupyter notebook

Jupyter notebook is a web-based tool to interactively execute Python programs. The name Jupyter notebook came into usage because in a Jupyter notebook, we can execute Julia, Python and R code, the three most popular languages for data science. The functionality has now been extended to execute code from many other languages as well. You can find more details at http://jupyter.readthedocs.io/en/latest/.

Once installed, in the OS command line, type *"jupyter notebook"* to launch Jupyter notebook. This will start the notebook server on the local machine and also open the web page in your default web browser. Some Python distributions allow opening and executing notebook without a browser and some distribution allow double-clicking on the file to launch the local web server and also the browser.

The instruction for running the cells in the notebook can be found at http://jupyter-notebook.readthedocs.io/en/latest/examples/Notebook/Notebook%20Basics.html.

In some cases, invoking or installing Jupyter notebook will generate error. Please follow the instruction in the error message to fix the problem. In most cases, it will involve installing modules such as pyzmq, tornado, Jinja2 etc., using pip.

How is the book organized?

The book is broken in to multiple chapters. Each chapter is self-contained and contains all the required explanation, figures, codes and outputs.

The code in the book is placed in shaded box as shown in the example below.

```python
x = int(input("Please enter a number: "))
if x < 50:
    print("You chose a number less than 50.")
else:
    print("You chose a number greater than 50.")
```

The output from running the code is identified with a vertical line on the right as in the example below.

```
Please enter a number: 1000
You chose a number greater than 50.
```

All the code samples you see in the book are available as Jupyter notebooks format. We recommend that you type the code yourself into a Python interpreter, a Jupyter notebook, or a Python file so that you become familiar with it instead of executing the supplied code in Jupyter notebook.

The best way to learn a language is to practice. So, we have peppered the chapters with practice questions that we call as *Learning Activities*. We recommend that you solve the activity before moving to the next section. The solution to these activities is available to the readers in the link below as

Jupyter notebook. It is recommended that you program the solution instead of looking at the answer directly.

The code is available as Jupyter notebook at https://goo.gl/N8vG5V

In the course of our teaching, our students asked some advanced level questions that we answer in the class. We also decided to answer them in the book as a benefit to the readers. These questions are identified with Python** in the title. If you are new to Python or you feel these topics are advanced, you can skip these sections and come back to them at a later point when you feel comfortable.

We strive hard to make the content and wording as accurate as possible. However, if there are any errors, we would like to hear from you, so that we can fix it in the future edition. Also, if you would like to propose a missing feature in the book, please feel free to add your comment. You can do so by filling the form available at https://goo.gl/H25BjW

Good luck in becoming a Pythonista!

Introduction

In this chapter, we will learn the basic Python statements and functions. We will begin with print function, as it is needed to output values stored in variables to screen for all the examples we will be using in the book. We will also learn about commenting, naming and creating variables and finally end with obtaining user input. All the code sample are available as Jupyter notebook available at https://goo.gl/N8vG5V

Print

A print function is the mechanism that is used to communicate the state of the program with the user of the software via the command line.

We will begin with a simple example where we output the string, "Put the string here". To do so, run the following line in the Python command prompt or in Jupyter notebook:

```python
print("Put the string here.")
```

```
Put the string here.
```

The string can be formatted using single quotes, double quotes, triple single quotes or triple double quotes. For example, the following variables are all of type string. The print function in all these four cases are printing the same string even though they are formatted with different quotes. We will learn details of string in a different chapter.

```
w1 = 'First method with single quotes'
w2 = "Second method with double quotes"
w3 = '''Third method with triple single quotes'''
w4 = """Fourth method with triple double quotes"""
```

Below we have four print function calls that prints the four strings we defined above.

```
print(w1)
print(w2)
print(w3)
print(w4)
```

```
First method with single quotes
Second method with double quotes
Third method with triple single quotes
Fourth method with triple double quotes
```

We can give valid mathematical expressions or string operations to a print function and the evaluated value will be printed in the output. In the example below, we have 6+10 in the print function and a formatted print with 6+10 and notice that the mathematical expression is evaluated in the output. Comma induces an extra space, for this reason, in the output there is a double space before 16. If you wish to have only one space avoid providing space after ":" .

```python
print(6 + 10)
print("The sum of the numbers is: ", 6+10)
```

```
16
The sum of the numbers is:  16
```

Learning Activity 1: *Print 'I am a Pythonista' using a print function. Try printing the string using single quotes and then using double quotes.*

We will continue discussion of the various options available in print function in a later chapter.

Comments

Comments are used to improve the readability of the code and to communicate the inner working of the code.

Python has single line comments and multiple line comments. Single line comments start with a hash, #. All the text placed after the # sign until the end of the line are considered to be part of the comment. Thus, single line comments cannot span multiple lines. Multiple line comments are placed between pair of triple single quotes or triple double quotes and as the name indicates can span over multiple lines.

Below code shows how to write single and multiple line comments.

```
a = 40 # This is a single line comment
# This is a different single line comment
'''
This is a multiple line comment. We are using three
single quotes
in this example.
'''
# or

"""
In this multiple line comment, we are using three double
quotes at the
start and at the end.
"""
```

Variables

Variables in Python are labels to identify objects stored in memory. Python is a dynamically typed language. So, we don't have to declare the variable type before we use them. Python infers the data type of a variable depending on the content being stored.

The syntax for storing values to a variable is given below

variable_name = value

In the example below, variable str1 holds a string value, 'Apple' and str2 holds a string value, ' is delicious'. We then printed the content of these two variables.

```
str1 = 'Apple' # str1 is a variable, it's current value
is 'Apple'
str2 = 'is delicious'
print(str1, str2)
```

```
Apple is delicious
```

To change the content of the variable str1, we assign a new object to it. In the example below, we are assigning a new object of type string, "Watermelon" to the variable str1.

```
str1 = "Watermelon"
print(str1, str2)
```

```
Watermelon is delicious
```

In the example above, we are printing the content of the variable using print function. Sometimes, in a larger piece of code, a series of print statements or functions with no labels will be hard to read.

We can instead use a formatted print so that instead of printing only the variable, we also add a string to improve the readability of the output.

For example, we can use,

print("We are trying to print: ", variable_name)

instead of

```
print(variable_name)
```

In the code below, we are providing a string in double quotes and after the string we have a comma that separates the string from the variable_name. The comma (,) is the delimiter that separates the string and the variable or variables. In the output, Python adds an extra space before the variable value for readability.

```
print("The variable value in this case is:", str1)
```

```
The variable value in this case is: Watermelon
```

We can supply as many variables as we wish to the print function. In the below example, we declare three variables, a, b and c. These variables are given to the print function separated by commas. The values will be printed horizontally in one line.

```
a = 4
b = 5
c = 7
print(a, b, c)
```

```
4 5 7
```

Naming variables

The hardest part of programming is naming variables appropriately. As Phil Karlton put it, 'There are only two hard things in Computer Science: cache

invalidation and naming things.' The first is a technical problem but the second one is just a human problem.

It also makes sense that it is harder to name variables as we have a dual responsibility of making a code both human readable and computer executable. Donald Knuth put it succinctly when he said, "Programs are meant to be read by humans and only incidentally for computers to execute."

When we have to name a variable, special care has to be taken. Let us say we want to name a variable that will contain a number associated with a user, then it is appropriate to call it as user_number, so that the code is readable.

When you name the variable, it is a good idea to follow some standards. In Python, it is recommended to follow the PEP 8 guidelines [https://www.python.org/dev/peps/pep-0008/]. The three guidelines are:

1. Everything in lowercase such as *usernumber*.

2. Underscore between words known as snake case such as *user_number*, to improve readability.

3. Though not listed in the guidelines, some programmers use mixed case or camel case such as *userName*.

Later, when we discuss functions, classes etc., we will discuss naming convention for those as well.

Python keywords

We will take a slight digression to discuss keywords in Python. Python has specific keywords, that are reserved for Python's use only. Make sure to avoid using Python keywords for naming your variables as this could create hard to detect and hard to fix bugs. In our years of teaching, we found that this was one of the first mistake students make.

Below is the list of Python reserved keywords.

False	in	continue	import	def
True	for	break	raise	from
None	while	pass	with	del
if	not	return	try	as
elif	or	yield	except	lambda
else	and	nonlocal	finally	
is	assert	global	class	

In the example below, we define a variable called def, which is a keyword to identify Python functions and assign it a value of 3. Since this is not allowed by Python, a SyntaxError exception will be raised. The error is obvious and produced immediately after the execution of the variable definition. Our next example will show that misuse of keywords can be complex for the code inspector to detect.

```
def = 3
```

```
  File "<ipython-input-10-f63003433ec4>", line 1
    def = 3
```

```
                        ^
SyntaxError: invalid syntax
```

We have not discussed lists and tuples yet, but in this example, we will create a tuple with values 1, 2 and 3 and identify it with the variable of name list, which is a Python keyword. Then we will attempt to use the list function to convert the tuple to a list. This will fail as the list is not a function anymore after redefining but rather is a tuple. A tuple is not callable like a function and hence the error.

```
list = (1, 2, 3,)
new_list = list(list)
```

```
----------------------------------------------------------------
-------------------

TypeError                           Traceback
(most recent call last)

<ipython-input-11-89ed9df17ed8> in <module>()
      1 list = (1, 2, 3,)
----> 2 new_list = list(list)

TypeError: 'tuple' object is not callable
```

These errors are subtle as the error is not generated until the user executes the list function.

Multi-line statements

It is generally recommended in any program to only have 80 characters in a line. Sometimes a statement might not fit into the 80-character limit. We can break a statement into multiple lines by having a trailing backslash at the end of each line except for the last line.

In the code below, the expression is broken into multiple lines. At the end of each line, a backslash is added to indicate to the interpreter that the statement is continued in the next line

```
a = 14 + 10 / 2 + \
    5 - 4 + \
    10
print(a)
```

```
30.0
```

Learning Activity 2: Break the following expression into multi-line statements with three lines:
$w = 4**2 + 2**4 - 3*2 + 8*2$

Learning Activity 3: In the output for the code below there is no space between is and me, insert a space between them and print?

```
a = "It is"
b = "me"
print(a + b) # string concatenation
```

```
It isme
```

38

Multiple statements on a single line

You can add multiple statements to a single line in a Python code, by putting a semicolon between the statements.

In the example below, we have two print statements separated by a ';', semicolon and notice that in the output each statement is printed in a different line. Even though it is possible, it is not generally recommended as it reduces readability.

```
a = 10
b = 4
print("The value of a is:",a); print("The value of b
is:",b)
```

```
The value of a is: 10
The value of b is: 4
```

Learning Activity 4: What will be the output of this statement: print ''*10*

Learning Activity 5: use print function to produce the following output:

------Printing Output------

Fetching user input from the command line

The input() function is used to get information from the user. This is also known as standard input function. The function takes the prompt as an argument and returns the value entered by the user as a string type.

In the example below, we supply the prompt, "Please enter your name" to the input function. When the code is run in the command line, the prompt is shown to the user. The prompt provides documentation, so that the user can enter the correct type of value or value itself.

```
s1 = input("Please enter your name: ")
print(s1)
```

```
Please enter your name: Leo
Leo
```

Learning Activity 6: Ask the user to enter name of the current month and the year. Then print it to the standard output.

Introduction

In this chapter we will learn the built-in data types such as numbers, strings and booleans. We will also learn about type conversion and checking the data type of variables.

Number

The numbers in Python can be further broken down to integers, floats, and complex numbers.

In Python, an integer is also referred as int. Integers can be positive, zero or negative and will not contain a decimal point. Examples of int are:

100

-100

0

069

In Python, a floating-point number is also referred as float. A float can be positive, zero or negative. A float must contain a decimal point. They can also be represented using the exponent notation such as 1e9. Examples of float are:

10.0

0.0

-11.9

-2e19 which is equal to $-2*10^{19}$

A complex number is a number of the form a + bj where $j = \sqrt{-1}$, the imaginary number. In mathematics, sometimes i is used in place of j.

Examples of complex numbers are:

2j

4e13+j

3.25e-7+j

32.0j

0.678j

Below, we assign integer value 12 to int1, floating point value -10.1 to float1, and a complex number to c1 and we print these values.

```
int1 = 12
print(int1)

float1 = -10.1
print(float1)

c1 = 1 + 0.678j
print(c1) # c1 is a complex number

print(3.25e-7j)
print(-2e19) # -2e19 means -2*10¹⁹
```

```
12
-10.1
(1+0.678j)
3.25e-07j
-2e+19
```

String

A string in Python is an immutable data type that consists of a contiguous set of Unicode characters enclosed in single, double or triple quotation marks. We have seen some string examples in the Basic Syntax chapter. Here we will see few more examples. The three examples below produce the same output, even though the string in the three cases are enclosed in single quote, double quote and triple single quote respectively.

```
s1 = 'Python is cool' # this is a string variable
print(s1)
```

```
Python is cool
```

```
s1 = "Python is cool"
print(s1)
```

```
Python is cool
```

```
s1 = '''Python is cool'''
print(s1)
```

Python is cool

In a later chapter, we will learn about the various string methods that can be used to manipulate a string.

Boolean

There are only two boolean values – True and False. Note that the first letter in both the booleans are uppercase.

In Python, an int, a float or a string can be converted into boolean. We will first learn some of these details from this video: https://goo.gl/h9ZyHr. Now that you have watched this video, we will summarize the points from the video below.

The bool of non-trivial values will result in True and bool of trivial values will result in False.

For integers, the trivial value is zero and non-trivial value is non-zero. Thus, the bool of integer 0, will return False and bool of any other integer returns a True as can be seen in the example below.

```
print(bool(0))
```

False

Bool of integer 100 will return True. In integers, any value other than 0 is a non-trivial value.

```
print(bool(100))
```

```
True
```

For floats, the trivial value is 0.0 and non-trivial value is any other number. Thus, the bool of float 0.0, will return False and bool of any other float returns a True as can be seen in the example below.

```
print(bool(0.0))
```

```
False
```

The bool of float 0.123 returns True. In floats, any value other than 0.0 is non-trivial.

```
print(bool(0.123))
```

```
True
```

For strings, the trivial value is an empty string and non-trivial value is non-empty string. Thus, the bool of string '', will return False and bool of any other string returns a True as can be seen in the example below.

```
print(bool(""))
```

```
False
```

The bool of a string with space returns True. In strings, anything other than an empty string is non-trivial. Below, we have another string with "Zebra", and the bool of "Zebra" also returns True.

```
print(bool(" "))
```

```
True
```

```
print(bool("Zebra"))
```

```
True
```

What is Truthiness in Python?

In the above examples, we have seen to obtain a boolean value of a variable, we need to pass it to the bool() function. Python has a handy little trick called truthiness that eliminates this extra step.

In the example below, we set a to 0, which when passed through bool() function would be a False. However, we do not pass it to the bool() function but instead use it in the if statement. When Python encounters the conditional statement in if, it converts the 'a' implicitly to a False. Hence the output will be the string "Zero". The if-statement can be replaced with 'if bool(a):' with the same outcome. However the implicit boolean conversion is more Pythonic.

```python
a = 0
if a:
    print("Non-zero")
else:
    print("Zero")
```

```
Zero
```

However, if we supplied a non-zero value for a, then the if-condition would be a True as in the example below.

```python
a = 1
if a:
    print("Non-zero")
else:
    print("Zero")
```

```
Non-zero
```

Truthiness comes handy when we are checking whether something is trivial or not. We will see more examples of this in the if-else condition section.

Meanwhile, to learn more about truthiness, check the following links:

https://www.udacity.com/wiki/cs258/truthiness-in-python,

https://docs.python.org/release/3.7.1/library/stdtypes.html,

https://www.youtube.com/watch?v=9OK32jb_TdI

Learning Activity 1: Compute the value of 5>1.

Learning Activity 2: Print the value of 5.0+2. What do you observe?

Learning Activity 3: Print the value of "Python"+2. What do you observe?

Constants

Conventionally in Python, constants are declared in capital case. Below, we are indicating that PI is a constant by using all capital case. Here radius is a variable (indicated in all lower case) and its value is float 5.0. We will use both the constant and the variable together. We compute the circumference of the circle and assign it to c.

```
PI = 3.1415
print(PI)
radius = 5.0
c = 2*PI*radius
print('The circumference of a circle of radius %0.2f is:
%0.2f' %(radius, c))
```

```
3.1415
The circumference of a circle of radius 5.00 is: 31.42
```

In the above code, we are using %f, which is a format specifier for variables that are float. By using %f, we are controlling the number of digits in the output. In this case, we have %0.2f which means we only want to consider two decimal places. The % after the string acts as a delimiter between the string and the variables. If we have more than one variable, then the variables are supplied in a tuple. We will discuss format specifiers in detail in another chapter.

Type function

One of the important functions that we will often use in this book and the one that you will often use to learn the type of a data is the type() function. The type() function will return the class type of the data.

The syntax for the type() function is:

type(variable)

Below, we are assigning an integer value to b. We print b and type of b. This prints 10 and class type int.

```
b = 10 # b is a variable that contains integer value.
print(b, type(b))
# b is a variable that means the value of b can change
or vary
# in the above line, b equals 10.
```

```
10 <class 'int'>
```

Below, we are assigning a float to b. Now the value of b has changed from 10 to 10.1. Printing the value of b and type of b returns 10.1 and class type float.

```
b = 10.1 # here b takes a new value that is float
print(b, type(b))
```

```
10.1 <class 'float'>
```

Since Python is a dynamically typed language, such reassignment of the same variable is possible. The variable b at one time was an int and subsequently become of type float.

Data type conversion

Data type conversion or typecasting is done to change the data type of a variable. For example, we can convert an int to a float or float to an int provided it is legally allowed by Python.

For example, if we want to convert an integer 5 to a float, we can use the following code. The variable a is assigned a value of integer 5. The variable b contains the output of the typecasting using the float function and hence b is of type float. The value of b is added to the integer 2 and the sum is then typecast back to an integer using the int() function. The output of the print function clearly indicates that b is a float as it has a decimal point and the output of c is an integer as it does not have a decimal point.

```
a = 5
b = float(a)
c = int(b+2)
print(a, b, c)
```

5 5.0 7

We can convert a string to an int or float using int() and float() functions respectively. Here A is a string enclosed in single quotes with a value of 14. The value of A is converted to int and is stored in B. Similarly, the value of A is converted to float and is stored in C. The output of the print function clearly indicates that B is an int and C is a float.

```
A = '14'
B = int(A) # int(A) we are type casting A to an integer
C = float(A) # float(a) we are type casting A to float
print(B, C)
```

14 14.0

Learning Activity 4: If D = '14', convert D to float and print that value and its type.

Will all typecasting be successful?

Let us check this by considering a couple of examples. Below we have A = "10h". When we try to typecast it into an integer using the int() function, Python raises ValueError exception as "h" is not a digit. This example proves that not all typecasting will be successful. Checking if the type conversion is successful is crucial especially when the data is coming from web or other sources and it has to be passed to a function or a method. We will later learn about handling these exceptions gracefully in a later chapter.

```
A = "10h"
print(int(A))
```

```
-----------------------------------------------------------
--------------------
ValueError                               Traceback
(most recent call last)
<ipython-input-2-c1783fb60c1e> in <module>()
      1 A = "10h"
----> 2 print(int(A))

ValueError: invalid literal for int() with base 10:
'10h'
```

In the below example F = "apple" we try to convert it into float and we again run into ValueError because the string has one or more non-digit characters which cannot be converted to float.

```
F = "apple"
print(float(F))
```


```
ValueError                              Traceback
(most recent call last)
<ipython-input-3-bf8e37fbaa09> in <module>()
      1 F = "apple"
----> 2 print(float(F))

ValueError: could not convert string to float: 'apple'
```

Learning Activity 5: b = 12 and c = 14.65, print b and c and their type. Type cast b to float and c to integer and save it to b and c respectively. Print the new values b and c and their type.

Learning Activity 6: A = "apple", print A and its type. Convert A to an integer. Read the message carefully.

Learning Activity 7: Add long1 = 19002756 with t1 = 123 and print the result.

None type

None is a special data type that is used to represent a no value. It is similar in idea to null or nil in other languages. Even though None stands for nothing, when we find the type(None), we will get the type as NoneType.

```
a = None
print(a)
print(type(a))
```

```
None
<class 'NoneType'>
```

4. Basic Operators

Introduction

Operators are symbols that are used to inform the interpreter to perform certain computations. For example, + is an operator that informs the interpreter that two objects should be added. The exact nature of the addition will depend on the objects being operated on.

Python supports most of the operators found in programming languages such as:

1.   Arithmetic Operators

2.   Comparison (Relational) Operators

3.   Assignment Operators

4.   Logical (Boolean) Operators

5.   Membership Operators

6.   Identity Operators

In this chapter, we will discuss each these in detail.

Arithmetic operators

Arithmetic operators are used to perform mathematical operations. They normally take two inputs and perform arithmetic operations on them. Since they take two inputs, they are sometime referred as binary operator. The + and – can be used as unary operators as well. If we have +3, then this means positive 3, whereas -3, means negative 3.

Here is a list of arithmetic operators. The expression under "Example" column demonstrates the arithmetic operation and is not a Python syntax.

Operator	Description	Example
+ Addition	Adds values to the left and right of the operator.	3+ 6 = 9
- Subtraction	Subtracts value to the right of the operator from the value to the left.	7– 5 = 2
* Multiplication	Multiplies values to the left and right of the operator.	7 * 3 = 21
/ Division	Divides the value to the left of the operator by the value to the right. The output is a floating-point value.	12/3 = 4.0
% Modulus	Divides the value to the left of the operator by the value to the right and will return the remainder.	11%3 = 2
// Floor Division	Divides the value to the left of the operator by the value to the right and only rounded values are returned.	8//3 = 2 8.0//3.0 = 2.0 -15//4 = -4

**	Raises the left operand by the right	$3**4 =$
Exponent	operand.	81

Let us consider some examples to understand arithmetic operations.

In the below example, we perform 5 moduli 3. Since 5 is not a multiple of 3, we obtain a non-zero remainder of 2 and a quotient of 1. Since the modulo operator only returns the remainder, a value of 2 is returned.

```
# % - modulus, a%b returns the remainder
print(5%3)
```

2

Below, we consider 3 raised to the power of 4. This is equal to 3*3*3*3. Hence, the value 81 is returned. Note that since base and exponent are integers, the output is also an integer. Even if one of them is a float, then a float would be returned.

```
# ** - exponent, a**b raises a to power b
print(3**4) #3^4
```

81

Instead of exponent, **, we can use the pow() function from the math module. In the below example, in the first statement, we import the math module. In the second line, we use the pow() function and provide the base with a value of 3 and the exponent with a value of 4. Notice that the output of the pow() function is a float with a value of 81.0 while the ** operator returned an integer of 81 in the previous example.

```
import math
print(math.pow(3,4))
```

```
81.0
```

Learning Activity 1: *Using the pow() function, compute 5**3.*

In Python 3, all divisions are floating point divisions. So, an integer divided by another integer will result in a float. Below, we divide integer 4 by integer 2 and the output is a float of value 2.0.

```
print(4/2)
```

```
2.0
```

While , division of 5 by 2 will result in 2.5.

```
print(5/2)
```

```
2.5
```

Dividing a float 7.1 by an integer 2, returns 3.55.

```
print(7.1/2)
```

```
3.55
```

Dividing a float 7.1 by another float 2.0, returns 3.55 as well.

```
print(7.1/2.0)
```

```
3.55
```

To obtain a float value rounded down after division, we need to use floor division operator (//). From the previous example we know that 7.1/2 yields 3.55 but since we wanted the answer to be floored with // operator, the result is 3.0

```
print(7.1//2)
```

```
3.0
```

Comparison operators

Comparison operators are used to compare variables (also called operands) placed on either side of the operator. Here is a list of comparison operators.

Operator	Description	Example
==	If value to the left of the operator is same as to the right, then True is returned otherwise False is returned.	3 == 4 will return False X == X will return True
!=	If the value to the left is not same as the value to the right, then True is returned. Otherwise False is returned.	4 != 4 will return False 3 != 4 will return True
<	If the value to the left is less than the value to the right, then True is returned. Otherwise False is returned.	3 < 4 will return True 4 < 3 will return False
>	If the value to the left is greater than the value to the right, then True is returned. Otherwise False is returned.	7 > 6 will return True 7 > 8 will return False
<=	If the value to the left is less than or same as the value to the right, then True	3 <=3 will return True 3 <=4 will return True 3 <=2 will return False

	is returned. Otherwise False is returned.	
>=	If the value to the left is more than or same as the value to the right, then True is returned. Otherwise False is returned.	4 >= 3 will return True 4 >= 4 will return True 2 >= 5 will return False

Let us consider some examples. As 3 is not 4, when we do a comparison between 3 and 4, it returns False.

```
print(3 == 4)
```

```
False
```

Since 3 is not 4 is true, the below comparison returns True.

```
print(3 != 4)
```

```
True
```

Since 3 is not greater than 4, below comparison returns False.

```
print(3 >= 4)
```

False

Since 3 is less than or equal to 4, below comparison returns True.

```
print(3 <= 4)
```

True

Assignment Operators

Assignment operators are used to assign values. An item on the right-hand side of the operator is stored in the left-hand side with or without any changes. Here is a list of assignment operators.

Operator	Description	Example
= is known as equal to	The value to the right is assigned to the variable on the left.	z = 10
+= is known as add and	Adds right operand to the left operand and assigns the result back to left operand.	b += a is same as b = b + a

-= is known as subtract and	Subtracts right operand from the left operand and assigns the result back to left operand.	b -=a is same as b = b -a
*= is known as multiply and	Multiplies left operand with the right operand and assigns the result back to left operand.	s *= t is same as s = s *t
/= is known as divide and	Divides left operand with the right operand and assigns the result back to left operand.	b /= a is same as b = b/a
**= is known as exponent and	Raises the left operand by the right operand and assigns the result back to left operand.	c **= a is same as c = c**a
%= is known as modulus and	Performs modulus operation on the left operand by the right operand and assigns the result back to left operand.	p %= t is same as p = p%t

//= is known as floor division and	Performs floor division on operators and assigns value to the left operand.	b //=a is same as b = b//a

To understand the assignment operators, let's consider the example below that contains the statement c = 7. The value of 7 is assigned to the variable c. In a later chapter, we will discuss the inner working of the assignment operation.

```
c = 7
print(c)
```

7

In the example below, we are adding 2 to c and assigning the result 9 back to c.

```
c += 2 # is same as c = c + 2
print(c)
```

9

In the example below, we are subtracting 2 from c and assigning the result 7 back to c.

```
c -= 2 # is same as c = c - 2
print(c)
```

7

In the example below, we are multiplying c with 2 and assigning the result 14 back to c.

```
c *= 2 # is same as c = c*2
print(c)
```

14

In the example below, we are dividing c by 2 and then assigning the result 7.0 back to c.

```
c /= 2 # is same as c = c/2
print(c)
```

7.0

In the example below, we are calculating c modulus 4 and assigning the remainder 3.0 back to c.

```
c %= 4 # is same as c = c%4
print(c)
```

```
3.0
```

In the example below, we are calculating c power 2 and then assigning the result 9.0 back to c.

```
c **= 2 # is same as c = c**2
print(c)
```

```
9.0
```

In the example below, we are performing floor division on c by 4 and assigning the result 2.0 back to c.

```
c //= 4 # is same as c = c//4
print(c)
```

```
2.0
```

Logical operators

Logical operators are used to combine logical statements (i.e.,) the statements that return Boolean True or False. Here is a list of logical operators.

Operator	Description	Example
and	Returns True if both the operands are true.	(x > 2) and (x%3 == 0) will return True if x = 6 (x>2) and (x%3 == 0) will return False if x = 0
or	Returns True if either of the operands are true.	(y < 10) or (y%4 == 0) will return True if y = 12 (y < 10) or (y%4 == 0) will return False if y = 17
not	True if operand is not True.	not z will return True if z = False

To understand logical operations, let us look at a few examples. Let's consider x = 6. We would like to check if x is a multiple of 3 and if x is greater than 4. The if-condition has two statements, x should be a multiple of 3 and x should be greater than 4. We will enter the if-block only when both the statements are True. Since 6 is divisible by 3 and is also greater than 4, the if condition returns True and we print the value of x.

```
x = 6
if x%3==0 and x>4:
    print(x)
```

6

Let's consider x = 9. We want to check if x is less than 3 or x is greater than 4. In the if-condition, we check these two conditions and use the logical "or". The first condition, x<3 is False. However, the second condition, x>4 is True. Hence when the two statements are combined with "or", the if-condition returns True and we print the value of x.

```
x = 9
if x<3 or x>4:
    print(x) # this statement is inside the if block
```

9

We start with x = False, since not False is True, the if-condition is satisfied and the x value is printed.

```
x = False
if not x:
    print(x)
```

False

Learning Activity 2: *Using the logical operators, check whether integer 10 is a multiple of 2 and 5.*

Membership operators

Membership operators are used to check whether an item is in a sequence such as string, list, dictionary, tuple etc. We will learn about some of these sequences in a later chapter.

Operator	Description	Example
in	Returns True if the item is in the sequence.	"a" in "apple" will return True "a" in "dog" will return False
not in	Returns True if the item is not in the sequence.	"b" not in "cat" will return True "t" not in "cat" will return False

To understand membership operators, let us consider a few examples. We assign, A1 = "ostrich". We use the "in" operator to check whether "o" is a member of A1. Since "ostrich" has "o", True is returned.

```
A1 = "ostrich"
print("o" in A1)
```

True

Since "r" is in "ostrich", when we check "r" not in "ostrich", False is returned.

```
print("r" not in A1)
```

False

Learning Activity 3: Check whether 4 is a member of list2 = [5, 6, 7].

Learning Activity 4: Check whether 9 is present in the integer 8673452.

Identity operator

Identity operator returns a unique number for the lifetime of an object. This number can be obtained by using the id() function. One important thing to remember is that the number is unique for a particular kernel. It means, there is no guarantee that id of an object will be same if we restart the kernel.

Operator	Description	Example
is	Returns True if operands point to the same memory location	x = 5 y = 5 x is y will return True
is not	Returns True if operands do not point to the same memory location	x = "lion" y = "king" x is not y will return True

Let us consider a few examples. In the example below, we assign x = 4 and y = 5. When we check if x is y, False is returned because x and y point to different memory locations as shown by the different values returned by the id() function.

```
x = 4
y = 5
print(x is y) # 'is'
print("ID of x is:", id(x))
print("ID of y is:", id(y))
```

```
False
ID of x is: 1914616368
ID of y is: 1914616400
```

In the example below, we assign a = 7 and b = 4. When we check a is not b, True is returned as a and b are pointing to different memory locations as shown by the different values returned by the id() function.

```
a = 7
b = 4
print(a is not b)
print("ID of a is:", id(a))
print("ID of b is:", id(b))
```

```
True
ID of a is: 1914616464
ID of b is: 1914616368
```

We have a = "Apple" and B = "Apple". When we check a is not b, False is returned because both a and b are pointing to the same memory location as shown by the output of id() functions.

```
a = "Apple"
b = a
print(a is not b)
print("ID of a is:", id(a))
print("ID of b is:", id(b))
```

```
False
ID of a is: 2058385528400
ID of b is: 2058385528400
```

Learning Activity 5: *If a = ' Mississippi' and b = ' mississippi', check if a equals b.*

Introduction

In this chapter, we will discuss branching statements such as if-else and looping statements such as for-loop and while-loop. In the process, we will also learn about the iterator called range.

If-else

In Python, branching can be achieved using if-else statement. When we have two branches, then we use if-else construct.

The syntax for if-else is shown below. The statements under an if-else block could perform any legal Python operations. The statements in the if- and else block must be indented to the right of the if and else statements.

if (condition 1):

> *execute statement(s) that are under this block*

else:

> *execute statement(s) that are under this block*

If the condition in the if clause is True, then the corresponding code block will be executed. If the condition is False, then the else code block will be executed. Notice that there is no condition checked needed for the else block. All the conditions that do not fall under "condition 1" will be captured by the else block.

If we have more than two branches then we use if-elif-else construct as shown in the syntax below. If the if-condition is True, then the code block will be executed. All the other clauses will be skipped and Python will execute the next statement after the if-elif-else statements. If any of elif clauses are True, then the corresponding code block will be executed and all the other clauses will be skipped and Python will execute the next statement after the if-elif-else statements. If neither if-clause nor the elif-clauses are True, then the else block will be executed.

The syntax for if-elif-else is shown below. The condition1, condition2 etc., can be either True or False. The statements under an elif block could perform any legal Python operations.

if (condition 1):

    execute statement(s) that are under this block

elif (condition 2):

    execute statement(s) that are under this block

else:

    execute statement(s) that are under this block

In the example below, we obtain input from the user, convert it in to an integer and store it in x. We then check if x is less than 50 in the if-statement. If it returns True, then the print("You chose a number less than 50.") will be executed. In the elif statement, we check if the number is between 50 and 100. If it returns True, then the print("You chose a number that is between 50 and 100.") will be executed. When condition 1 and condition 2 fail, then the code in the else block will be executed.

When we execute the code, we supply a number 1000 at the prompt. Since x=1000 is not less than 50, the if condition will return False. Python will then check the elif condition, which will also return False. Finally, Python will execute the code under the else statement.

```
x = int(input("Please enter a number: "))
if x < 50:
    print("You chose a number less than 50.")
elif x > 50 and x < 100:
    print("You chose a number that is between 50 and
100.")
else:
    print ("You chose a number greater than 100.")
```

```
Please enter a number: 1000
You chose a number greater than 100.
```

Truthiness

In the previous example, we check the condition x<50 which can either be True or False. This is generally referred as an explicit Boolean, as we will obtain a True or False when x<50 is executed.

Python also has the concept of implicit Boolean generally referred as truthiness. In truthiness, all trivial value returns a False and non-trivial value return True. The trivial value of int is 0, float is 0.0 and string is "", a string with no characters inside. Each of these will be False in truthiness. All other values will be True.

We will begin the discussion of truthiness by using the bool() function to convert int, float and string to boolean. Later, we will skip the use of bool()

function and demonstrate that Python will automatically convert trivial values to False and non-trivial to True.

In the example below, we are converting a trivial value of 0 stored in A in to boolean. In line 3, we are converting the non-trivial value of 1 stored in B to Boolean. The former prints False while the latter prints True, as we had discussed previously.

```
A = 0
print("The Boolean value for trivial integer is:",
bool(A))
B = 1
print("The Boolean value for non-trivial integer is:",
bool(B))
```

```
The Boolean value for trivial integer is: False
The Boolean value for non-trivial integer is: True
```

Likewise, bool for non-trivial values of string and float will result in True as shown below. Notice that a string with a space is a non-trivial string, so bool of it will be True. A string with no characters in it including space is a trivial string and will return False.

```
f1 = 0.0
print("The bool of trivial value of float is:",
bool(f1))
f2 = 0.001
```

```
print("The bool of non-trivial value of float is:",
bool(f2))
```

```
The bool of trivial value of float is: False
The bool of non-trivial value of float is: True
```

```
s1 = ""
print("The bool of trivial value of string is: ",
bool(s1))
s2 = " " # a string with a space is a non-trivial string
print("The bool of non-trivial value of string is: ",
bool(s2))
s3 = "Apple"
print("The bool of non-trivial value of string is: ",
bool(s3))
```

```
The bool of trivial value of string is:  False
The bool of non-trivial value of string is:  True
The bool of non-trivial value of string is:  True
```

However, if we are only checking if the value is empty or not, then we can implicitly obtain the boolean of the value using if statement. To do this, we can simply say:

if A:

if block statements

else:

    else block statements

By doing so, we have made the if construct simple. If the value of A is non-trivial, then implicitly the if statement will be evaluated as "if bool(A)" is True and the "if block" will get executed. If the value of A is trivial, then implicitly the if statement will be evaluated as "if bool(A)" is False and the "else block" will get executed. Thus, in all the examples below, we can replace 'a' in the if-statement with 'not bool(a)' with the exact same result.

```python
a = -1
if a:
    print("a is non-zero integer")
else:
    print("a is zero")
```

```
a is non-zero integer
```

```python
a = 0.0001
if a:
    print("a is non-zero float")
else:
    print("a is 0.0")
```

```
a is non-zero float
```

```
a = ''
if a:
    print("a is a non-empty string")
else:
    print("a is an empty string")
```

```
a is an empty string
```

When we discuss lists, dictionary, sets etc., we will discuss truthiness of those data structures.

range

We will learn about an iterator called range(), as we will be using it for introducing loops. Iterators are memory efficient cousins of a Python list. We will learn more about them at a later chapter.

The range function can be used in three ways.

range function	Description
range(n)	The range(n) will create an iterator that generates values from 0 to n-1 as we loop through the iterator.
range(n1, n2)	The range(n1, n2) will create an iterator that generates values from n1 to n2-1 as we loop through the iterator.

range(n1, n2, incr)	The range(n1, n2, incr) will create an iterator that generates values from n1 to n2-1 in steps of incr as we loop through the iterator.

Let us consider some examples.

A call to the print function with the range(5) as an input prints range(0, 5). We will print the five values in a later example.

```
a = range(5)
print(a)
```

```
range(0, 5)
```

In the below example, our start value is 2 and stop value is 9. When we loop through the iterator later in the next section, the output would be 2, 3, 4, 5, 6, 7 and 8.

```
print(range(2, 9))
```

```
range(2, 9)
```

Below, the start value is 2, the stop value is 9 and the step size is 3. So, when we loop (in a later example) through the iterator range(2, 9, 3), the output would 2, the next value will be 5 and then the next value will be 8. For iterator range(3, -3, -2), the start value is 3, the stop value is -3 with a step size of -2. Looping through range(3, -3, -2) would output 3, 1 and -1.

81

```
print(range(2, 9, 3))
print(range(3, -3, -2))
```

```
range(2, 9, 3)
range(3, -3, -2)
```

for-loop

In Python, a for-loop provides a convenient mechanism for looping through finite sized sequences such as list, dictionary, tuple, iterator etc. In the examples below, we will demonstrate a for-loop with the range() function. In the data structures, we will learn about for-loop mechanism the individual data structures.

The syntax of a for-loop is

for i in iterable_name:

    code to be executed in each iteration

At every iteration of the for-loop, the value in the iterable object will be stored in the variable, i. The ':' at the end of the for statement indicates that we are entering the for-block. For every iteration, the statements under the for statement will be executed.

In the example below, we are assigning range(5) to variable arange and then using for-loop to iterate through arange. In the first iteration of the loop, the value of i will be 0, as the first value of range(5) is 0. In the second iteration, the value of i will be 1, as the next value of range(5) is 1. The iteration continues until the last element in range(5), which is 4 is returned.

```python
arange = range(5)
for i in arange:
    print(i)
```

```
0
1
2
3
4
```

Note: The variable, i in the for-loop is local to the for-loop.

Loop control statements

In the example above, we are obtaining a sequence of values from the iterator range function until it is exhausted. In some scenarios, we might be interested in changing this normal course of execution by either skipping some iteration, passing the turn to process the loop or break off the loop. These are called loop controls and Python has three such loop control statements. They are described in the table below.

Control Statements	Description
break	This statement terminates the loop and transfers the execution to the statement after the loop.

continue	This statement suspends execution of remaining statements in the loop and goes back to the next loop iteration.
pass	This statement does nothing. The control goes to the next line. Used mostly as a place holder

We will begin the discussion with the break statement. In the code below, we have an if-statement inside the for-loop. In the first iteration of the loop, the value of i is 1. The if-statement returns False and the loop continues. Only when i is 5, the if-statement returns True and the value 5 will be printed. The break statement will be executed, which causes the for-loop to end.

```python
b = range(1, 7)
for i in b:
    if i%5 == 0:
        print(i)
        break
    else:
        print(i, "is not 5!")
```

```
1 is not 5!
2 is not 5!
3 is not 5!
4 is not 5!
```

5

In the below code, we demonstrate the use of continue statement that allows skipping execution of remaining statements in a loop and the control statement goes to the header of the loop and to the next item in the iteration.

Let's take a scenario where we want to find all the numbers in the range(22, 30) that are not multiples of 6. and for all other cases, we need to print that the number we processed . In the first iteration of the loop, the value of n is 22. Since 22 is not a multiple of 6, the if-statement returns False and hence we print that 22 is not a multiple of 6. Then the control goes to the header of the loop. The same applies to n=23 as well. In the third iteration, n is 24 which is a multiple of 6. Hence the if-statement returns True. When Python encounters the 'continue', it skips all the lines below it and returns to the header of the loop. Thus, the second print statement in the for-loop is skipped when the if statement is True. The loop then continues with subsequent values 25, 26, 27, 28 and 29 for which the if statement returns False. Of course, we can have the print function in an else statement, however, having continue makes the code more readable. We avoid having multiple branches.

```python
for n in range(22, 30):
    if n%6 == 0:
        continue
    print(n, "is not a multiple of 6")
```

```
22 is not a multiple of 6
23 is not a multiple of 6
25 is not a multiple of 6
```

```
26 is not a multiple of 6
27 is not a multiple of 6
28 is not a multiple of 6
29 is not a multiple of 6
```

In the code below, we demonstrate the use of pass, a syntactical mechanism to inform the interpreter to perform no operations. It is generally used in places where the programmer has not yet written the code but would like to keep the code syntactically correct. In languages such as C, C++ etc., the empty curly braces are used to indicate block of code not yet written.

In the for-loop below, we iterate over items in range() function. If the programmer is not sure about the code to be written under the for-loop, they can use the pass statement. When Python interpreter encounters it, Python continues with other statements below pass. Since in this case, there are no statements below pass, there will be no output.

```
for item in range(3):
    pass
```

Note: The pass keyword is useful not only in loops but also in functions, classes and methods.

Learning Activity 1: If nlist = [12, 4, -6, 8, -20, 10]. Iterate through the list, stop when you hit the first negative value.

Learning Activity 2: Ask the user to input a year and if the input is the string '2000', then print "You are right." If user enters any other year, prompt the user to enter the correct year.

Learning Activity 3: *Create a list that starts with -10 and goes all the way up to 10 (inclusive). Find all the multiples of 4.*

Learning Activity 4: *Create a list that starts with -10 and goes all the way up to 10 (inclusive). Then find the first multiple of 4.*

while-loop

A while-loop offer another looping mechanism in Python. It is not as frequently used as for-loop. Yet it has good use cases that we will discuss in this section.

The flowchart for a while-loop is shown below.

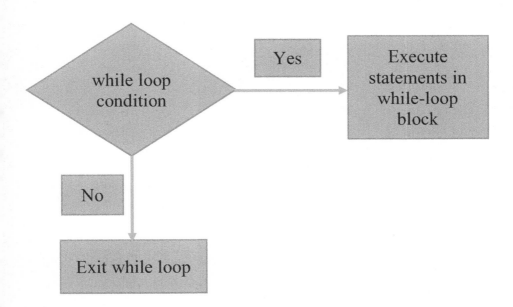

The while loop will be executed only when the condition is True. The loop terminates when the condition is False.

The syntax for a while-loop is:

while (condition):

> *statements*

Below we start with n = 5 and the while condition is n > 0. Since n is greater than 0, we enter the while block. We print n and the value of n is decreased by 1 in every iteration. When n = 0, then the while condition returns False and we terminate the loop.

```
n = 5
while (n > 0):
    print("The value of n is: ", n)
    n -= 1 # n = n-1
```

```
The value of n is:  5
The value of n is:  4
The value of n is:  3
The value of n is:  2
The value of n is:  1
0
```

We can of course replace the comparison statement with True in the while statement and that would guarantee that the while condition is always true, making the loop run infinite times. To exit this loop, we need to have a break statement inside the while-block and also ensure that the break statement is executed when certain conditions are met.

Below is an example of an infinite while-loop that is achieved by making the condition True. Outside the while-loop, the value of n starts at 0 and inside the while-loop n is incremented at every iteration. When n reaches 4, the if-statement returns True. This causes the loop to break.

```
n = 0
while True:
    if n == 4:
        print(n)
        break
    n += 1
print("I am out of while loop")
print(n)
```

```
4
I am out of while loop
4
```

Learning Activity 5: Write a code that continuously loops and obtains names from the user until the user decides to quit by entering q or Q. Also perform a check to see whether the user entered anything. If the user didn't enter anything, ask them to enter a name.

Python**: for-else

The else block in the for-else loop is executed only when the loop exits normally without any break.

Below, we have a list, list1 with three items. In the for-loop we have an if statement. If the item is "Orange" then we print and break. In this case, since the string "Orange" is present in the list and hence the break statement in the if block will be executed. Consequently, the else block will not be executed.

```python
list1 = ["Apple", "Orange", "Apricot"]
for item in list1:
    if item == "Orange":
        print("We found an Orange!")
        break
else:
    print("We didn't find Orange!")
```

```
We found an Orange!
```

In the below code, list2 does not have Orange, so the else block will not be executed and so the else block will be executed.

```python
list2 = ["Apple", "Kiwi", "Apricot"]
for item in list2:
    if item == "Orange":
        print("We found an Orange!")
        break
else:
    print("We didn't find Orange!")
```

```
We didn't find Orange!
```

Python**: while-else

The else clause in the while-else construct will get executed when the while condition is False.

In the code below, notice that since the while condition is False, the else clause gets executed.

```python
n = 5
while False:
    if n == 4:
        print(n)
        break
    n -= 1
else:
    print("The while condition is False!")
```

```
The while condition is False!
```

Python**: Value bleeding outside for-loop

The scope of a variable means the portion of code in which the variable is available for use. The scope of loop-variables in most languages are limited to their work inside the loop. However, in the case of Python, the loop variable defined only in the scope of the loop can bleed outside (i.e., the loop variable can be accessed outside the loop). The loop variable will retain its last value when it exits the loop.

The example below demonstrates value bleeding. The variable 'item' does not exist before the loop. It is created inside the loop and its value is assigned at every iteration of the loop. The print function in the loop is called 4 times and prints values in the range 0 to 3. However, the variable item continues to exist outside the loop with a value equal to 3, its last assigned value inside the loop. Hence the last print function outputs the value 3.

The value bleeding could become an issue if this variable is accessed outside the loop without paying attention to the fact that its value was assigned inside the loop.

```python
for item in range(4):
    print('Items inside loop is {0}'.format(items))
# The value of item is available outside for-loop
print('Item outside loop is {0}'.format(item))
```

```
Item inside loop is 0
Item inside loop is 1
Item inside loop is 2
Item inside loop is 3
Item outside loop is 3
```

An even greater danger exists if the variable is accessed outside the loop when it has not even been created yet as shown in the example below.

In the example below, some_list is an empty list. Since some_list is empty, the loop is never executed and hence the variable items_empty is never created or initialized. Hence if the variable is accessed outside the loop as shown in the print statement, the program will crash with NameError exception, as the variable is not yet in existence.

In this simple example, it is obvious the error occurred. But if the some_list is a list returned by a function which at run-time may or may not be empty, then the program may crash only at run-time making it difficult to debug and make users run into problems.

```
some_list = []
for items_empty in some_list:
    print('Items inside loop is
{0}'.format(items_empty))
print('items outside loop is {0}'.format(items_empty))
```

```
----------------------------------------------------------------
----------------
NameError                        Traceback (most
recent call last)
<ipython-input-24-0ef6c4d1d4ab> in <module>()
      2 for items_empty in some_list:
      3     print('Items inside loop is
{0}'.format(items_empty))
----> 4 print('items outside loop is
{0}'.format(items_empty))

NameError: name 'items_empty' is not defined
```

What is the solution for value bleeding?

1. Avoid using the loop variables outside the loop even though the language does not prevent its usage.

2. Use variable names like items, i or j as loop variable and do not use them in other places.

Introduction

In all the previous chapters, we used print() function to output the value stored in variables on to the screen. We used print() in two different ways. In the first one, we passed a name of the variable to print() and produced an output corresponding to the value stored in the variable. In the second method, we passed not only a variable but also a string, so that the output is more readable. The string became the label that identified the value being printed. In this chapter, we will discuss formatted print, an elegant method to produce a nicer output.

Formatting output

The formatting of output is done based on the data type. For example, to print an integer using a formatted printing, we need to specify the type using the symbol %d where % is known as the conversion specifier and d to indicate an integer.

In the example below, we assign a value of 10 to the variable N. In the print function, the position where the value of N will be placed is indicated using %d. The second % sign is the delimiter that separates the string from the variable(s) that need to be printed. The parenthesis around the variable N in the print statement is optional if there is only one variable. If there are more than one variable, then the parenthesis is mandatory.

```
N = 10
print("The value of N is: %d" %(N))
```

```
The value of N is:   10
```

Python has many other conversion types as well. They are:

Conversion	Meaning
d	Signed integer decimal.
i	Signed integer decimal.
u	Unsigned decimal.
f	Floating point decimal format.
F	Floating point decimal format.
e	Floating point exponential format in lowercase.
E	Floating point exponential format in uppercase.
g	e, if exponent > -4 or less than precision, f, otherwise.
G	e, if exponent > -4 or less than precision, f, otherwise.
c	Single character, can be integers or strings.

r	String, converts any Python object using repr() function.
s	String, converts any Python object using str() function.
o	Unsigned octal.
x	Unsigned hexadecimal in lowercase.
X	Unsigned hexadecimal in uppercase.

Conversion specifier

In the example below, we have B = 12, an integer. In the print(), we use %f conversion specifier to print B as a float. Hence the output is 12.000000. The default number of digits after decimal point is 6.

```
B = 12
print("Printing B as a floating point:%f" %B)
```

```
Printing B as a floating point:12.000000
```

In the example below, D = 23.76, a floating-point number. If we use %d, which indicates integers, in the print() then only the digits to the left of the decimal will be printed as the float is rounded off to an int.

```
D = 23.76
print("Printing D as an integer:%d" %D)
```

```
Printing D as an integer:23
```

In the example below, we try to express 790189012 in scientific notation.

```
t = 790189012
print("Using e conversion specifier: %e" %t)
```

```
Using e conversion specifier: 7.901890e+08
```

In the example below, H is 144 in decimal number system. To print H in hexadecimal we are using %x.

```
H = 144
print("The value of h1 as hexadecimal is: %x" %H)
```

```
The value of H is: 90
```

In the example below, oct1 is 871 in decimal system. To print oct1 in octal system, we are using %o.

```
oct1 = 871
print("The value oct1 as octal is: %o" %oct1)
```

```
The value oct1 as octal is: 1547
```

Width and Precision

Using the conversion specifiers, we can specify the width of a number and its precision. Width controls the minimum number of characters required for formatting. Precision controls the number of digits that need to be considered after the decimal point.

In the example below, we consider w = 10.1234567 to demonstrate precision. We want to only print 2 digits after decimal point. In the formatted print(), we write %0.2f to have two digits after the decimal point. The 2 in 0.2 indicates the number of values to the right of the decimal point.

```
w = 10.1234567
print("Only printing two digits after decimal point:
%0.2f" %w)
```

```
Only printing two digits after decimal point: 10.12
```

Below is an example of width. We have D1 = 37. If we would like to express D1 in terms of three digits then we use %03d in the formatted print statement.

```
D1 = 37
print("The value of D1 is: %03d" %D1)
```

```
The value of D1 is: 037
```

Let us combine width and precision. Below we have gr = 1.6180339, which is the golden ratio. The total number of characters in gr including the decimal point are 9. Let us make the width 12 and consider only 6 digits after the decimal point.

```
gr = 1.6180339
print("The width for gr is 12 and the precision is six:
%012.6f" %gr)
```

```
The width for gr is 12 and the precision is six:
00001.618034
```

f-strings

One of the problems with formatted printing is that the expression is outside the string that is being templated. In the previous example, the value gr is evaluated and then substituted in to the position where the formatting %012.6f is located.

The f-strings which were introduced in Python 3.6 allows combining the position for substitution and the variables or expressions to be substituted in to the string. The f-strings are evaluated at run-time and hence it is possible to add expressions inside them.

The f-strings have f at the beginning of the string. Any value or expression that needs to substituted must be placed inside curly braces. Programmers who have used template tools like Jinja, Django template will be familiar with this syntax.

In the code below, we assign a value 5 to variable a. In the string inside the print function call, we perform two operations. The first operation we substitute the value of a and in the second operation, we calculate the expression a**2 and substitute its value.

```
a = 5
print(f"The value of {a} power 2 is {a**2}")
```

```
The value of 5 power 2 is 25
```

The expressions inside the f-string can include calls to methods or functions including user-defined. In the example below, we define a function called mylen. This function takes a list and return the number of elements in the list. In the print function, the expression mylen(lst) is evaluated and substituted.

```
lst = [3, 4, 5]
def mylen(lst):
    return len(lst)
```

```
print(f"The length is {mylen(lst)}")
```

```
The length is 3
```

Thus, we can see that f-strings compared to formatted strings are readable. Moreover they have been optimized to be faster than other string creation mechanism. You can learn more about f-strings in the following links: https://www.python.org/dev/peps/pep-0498/, https://realpython.com/python-f-strings/ and https://cito.github.io/blog/f-strings/

7. Strings

Introduction

In this chapter, we will learn about some of the methods used to manipulate a string. In Python, a string is a sequence or collection of characters. The power of the string does not lie in the fact that it contains zero or more characters but the fact that these characters can be easily manipulated. We will discuss each of the methods in detail with examples.

String Methods

Here is a list of some of the most popular string methods.

Method	Syntax	Description
capitalize()	string.capitalize()	Capitalizes the first letter of the string.
count()	string.count(pattern, beginning index, end index)	Returns the number of times a pattern appears in the string.
find()	string.find(pattern, beginning index, end index)	Determines whether a pattern occurs in the string. The beginning and end indices are used to find a substring. Find returns the index if the pattern

		or substring occurs otherwise returns -1.
isalnum()	string.isalnum()	Returns True if the string has at least one character and all characters are alphanumeric and False otherwise.
isdigit()	string.isdigit()	Returns True if string contains only digit(s) and False otherwise.
istitle()	string.istitle()	Returns True if the string is title cased and False otherwise.
join()	join_character.join(sequence)	Joins items in the sequence with the specified join_character.
lower()	string.lower()	Converts all the characters in string to lowercase.
lstrip()	string.lstrip([chars])	If [chars] is not given, then lstrip removes leading whitespaces, newline character, carriage return and tab from string. If [chars] is provided then the lstrip will remove all

		combinations of chars from leading end of the string.
replace()	string.replace(old, new)	Replaces the old substring with new substring in the string.
rstrip()	string.rstrip([chars])	If [chars] is not given, then rstrip removes trailing whitespaces, newline character, carriage return and tab from string. If [chars] is provided then the rstrip will remove all combinations of chars from trailing end of the string.
split()	string.split(delimiter)	Splits the string according to the delimiter and returns a list that consists of all the substrings.
splitlines()	string.splitlines(delimiter)	If delimiter is specified, splitlines will split the lines at the delimiter. Otherwise the lines will be split at newlines. Returns a list with the lines.
strip()	string.strip([chars])	If [chars] is not given, then strip removes leading and trailing

		whitespaces, newline character, carriage return and tab from string. If [chars] is provided then the strip will remove all combinations of chars from leading and trailing end of the string.
title()	string.title()	Returns a title cased string, where the first character in each word will be uppercase and rest will be lowercase.
upper()	string.upper()	Converts all the characters in string to uppercase.
zfill()	string.zfill(width)	Returns the original string along with zeros left padded to a total of width. If a sign is specified in the string, then zfill() retains it.
isdecimal()	string.isdecimal()	Returns True if the string contains only decimal characters and False otherwise. The method isdigit() on the other hand can handle Unicode characters.

Let us consider a few examples. In the code below, string1 = 'programming'. We then use upper() method to convert all the characters in string1 to uppercase.

```python
string1 = "programming"
print(string1.upper())
```

PROGRAMMING

In the code below, we use capitalize() on string1 to capitalize only the first character in string1.

```python
string1 = "programming"
print(string1.capitalize())
```

Programming

In the code below, string2 = "POWERFUL". We use lower() method to convert all the characters in string2 to lowercase.

```python
string2 = "POWERFUL"
print(string2.lower())
```

powerful

Learning Activity 1: If A = 'I know' and B = 'Python' can you convert A into uppercase and B into lowercase and then concatenate them?

In the code below, stringA = "the life of pi". We use title() method to convert stringA to title case, where the first character in each word will be converted to uppercase and rest will be lowercase.

```
stringA = "the life of pi"
print(stringA.title())
```

```
The Life Of Pi
```

Learning Activity 2: Ask the user to enter their favorite book. Convert their input into title case.

In the code below, we have string3 = "34". We use isdigit() to check whether all characters in string3 are digits. In this case, True is returned.

```
string3 = "34"
print(string3.isdigit())
```

```
True
```

The isdigit() on string4 = "3apples" will return False as all the characters in string4 are not digits.

```
string4 = "3apples"
print(string4.isdigit())
```

False

In the code below, we have string5 = "pamphlet" and we use find() to check if the string "ph" is in string5. Since "ph" exists in string5, the index where the match occurs is returned. Note that the index starts at 0.

```
string5 = "pamphlet"
print(string5.find("ph"))
```

3

In the code below, we provide the beginning index as 4 and the end index as 6 to the find() method to ensure that find() only searches between index 4 and 6. Since "p" in "ph" occurs at index 3 and since 3 does not fall under 4 and 6, -1 is returned.

```
string5 = "pamphlet"
print(string5.find("ph", 4, 6))
```

-1

In the code below, string5="pamphlet". We use replace() method to replace "ph" with "PH. "

```
string5 = "pamphlet"
print(string5.replace("ph", "PH"))
```

```
pamPHlet
```

Learning Activity 3: If string1 = 'Amazon has the biggest rainforest' use the split function to split string1 at space and print..

Learning Activity 4: In string1 = 'Amazon has the biggest rainforest', replace 'biggest' with 'BIGGEST'.

In the code below, we use join() method to join all the items in list1 using s1 as the delimiter between the items. The join() operation returns a single string. The first item 'I' and 'can' are joined with a space (provided by s1) between them. To this string, the third item, "code!" is joined with a space between the previous string and the third item. If there are more items, they will be joined to form a larger string.

```
s1 = " "
list1 = ['I', 'can', 'code!']
print(s1.join(list1))
```

```
I can code!
```

Instead of providing a space between two items, we could use any other string. For example, in the code below, we use s2 which contains a hyphen to join items in list1.

```
s2 = "-"
list1 = ['I', 'can', 'code!']
print(s2.join(list1))
```

```
I-can-code!
```

Learning Activity 5: Create a list that contains the following strings: grapes, can, be, sour. Join the items in the list with space, ' ' and print them.

We can perform formatted printing of a string using zfill() method. In the example below, string6 = "3.1415". We use zfill() method and specify a width of 8. Since there are only 6 characters in string6 including the decimal point, in the output two zeros are added to the left of the string.

```
string6 = "3.1415"
print(string6.zfill(8))
```

```
003.1415
```

If string7 = "-3.1415", then zfill(8) will add only one zero to the left because including -, string7 has 7 characters.

```
string7 = "-3.1415"
print(string7.zfill(8))
```

```
-03.1415
```

String Functions

In the previous section, we have seen string methods, which are functions associated with a string. These methods are called by referencing the string followed by a . (dot) followed by the name of the method. In this section, we will consider string functions that take string as an input.

Syntax	Description
max(string)	Returns the maximum alphabetical character from the string.
min(string)	Returns the minimum alphabetical character from the string.
len(string)	Returns the number of characters in the string.

In the code below, we have string8 = "xylophone". The max() function on string8 will return the character with maximum value, which is "y" in this case.

```
string8 = "xylophone"
print(max(string8))
```

y

The min() function on string8 will return the character with the minimum value, which is "e" in this case.

```
string8 = "xylophone"
print(min(string8))
```

e

The len() function on string8 will return the number of characters in string8. In this case, it will return 9.

```
string8 = "xylophone"
print(len(string8))
```

9

In the code below, apart from the characters, string9 also has 3 spaces. When we perform len() on string9, it will return 25 which includes 22 characters and 3 spaces.

```
string9 = "I am learning programming"
print(len(string9))
```

25

Learning Activity 6: If stringA = "interpreter", find the length of stringA. Check whether the length is greater than 4. If it is then, print stringA, otherwise print "It is a short string".

Slicing a string

Since a string is a sequence or collection, we can slice it and create a new string. In the below example, string1 has 11 characters. The first character p is located at index 0 or position 0, r is located at index 1 or position 1 etc. The last character g is located at index 10.

string1 = "programming"

string1[start:stop] will return characters from string1 that are located at the index start to stop index – 1.

string1[3:7] will return gram

string1[5:] will return characters from index 5 till the end of the string since the stop is not specified. This will return amming.

string1[:4] will return characters from index 0 as the start index is not specified till end index 3, which is obtained by subtracting 4 from 1.

If we say string1[:] will return all the characters from string1 as start and stop indices are not specified.

***Learning Activity* 7:** *If h = "quintessential", then slice h and do the appropriate operations to obtain QuinTESSential.*

8. Data structures

Introduction

In computer science, data structure is a particular way of organizing data in a computer so that it can be used efficiently. There are many different methods for storing data and they differ based on the arrangement of the individual elements in memory, the speed of access to the individual element, and the indexing technique used to access the individual elements etc. In Python, data structures can be classified further into two categories: mutable and immutable. Mutable data structures can be modified, that means, elements can be added to them or elements can be removed. On other hand, immutable data structures cannot be modified, that means, once an immutable data structure is defined, no changes be performed on it.

The built-in data structures in Python are:

1. **List** is an ordered sequence of objects. Elements in the list can be any Python objects. They are mutable.

2. **Tuple** is an ordered sequence of objects. Elements in the tuple can be any Python objects. Tuples are immutable.

3. **Dictionary** is a sequence of key and value pairs. Dictionary is mutable as new key-values can be added and existing key-values can be modified. In a dictionary, the keys have to be immutable.

4. **Set** is an unordered sequence of unique elements. Sets are mutable but its elements are immutable.

5. **String** is an ordered sequence of characters. Strings are immutable. We discussed strings in the last chapter.

116

Each Python data structure serves a purpose. It is necessary to understand the time and space complexity of these data structures, so that code can be written that runs efficiently both in terms of time and memory. It is also a good programming practice that future programmers reading your code would appreciate and understand. In this chapter, we will learn the syntax, associated methods, their design including its time and space complexity and along the way we will suggest good practices.

Lists

Syntax

A list is collection of items. These items can be of any Python data type. Thus, we can create a list of integers, floats, strings, tuples, lists etc. You can also have items of different type in the same list. However, it is not recommended.

The syntax for list is A = [element1, element2, element3]

Note that list starts with an open square bracket, [and ends with a closed square bracket,] and elements in a list are separated by a comma. The index of the list starts from zero. In the image below, we have List1 with four elements. The table shows the value of the element and the associated index or position of that element in the list. The element 'any' is at index 0, 'banana' is at index 1, 'is' at index 2, and 'fine' is at index 3.

List1 = ['any', 'banana', 'is', 'fine']

Values	'any'	'banana'	'is'	'fine'
Index, position of the value in the list	0	1	2	3

Let us consider some examples. Below, we define goodFruits and assign it a list with three elements. The print(goodFruits) will print the content of the list.

```
goodFruits = ['apricot', 'banana', 'grapes']
print(goodFruits)
```

```
['apricot', 'banana', 'grapes']
```

We can loop through goodFruits list and access one element at a time using the for-loop. Here gf is the for-loop variable. For every iteration, gf will take a value from goodFruits. In the first iteration, its value will be apricot, in the second iteration its value will be banana etc. When all the elements in the goodFruits have been accessed, then Python will exit the for-loop block.

```
for gf in goodFruits:
    print('We are printing one element at a time:', gf)
```

```
We are printing one element at a time: apricot
We are printing one element at a time: banana
We are printing one element at a time: grapes
```

List Methods and Functions

Here are a few list functions that take a list as an input.

Function	Description	Example
len(A)	Returns the number of items in A.	If A = [4, 2, 6], then len(A) will return 3.
min(A)	Returns the minimum value in A.	If A = [4, 2, 6], then min(A) will return 2.
max(A)	Returns the maximum value in A.	If A = [4, 2, 6], then max(A) will return 6.

Let's see a few examples. In the first example, we will determine the length of the list.

```
A = [4, 7, 5]
print('number of elements is:', len(A))
```

```
number of elements is: 3
```

In the example below, we will calculate the max and min value of a list.

```
A = [4, 7, 5]
print('the max and min are: ', max(A), min(A))
```

```
the max and min are: 7 4
```

Here is a table that lists a few methods.

Method	Description	Example
A.append(x)	Will append x to the end of the list.	If A = [4, 5], A.append(-7) will add -7 to the end of A, the result is [4, 5, -7]. If A = [4, 5], A.append([3,-3]) will add [3,-3] to the end of A, the result is [4, 5, [3, -3]].
A.extend(y)	Will extend the list A by appending all the elements in list y. y has to be a list or an iterable (which we will discuss later).	If A = [10, 11], then A.extend([-7, 7]) will result [10, 11, -7, 7].

A.insert(i, v)	Will insert item v at index i.	If A = [4, 5], A.insert(1, 7) will insert 7 at index 1, the result will be [4, 7, 5].
A.count(x)	Will return the frequency of occurrence of x.	If A = [3, 4, 3, 2]. Then A.count(3) will return 2, because 3 occurs 2 times in the list.
A.remove(y)	Will remove the first y from A. Will raise a ValueError, if there is no y.	If A = [1, 2, 3, 4, 3], A.remove(3) will return [1, 2, 4, 3].
A.pop([i])	Will remove and return the item at index i. If no index is provided, the last item will be removed and returned.	If A = [1, 5, 9], then A.pop(1) will return [1, 9]. If A = [1, 5, 9], then A.pop() will remove the last item 9 and the result will be [1, 5].
A.sort()	Will sort the items in A in-place.	If A = [3, 2, 6] then A.sort() will result in A = [2, 3, 6].

Let us consider examples. In the code below, A is a variable that points to a list with three elements. We insert the value of -3 at index 2 and then print A. Notice that now A has four elements.

```
A = [4, 7, 5]
A.insert(2, -3)
print(A)
```

```
[4, 7, -3, 5]
```

In the code below, we use pop() to remove element that is located at index 1 from the list.

```
A.pop(1) # will pop 7 that is located at index 1
print(A)
```

```
[4, -3, 5]
```

In the code below, we use pop() without any specific index to remove the last element from the list.

```
A.pop()
print(A)
```

```
[4, -3]
```

In the code below, we use remove() to remove the element -3 from the list. Notice that -3 is not the index but the value in the list.

```
A.remove(-3) # will remove -3 from the list A
print(A)
```

```
[4]
```

In the code below, we use append() to add 3.14 to the end of A. Note that 3.14 is a single value.

```
A.append(3.14) # 3.14 will get appended to A
print(A)
```

```
[4, 3.14]
```

In the code below, we append a list [-6, -7] to A. Note that the list [-6, -7] will be appended to A.

```
A.append([-6, -7]) # list [-6, -7] will be appended to A
print(A)
```

```
[4, 3.14, [-6, -7]]
```

A.extend(list2) appends individual items from list2 to the end of A. So, unlike append of a list, extend of a list separates each element and adds them to the end of the list.

In the code below, we use extend and provide a list [-9, -8]. Notice that individual elements -9 and -8 are added to the list.

```
A.extend([-9,-8]) # values -9 and -8 will be appended to A
print(A)
```

```
[4, 3.14, [-6, -7], -9, -8]
```

It is important to note that the extend function takes only a list or any other iterable object. Hence, you cannot provide a value such as a single integer to extend, as a single value is not iterable. If you need to provide a single value, first convert it into a list or some other iterable object.

```
A = [4, 3.14, [-6, -7], -9, -8]
A.extend([4])
print(A)
```

```
[4, 3.14, [-6, -7], -9, -8, 4]
```

In the code below, we use extend and provide a tuple (91, 92). Since tuple (will be discussed later in this chapter) is an iterable, the individual values 91 and 92 will be added to A.

```
A = [4, 3.14, [-6, -7], -9, -8]
A.extend((91,92))
print(A)
```

```
[4, 3.14, [-6, -7], -9, -8, 91, 92]
```

Use case for extend: Let's consider a case, where you call a function that returns a list and the elements in that list have to be added to the end of a master list. One approach would be to loop through elements in the list that was returned by the function and append them one at a time to the master list or one can simply use extend.

To check for membership of an element in a given list, we use 'in' as shown below. Since 4 is a member of A, True will be returned.

```
print(4 in A)
```

```
True
```

The sort function sorts elements in list A in-place. That means, after the sort operation, the variable A contains a sorted list and the unsorted version is no longer accessible. In the following code, the list A is sorted. The original values in A are lost and they are replaced with the sorted elements. The output of the sort function is stored into the variable sortout. The print function demonstrates that the value in sortout is None. This is due to the fact that sort is inline and it replaces the original list with the sorted list. Hence, it does not have to return a new list.

```
A = [1, 5, 4, 7, 3]
sortout = A.sort()
print(A, sortout)
```

```
[1, 3, 4, 5, 7] None
```

If we have a list of lists, then sort() will sort with respect to the value at the zero index in the inner lists. But, if the value at the zeroth index is same for both inner lists, then the values at first index will be considered. In the example below, since lista is a list of lists. When sorting the inner list, Python will check the values at the zeroth index of the inner lists. Since we have 5 in the first inner list and 2 in the second inner list, sort() will move [2, 9] list to the first index and [5, 7] to the second index in lista.

```
lista = [[5, 7], [2, 9]]
lista.sort()
print(lista)
```

```
[[2, 9], [5, 7]]
```

Below, both the inner lists in lista have 5 in the first index, so, Python will consider the value at the second index in the inner lists to sort.

```
listb = [[5, 7], [5,4]]
listb.sort()
print(listb)
```

```
[[5, 4], [5, 7]]
```

List concatenation is a process of extending a list using another list similar to the effect achieved using the extend() method. List concatenation is achieved by using '+' operator.

```
list1 = [-10, -9]
list2 = [9, 10]
list3 = list1 + list2
print(list3
```

```
[-10, -9, 9, 10]
```

Learning Activity 1: Consider listA = [12, 14, 16, 19, 20, 24].

1) To listA, add 18 at index 3.

2) From the list that was obtained from #1, remove 19.

3) To the list that was obtained from #2, extend with the list [28, 30]. Print the output after each case.

Learning Activity 2: Consider list B = [14, 21, 24, 27, 32].

127

1) Create a list that contains the multiples of 4 from B.

2) Create a list that contains the multiples of 3 and 6. Print the output after each case.

List comprehension

In Python, list comprehensions provide an efficient and elegant way to create lists from a list or other iterable object. It is faster compared to looping through each element in the list. It also provides a very succinct syntax making the code readable. It can also prevent modifying the existing list in the process of creating a new list and hence makes the code "functional".

List comprehension uses square bracket with an expression followed by for-loop with an optional if statement.

Syntax for list comprehension:

List2 = [a for a in iterable if statement]

Let's say we want to square every element in list1 = [-9, 2, 5]. To accomplish this in a traditional way, we create an empty list called list2. We loop through elements in list1 using the for-loop and for every iteration we square the element and append it to list2. Finally, we exit the for-loop and print list2. Excluding the initialization of list1 and print function, we needed three lines of code.

```
list1 = [-9, 2, 5]
list2 = []
for x in list1:
```

```
    list2.append(x*x)
print(list2)
```

```
[81, 4, 25]
```

The three lines of code can be replaced with the one-line of list comprehension as shown below. After the opening square bracket [, we describe the output, which in this case is x*x and then we inform the interpreter that x must be fetched serially from list1. We close the list comprehension with a closing square bracket,]. We then print the content of list2.

```
list1 = [-9, 2, 5]
list2 = [x*x for x in list1]
print(list2)
```

```
[81, 4, 25]
```

We can use list comprehension to filter elements from the input list before creating a new list. Let's consider the case where we want to obtain another list with elements from list1 = [10, 15, 18, 20]. The new list must only contain the multiples of 3 from the original list. The first part of the list comprehension is similar to the one above. To filter only the multiples of 3, we added the if statement.

```
list1 = [10, 15, 18, 20]
list2 = [a for a in list1 if a %3 == 0]
print(list2)
```

```
[15, 18]
```

Learning Activity 3: *Given list C = [7, 9, 15, 18, 24, 28]. Use list comprehension to:*

1) Create a list that comprises of multiples of 7 from list C.

2) Create a list that comprises of multiples of 4 or 7 from list C.

Python**: List internals

In Python, a list is implemented as a C array that contains pointers to elements in the list, [https://github.com/python/cpython/blob/master/Objects/listobject.c]. The C array is over-allocated, so that elements can be added to the list without the need for constant expansion.

For example, in the figure below, we create a list of four elements. The C array contains the pointer to the four items stored in memory.

mylist = ["a","b","c","d"]

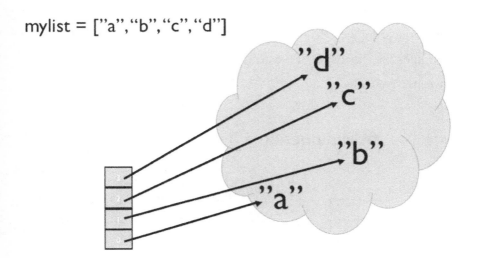

When a new element is appended, as shown in figure below, the array expands to size 8. The new element is added to index 4. Since there may not be enough memory to expand the array in the above figure, CPython will create a new array at another location and copy the content of the original list to the new location. Thus, it can be imagined that the expanding a list dynamically is expensive in terms of CPU.

To reduce this cost over the lifetime of a list, CPython adopts the following strategy. The new array size is dependent on the size of the old array based on the following formula [https://github.com/python/cpython/blob/master/Objects/listobject.c].

new_allocated = (size_t)newsize +

(newsize >> 3) +

(newsize < 9 ? 3 : 6);

The first term is the size of the old array, the second term is equivalent to dividing the size of old array by 8 (using the bit right shift operator) and the

131

third term is returns either 3 or 6 depending on the size of the old array. For a really large array the effect of the third term in minimal. So, the second term determines the expansion of the array and it grows approximately 12.5% between expansions.

mylist.append("e")

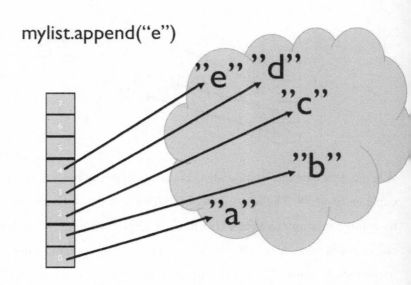

Based on its construction, we can say that appending to a list will add the element to the end of the array. If there is enough room to add elements in the array, it should take only constant time. Hence, this operation is O(1). Also, removing the last element in a list using pop() with no index is also O(1).

However, pop at any other index is inefficient. For example, in the figure below, we pop element at index 2. To keep all elements contiguous, the pointer at index 3 has to be moved to index 2 and the pointer at index 4 must be moved to index 3 and so on. The worst-case scenario happens when we pop at 0th index in which case all the pointers must be moved one level down resulting in O(n) operation where n is the number of elements in a list.

Similarly, adding an element to the list using insert to index 1(say) would need moving all the pointers from 1 to the end of the list by 1 index. The worst-case scenario happens using insert to 0th index which is O(n) operation.

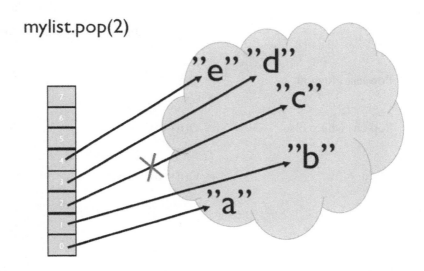

The 'in' operation is O(n) as all elements have to be visited in order to determine if an element is in the list.

To fetch an element given its position using the [] operator requires only O(1) operation, as only one element corresponding to the index needs to be visited.

The big-O values for various operations is summarized in the table below.

Operation	Time
Append	O(1)
Extend	O(k) where k is the length of the iterable supplied as argument to extend.
Pop last element	O(1)
Pop anywhere else	O(n) worst case
Insert	O(n) worst case
Index	O(1)
Slice	O(k) where k is the number of elements returned by the slice.
in operator	O(n)
Sort	O(nlogn)

Tuples

In Python, a tuple is another sequence just like a list. Unlike lists, tuples are immutable. So, the elements of a tuple cannot be modified after they have been created.

Syntax

A tuple starts with an open parenthesis, (and ends with a closed parenthesis,). Elements in a tuple are separated by comma. In the following example, we create a tuple with 3 elements in it.

```
tuple1 = (1, 2, 3,)
print(tuple1)
```

```
(1, 2, 3)
```

You probably noticed the last comma (,) in the tuple. It is customary to put a comma after the last element. This will be especially useful when we have only one element in a tuple. Why? In the following example, we follow the tuple syntax and created a tuple with only one element. When we printed the type, notice that the type is str and not tuple.

```
tuple1 = ('one')
print(tuple1, type(tuple1))
```

```
one <class 'str'>
```

By adding a comma, we are indicating to the Python interpreter that we want the object to be treated as a tuple and not a string. It is mandatory to have a comma at the end for tuples with one element. However, it is optional when there is more than one element. Still it is customary to add comma at the end to all tuples. In the example below, the type(tuple1) is tuple and not string.

```
tuple1 = ('one',)
print(tuple1, type(tuple1))
```

```
('one',) <class 'tuple'>
```

Elements in a tuple are accessed using [ ] just as in case of a list. The index starts at 0. In the code below, we access the elements in tuple2.

```
tuple2 = (13, 19, 25,)
print(tuple2[0]) # accessing the first element in tuple2
print(tuple2[1]) # accessing the second element in tuple2
```

```
13
19
```

Since tuples are immutable, we cannot alter elements in a tuple after the tuple is defined. In the below code, we try to modify an element in tuple2. We get a TypeError: 'tuple' object does not support item assignment. Python provides a clear error messages that explains that tuple objects do not support any assignment operator.

```
tuple2[1] = 29
```

```
----------------------------------------------------------
-----------
TypeError                          Traceback (most recent
call last)
<ipython-input-79-a7e0dd770193> in <module>()
----> 1 tuple2[1] = 29
TypeError: 'tuple' object does not support item
assignment
```

Just like in lists, we can loop through elements in a tuple using a for-loop.
Below is an example.

```
for t in tuple2:
    print(t)
```

```
13
19
23
```

Just like in case of lists, len() function can be used to determine the number
of elements in a tuple.

```
print(len(tuple2))
```

```
3
```

min() and max() functions can be used on tuples to find minimum value and maximum value in a tuple as shown in the example below.

```
print(min(tuple2))
print(max(tuple2))
```

13
23

If we have two tuples t1 and t2 and we want to create another tuple t3 with t1 and t2 as its elements then we have to do the following:

```
t3 = (t1, t2)
```

An example of creating tuple of tuples is shown below.

```
t1 = ('the good', 'the bad', 'the ugly',)
t2 = ('Clint Eastwood',)
t3 = (t1, t2)
print(t3)
```

```
(('the good', 'the bad', 'the ugly'), ('Clint
Eastwood',))
```

Concatenation of the tuples can be done by using '+' operator. The concatenation produces a new tuple. The elements of t2 are separated and added to the right of the elements of t1 similar to the extend method in list.

```
t1 = ('the good', 'the bad', 'the ugly')
t2 = ('Clint Eastwood',)
t5 = t1 + t2
print(t5)
```

```
('the good', 'the bad', 'the ugly', 'Clint Eastwood')
```

Using '*' repetition of elements can be created as shown below.

```
t6 = ('Good morning',)
print(t6*3)
```

```
('Good morning', 'Good morning', 'Good morning')
```

Membership of an element in a tuple, can be checked by using 'in' keyword as shown below. Since 'there' is not an element of the tuple t1, the 'in' operator will return a False.

```
print('there' in t1)
```

```
False
```

A tuple can be converted to a list by using list() function. In the code below, we convert tuple t5 into a list and then print the tuple_to_list and its type.

```
tuple_to_list = list(t5)
print(tuple_to_list, type(tuple_to_list))
```

```
['the good', 'the bad', 'the ugly', 'Clint Eastwood']
<class 'list'>
```

Similarly, a list can be converted into a tuple by using tuple() function.

In the code below, we are converting a list into a tuple and then printing the list_to_tuple and its type

```
list_ratings = ['bad', 'okay', 'excellent']
list_to_tuple = tuple(list_ratings)
print(list_to_tuple, type(list_to_tuple))
```

```
('bad', 'okay', 'excellent') <class 'tuple'>
```

Learning Activity 4: If tuple1 = (-4, -2, -1). Change the value at index 0 to 5 in tuple1. Read the output message carefully.

Learning Activity 5: Convert tuple1 = (-4, -2, -1, 1) to a list and perform the following operations:

1) To the list, change the value index 0 to -5.

2) To the list that was obtained in #1, pop the value at index 1.

3) To the list that was obtained in #2, append -3.

4) Convert the list that was obtained in #3 to a tuple.

Python**: Tuple internals

In Python, a tuple is implemented as a C array that contains the pointer to the element [https://github.com/python/cpython/blob/master/Objects/tupleobject.c].

In the figure below, a tuple of four elements is assigned to the variable t1. Internally, CPython creates an array of size 4 that can hold the pointers to the four elements.

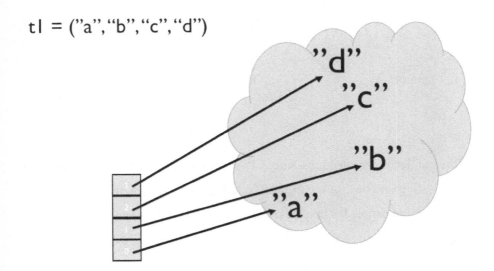

Since the C array is designed only to contain the pointers to elements of the tuple and since the array is not designed for reallocation at run-time, tuple by design cannot add new elements. Hence, its immutability. For the exact same reason, it is not possible to reassign a specific element either.

The 'in' operation is O(n) as all elements have to be visited in order to determine if an element is in the tuple.

To fetch an element given its position using the [] operator requires only O(1) operation, as only one element needs to be visited.

The big-O values for various operations is summarized in the table below.

Operation	Timez
Index	O(1)
Slice	O(k) where k is the number of elements returned by the slice.
in operator	O(n)

Since tuples do not need resizing, CPython has some built-in optimization for creating and destroying tuples. To reduce memory fragmentation and for better performance, Python tuples are reused (i.e.,) the memory id of the previously cleared tuples of the same size is used for a new tuple.

In the following code, a tuple t1 is created with three elements. Later t1 is reassigned to integer 6. CPython will eventually clear the first tuple object. Later, when a new tuple t2 is created, CPython may use the same memory location to store the second tuple and hence the memory id may be the same.

You can learn more about this in the link: https://rushter.com/blog/python-lists-and-tuples/.

```
t1 = (3, 4, 67)
print(id(t1))
t1 = 6
t2 = (1, 2, 423)
print(id(t2))
```

```
4590801976
4590801976
```

Usage

If tuples are a more restrictive cousin of a list, why would we need one? Tuples might have restrictions but they are memory efficient. A list needs an array of pointers that is not fully utilized. A tuple on the other hand use a fully populated array that is not resized at run-time. Since it cannot be resized or reassigned, it does not have to be copied like a list. It is very useful in scenarios where a collection should not or will not be modified. For example, it can be used to store a collection of constants, return value from a function or method etc. It is also used to pass a series of values to a function.

Dictionary

In Python, a dictionary is a sequence of key-value pairs. Dictionaries are mutable and they start with curly braces and end with curly braces. The keys and the values are separated by a : (colon) as shown in the example below.

Syntax for dictionary is d1 = {key1: value1, key2: value2}

In a dictionary, the keys have to be unique and should be of immutable type such as integer, string, tuple etc. The values can be any Python object.

In the example below, we create a dictionary with three key-value pairs. The first key is 'b' and the corresponding value is 'ice', the second key is 'c' and its values is 'steam' and the third key is 'a' and its value is 'water'.

```
D1 = {'b': 'ice', 'c': 'steam', 'a': 'water'}
print(D1)
```

```
{'b': 'ice', 'c': 'steam', 'a': 'water'}
```

The dictionary in Python 3.5 and below do not maintain the order of the entries while dictionary in Python 3.6 and above maintain the order. This is only true for CPython 3.6 and not for Jython, IronPython, Pypy etc. at the time of writing this book. Elements in a dictionary are generally accessed either by looping through all key-value pairs or by accessing a single value given its key. In both cases, the order is not critical and hence the unordered dictionary prior to 3.6 is not a big concern for a typical programming case.

Another way to define a dictionary using dict() function is shown below. Note that the key 'a' is not supplied as string a but as a variable name to this function.

```
any_fruit = dict(a='mango', b='pear')
print(any_fruit)
```

```
{'a': 'mango', 'b': 'pear'}
```

Let's create another dictionary city_temp.

```
city_temp = {'San Francisco': 72, 'New York': 51}
print(city_temp)
```

```
{'San Francisco': 72, 'New York': 51}
```

If we want to add another city, Austin and its corresponding temperature to the city_temp, we can use the assignment operation.

```
city_temp['Austin'] = 80
print(city_temp)
```

```
{'San Francisco': 72, 'New York': 51, 'Austin': 80}
```

Notice that key 'Austin' and its corresponding value are now added to city_temp.

For a dictionary, the keys() method will return a list of all the keys while the values() method returns a list of all the values. city_temp.keys() will return a list of keys from city_temp dictionary while city_temp.values() will return a list of values.

```
print(city_temp.keys())
print(city_temp.values())
```

```
['San Francisco', 'New York', 'Austin']
[72, 51, 80]
```

Notice how both the keys() function and values() function preserve the index of key-value in the city_temp dictionary.

Let us loop through the keys in city_temp and print one key and its corresponding value. In the for-loop below, we use the loop variable, 'key' to access the keys one at a time. Using the key and the [] operator, we can obtain the value for that particular key.

```
for key in city_temp:
    print(key, city_temp[key])
```

```
San Francisco 72
New York 51
Austin 80
```

Alternately, you can access the contents of a dictionary as an iterable object using the items() method. In every iteration, the iterable object will return a tuple with two values namely the key and value in that order. We assign this tuple to the variables key and value respectively

```
for key,value in city_temp.items():
    print(key, value)
```

```
San Francisco 72
New York 51
Austin 80
```

To check whether a particular key is in the dictionary, we can use the 'in' membership operator. In the below code, we check if Boston is a key in city_temp. Since it is not in the dictionary, False is returned.

```
print('Boston' in city_temp)
```

```
False
```

We can check if Austin is a key in city_temp. Since it is, True will be returned.

```
print('Austin' in city_temp)
```

```
True
```

Dictionary Comprehension is similar in idea to list comprehension. It is a fast and efficient way to create a dictionary from any iterable object. Dictionary comprehension uses curly brackets with an expression followed by for-loop with optional if statements.

Syntax for dictionary comprehension:

D2 = { a: a*a for a in list1 if statement}

In the below code, we create a dictionary whose key is the element in the list and the value in the dictionary is the cube of the corresponding element. The key in the new dictionary is to the left of the : (colon) while the value is to the right of the : (colon). In the for-loop, we mention that x values are from the list, list1.

```
list1 = [-9, 10, 14]
cubed = {x: x**3 for x in list1}
print(cubed)
```

```
{10: 1000, 14: 2744, -9: -729}
```

In the below example, we will create a dictionary using dictionary comprehension that takes the iterable object range().

```
rangeiter = range(10)
cubed = {x: x**3 for x in rangeiter}
print(cubed)
```

```
{0: 0, 1: 1, 2: 8, 3: 27, 4: 64, 5: 125, 6: 216, 7: 343,
8: 512, 9: 729}
```

148

List comprehension provides the ability to filter elements that satisfy a certain requirement. Similarly, dictionary comprehension also provides similar functionality as seen in the example below. Unlike the previous example, in the example below, we are interested in creating key-value pairs only if the elements in the iterable objects are odd numbers. The test for odd number is done in the if statement using the % (modulo) operator.

```
rangeiter = range(10)
cubed = {x: x**3 for x in rangeiter if x%2==1}
print(cubed)
```

```
{1: 1, 3: 27, 9: 729, 5: 125, 7: 343}
```

Learning Activity 6: *Define a dictionary with the following key value pairs:*
'France': 1789, 'India': 1947, 'USA': 1776, 'Brazil': 1822

Learning Activity 7: *Given D2 = {'apples':25, 'bananas': 76}, then add {'kiwi': 56} to D2.*

Learning Activity 8: *listA = [2, 14, 16, 38]. Use dictionary comprehension to create a dictionary with elements from listA as the key and its square as the value.*

Python**: Dictionary internals

A Python dictionary is implemented as a hash-table
[https://en.wikipedia.org/wiki/Hash_table] as can be seen in the CPython
source code for a dictionary at
https://github.com/python/cpython/blob/master/Objects/dictobject.c. We
already discussed that prior to CPython 3.6, the order of the insertion was not
maintained. Beginning with CPython 3.6. the insertion order is maintained.
In this discussion, we will focus on the CPython 3.6 version of the
dictionary.

The dictionary hash-table consists of two moving parts.

1. A sparse array of indices

2. A dense array containing a struct that consist of the hash value,
    the pointer to the key and pointer to the value.

Let's assume that we begin with an empty dictionary. This will create a
sparse array and dense array. When the first key is inserted in to the
dictionary, the key will be sent to a hash function which will return a long
int. Assuming that the indices array is of size 8, then a new int called an
index is calculated by using the following formula:

index = hashvalue mod arraysize

At that index in the indices array, a value of 0 (indicating the first dictionary
entry) will be stored and in the dense array, a struct containing the hash
value, the pointer to the key and pointer to the value will be stored.

When a second key is inserted, the hashvalue and the index will be computed and the corresponding struct will be stored in index 1 (indicating the second dictionary entry) of the dense array.

In some cases, two keys may have the same hashvalues even though their keys may be different and hence the same index. In such cases, CPython uses open addressing to quadratically probe [https://en.wikipedia.org/wiki/Quadratic_probing]for an unoccupied index in the indices array.

The indices array is resized whenever the number of occupied slots in the array to the number of slots in that array is 2/3 or more. If the ratio is smaller, it indicates that the indices array is sparse which indicates lower chance of collision. However, if the ratio is higher, it will result in a dense array but with more collision and consequently more calculation for probing.

The elements in the dense array are in the insertion order and hence the dictionary in CPython 3.6 maintains the order. The indices array may be sparse but does not consume too much memory as it only needs to hold integers. Hence dictionary in CPython 3.6 is also compact compared to the older implementation.

You can learn more about the CPython 3.6 dictionary check out the following links: https://mail.python.org/pipermail/python-dev/2012-December/123028.html and https://morepypy.blogspot.com/2015/01/faster-more-memory-efficient-and-more.html.

The keys need to be immutable because mutable objects are not hashable in Python.

To insert a value in to a dictionary using a key requires O(1) operation that consist of hashing, masking to get index, probing if needed and adding the struct.

To fetch a value in a dictionary using a key requires O(1) operation that consist of hashing, masking to get index, probing if needed and finally fetching the struct.

To check if a key exists in a dictionary is also O(1) that consist of hashing, masking to get index, and probing if needed.

The big-O values for various operations is summarized in the table below. As can be seen, most of the common operations are O(1). Hence dictionaries are used extensively inside CPython for storing global variables, modules, variables in classes etc.

Operation	Time
Add value based on key	O(1)
Fetch value based on key	O(1)
in operator	O(1)

Sets and Frozen Sets

In Python, a set is an unordered collection of unique items. Based on this definition, the following characteristics can be observed.

- Set is a collection and hence can contain one or more elements and hence it is like a list.

- A set is unordered. Hence, the order in which the elements are added to the set will not be maintained. Since the order is not maintained, operations that require maintenance of order such as indexing (setv[0]), which are possible in list are not allowed in set. The correct usage of set does not require order of items anyway.

- It contains unique items. The correct usage of set does not require duplicate items.

The set() function can be used to convert a list or a tuple to a set. In the below example, we convert a list to a set. Notice that the output of a set has 'set' keyword in front of it. The fruits_set consists only of unique elements from the list fruits and thus only one 'grapes' is present in the set even though there are 2 grapes in the list. Also, notice that elements in fruits_set are unordered. In sets, uniqueness is more important than the order.

```python
fruits = ['grapes','apple','grapes','oranges'] # A list
fruits_set = set(fruits)
# set command returns only unique items
print(fruits, type(fruits))
print(fruits_set, type(fruits_set))
```

```
['grapes', 'apple', 'grapes', 'oranges'] <type 'list'>
{'oranges', 'apple', 'grapes'} <type 'set'>
```

Just as in lists and tuples, we can iterate through a set and print one element at a time. In the below code, we are looping through elements of fruits_set (that we created above) and we are printing one element at a time.

```
for item in fruits_set:
    print(item)
```

```
oranges
apple
grapes
```

The second and a newer method for initializing a set involves using { } to create set as in the example below. The usage of { } is similar to the syntax in a dictionary except that set doesn't have key-value pairs. This functionality is available only in Python 2.6+.

A = { } will create an empty dictionary. To create an empty set, we still have to use set( ) function. Below examples show how to define an empty set.

```
A = {}

print(type(A))
```

```
<class 'dict'>
```

```
B = set()

print(type(B))
```

```
<class 'set'>
```

Below, we define a set s2 with three elements.

```python
s2 = {'CPython', 'Jython', 'IronPython'}
print(s2)
```

```
{'CPython', 'IronPython', 'Jython'}
```

A set can be converted into a list by using list() function. Similarly, we can convert a set to a tuple using the tuple() function. Below is an example where we are converting fruits_set into a list and into a tuple.

```python
set_to_list = list(fruits_set)
print(set_to_list, type(set_to_list))

set_to_tuple = tuple(fruits_set)
print(set_to_tuple, type(set_to_tuple))
```

```
['oranges', 'apple', 'grapes'] <class 'list'>
('oranges', 'apple', 'grapes') <class 'tuple'>
```

Just as in the case of lists and tuples, len() can be used on sets as well to obtain the number of elements in a set. In the below example, we are using len() on fruits_set. Since fruits_set has three elements, and hence 3 is returned.

```python
print(len(fruits_set))
```

Membership can be determined by using the 'in' operator. Below we are checking if 'avocado' is a member of fruits_set. Since 'avocado' is not a member, False is returned. In the next call, we are checking if 'grapes' is a member, since it is, True is returned.

```python
print('avocado' in fruits_set)
```

```
False
```

```python
print('grapes' in fruits_set)
```

```
True
```

Frozen set

An immutable set is known as a frozen set [https://docs.python.org/3/library/stdtypes.html#frozenset]. Hence, we cannot add or remove elements in a frozen set.

Below is the syntax to define an empty frozen set. To the frozen set function, we supply an empty list.

```python
fs = frozenset([])
```

```
print(fs)
```

```
frozenset()
```

A frozen set with no elements may not have programming value. So, let's look at an example of a frozen set with elements. To the frozenset function, the elements are supplied as a list. The frozenset returns an unordered list of unique elements.

```
fs = frozenset([-1, 2, 4, 2, -1])
```

```
print(fs)
```

```
frozenset({2, 4, -1})
```

An important power of Python set is its ability to perform set algebra. There are several operations that can be applied to sets and an extensive list can be found at https://docs.python.org/3/library/stdtypes.html#set. The table below describes a few set methods.

The following methods can be used both on sets as well as frozen sets. If the inputs are sets, then the output will be a set. However, if the inputs are frozenset, then the output will be a frozenset.

Method	Description	Example
A.subset(B)	Checks whether every element in A is in B. Returns True or False.	A = {1, 2} B = {2, 4} A.subset(B) returns False because 1 is in A but not in B.
A.superset(B)	Checks whether every element in B is in A. Returns True or False.	A = {1, 2} B = {2, 4} A.superset(B) returns False because 4 is in B but not in A.
A.union(B)	Returns a new set with elements from A and B.	A = {1, 2} B = {2, 4} A.union(B) returns {1, 2, 4}.
A.intersection(B)	Returns a new set with elements that are common to A and B.	A = {1, 2} B = {2, 4} A.intersection(B) returns {2}

A.difference(B)	Returns a new set with elements in A that are not in B.	A = {1, 2} B = {2, 4} A.difference(B) returns {1}.
A.clear()	Will clear all elements from A.	A = {3, 5} A.clear() will return set().

These methods can only be used on sets. The output in each case will be a set.

A.update(B)	Updates A by adding elements from B.	A = {1, 2} B = {2, 4} A.update(B) updates A to {1, 2, 4}.
A.remove(x)	Will remove x from A. If x is not in A, a KeyError exception will be raised.	A = {1, 3, 4, 5} A.remove(3), removes 3 from A and updates A to {1, 4, 5}.
A.discard(y)	Will remove y from A if it is present. If y is	A = {1, 3, 4, 5}

	not present, the discard method does not throw any error.	A.discard(1), discards 1 from A and updates A to {3, 4, 5}.
A.add(n)	Will add n to A.	A = {3, 5} A.add(-7), adds -7 to A and updates A to {-7, 3, 5}.

Let us consider a few examples. The set2.issubset(set1) can be used to check if set2 is a subset of set1. Since every element of set2 is an element of set1, True is returned.

```
set1 = {4, 5, 7}
set2 = {5, 7}
print(set2.issubset(set1))
```

```
True
```

We can check if set1 is a superset of set2 and using set1.issuperset(set2). Since set1 contains all the elements of set2, True is returned.

```
print(set1.issuperset(set2))
```

```
True
```

set1.difference(set2) will create a new set that only has elements from set1 and not set2. Since 4 is the only element that is in set1 and not set2, it is returned as a set.

```
print(set1.difference(set2))
```

```
{4}
```

Let us define two new sets, s1 and s2 and then use update() function to add elements from one set to another. s1.update(s2) will add elements in s2 to s1 as shown below. In the process, it will remove duplicate elements.

```
s1 = {3, 5, 7}
s2 = {2, 4, 6}
s1.update(s2)
print(s1)
```

```
{2, 3, 4, 5, 6, 7}
```

The s1.remove(6) will remove 6 from s1 and s1 is updated.

```
s1.remove(6)
print(s1)
```

```
{2, 3, 4, 5, 7}
```

If the element that we want to remove is not in the set, then we would get a KeyError exception. So, if we say s1.remove(10), then Python will raise a KeyError because 10 is not an element in s1.

```
s1.remove(10)
print(s1)
```

```
--------------------------------------------------------
--------------

KeyError                              Traceback (most recent
call last)
<ipython-input-44-0c74a05278e9> in <module>()
----> 1 s1.remove(10)
      2 print(s1)
KeyError: 10
```

The discard() method is similar to remove() method but with a small difference. s1.discard(9) will remove 9 if it's an element in s1 otherwise, it will fail silently. That means no exceptions will be raised. In the below code, we want to discard 9 from s1 even though 9 does not exist. Yet Python doesn't raise any error.

```
s1.discard(9)
print(s1)
```

```
{2, 3, 4, 5, 7}
```

s1.add(-12) will add -12 to s1 as shown below.

```
s1.add(-12)
print(s1)
```

```
{2, 3, 4, 5, 7, -12}
```

s1.clear() can be used to clear all the contents in s1 and obtain an empty set.

```
s1.clear()
print(s1)
```

```
set()
```

Since items in a set are used for finding presence or absence and it is also unordered, set does not provide a functionality to slice or index to a particular location in a set. Thus, operations such as s4[0] or s4[2:5] that are possible in a list are not allowed in a set as shown in the example below.

```
print(s4[0])
```

```
-----------------------------------------------------------------
------------
```

```
TypeError                          Traceback (most
```

```
recent call last)
<ipython-input-5-2128c94ea31d> in <module>()
----> 1 print(s4[0])
TypeError: 'set' object does not support indexing
```

Set comprehension

Set comprehension like list comprehension and dictionary comprehension provides a convenient syntax for creating a set from a collection of items. Set comprehension also uses curly brackets with an expression followed by for-loop with optional if statements.

Syntax for set comprehension:

set1 = {a for a in list1}

In the example below, every element from the range() function is squared and is placed in the set.

```
s4 = {i**2 for i in range(5)}
print(s4)
```

```
{0, 1, 4, 9, 16}
```

As in list and dictionary comprehension, items from the iterable object can be filtered before a set is created. Below we want to consider squaring the element only if the element is odd. This condition is specified in the if statement.

164

```
s4 = {i**2 for i in range(5) if i%2==1}
print(s4)
```

```
{1, 9}
```

Learning Activity 9: *Given listB = ['iron', 'copper', 'iron', 'aluminum',*
'copper', 'iron'].

1. *Create a set for listB.*

2. *Create a dictionary with the item from the set as the key and its*
    frequency of occurrence in listB as the value.

Learning Activity 10: *If listC = [-7, -11, -9, -7]. Use set comprehension to*
compute square of each item in listC.

Python**: Set internals

A Python set is implemented as a hash-table
[https://en.wikipedia.org/wiki/Hash_table] as can be seen in the CPython
source code for a set at
https://github.com/python/cpython/blob/master/Objects/setobject.c. The
Python set borrows many of the code from Python's dictionary as they are
both hash-table.

Let's assume that we begin with an empty set. An array will be created to
hold the pointers to the values in the set. When the first value is inserted in to

the set, the value will be sent to a hash function which will return a long int. Assuming that the array is of size 8, then a new int called an index is calculated by using the following formula:

index = hashvalue mod arraysize

At that index in the array, the element and its hash will be stored. When a second value is inserted, the hashvalue and the index will be computed and the corresponding value and hash will be stored.

In some cases, two different values may have the same hashvalues (even though their values might be different) and hence the same index. In such cases, CPython uses open addressing to quadratically probe for an unoccupied index.

The array is resized as needed. If the number of used elements in the array is less than 50000, then the array grows to 4 times its previous size else it grows 2 times.

To insert a value in to a set requires $O(1)$ operation that consist of hashing, masking to get index, probing if needed and adding the data.

To check if a value exists in a set is also $O(1)$ that consist of hashing, masking to get index, and probing if needed. The corresponding time for a list to locate an element by value is $O(n)$. **So when searching through a large collection, a set will be orders of magnitude efficient compared to a list.**

The big-O values for various operations is summarized in the table below. As can be seen, most of the common operations are $O(1)$.

Operation	Time
Add value	O(1)
in operator	O(1)

The values need to be immutable because mutable objects are not hashable in Python and hence cannot be added to a set. If mutable types such as list is supplied, Python will raise a TypeError as it cannot hash the element as seen in example below. The two elements of the set are of type list, which are mutable, these cannot be hashed in Python, so Python raises TypeError.

```
s3 = {[1, 2], [3, 4]}
print(s3)
```

```
---------------------------------------------------------------

------------
TypeError                                  Traceback (most
recent call last)
<ipython-input-3-7cf4a10264fb> in <module>()
----> 1 s3 = {[1, 2], [3, 4]}
      2 print(s3)
TypeError: unhashable type: 'list'
```

Because elements can be added or removed from sets (i.e., mutable), a set cannot be a key in a dictionary or value in another set. However, frozenset can be a key in a dictionary or value in another set as they are immutable.

Usage

Python set like mathematical set is useful for determining the presence or absence of items in a group of items. A search for an item in a Python list is an O(n) operation, implying that a visit to every item is needed to determine if it is present or not. However, in the case of the set, a search for an item is O(1), implying that we need to visit only one item. For a list with million items, a list search will visit all million items whereas a set search will visit only one item, a mere 1/million calculation, thus resulting in significant savings in computation and time.

In addition to performing quick searches, Python set can be used to perform mathematical set operations such as union, intersection, issubset, issuperset etc.

Deep copy of data structures

In Python assigning a value to a variable that contains mutable objects such as list, dictionary etc., to another variable does not create a brand-new copy. Instead both the new and the old variable point to the same object. Remember that in Python all variables are objects including list, set, dictionary etc.

Let us consider a list A and then make a copy of A and call it C. We print both A and C as well as their location in memory by using the id() function. Note that in the output, id for A and id for C is same. This type of copy is known as a shallow copy. In other words, we have two variables A and C both pointing to the same object in memory as illustrated by the figure below.

```
A = [12, 9, 14]
C = A
print(A, id(A))
print(C, id(C))
```

```
[12, 9, 14] 2744535086664
[12, 9, 14] 2744535086664
```

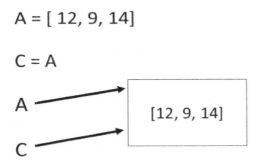

By doing a shallow copy, any changes to A will affect C and vice-versa. Below, we are appending -11 to A and print both A and C. Notice that -11 is appended to both A and C while we performed the append operation only on A.

```
A.append(-11)
print("A is:", A)
print("C is:", C)
```

```
A is: [12, 9, 14, -11]
C is: [12, 9, 14, -11]
```

You can imagine Python variables as convenient labels needed for programmers to reference objects in memory. However, from Python perspective it is manipulating objects in memory and not the labels. We can have multiple labels pointing to the same object and thus when Python manipulates the object, its effect is felt in all labels.

If we made shallow copy of a list which doesn't comprise of lists, then modifications to one variable will not affect another. In the code below, we make a shallow copy of A by using the colon (:). Since no indices are given before and after : (colon) using the [ ] operator will create a shallow copy of A by copying every element in A to the corresponding element in C. When we print A and C along with their ids, notice that their ids are different.

```
A = [12, 9, 14]
C = A[:] # using slicing technique to do a shallow copy
print(A, id(A))
print(C, id(C))
```

```
[12, 9, 14] 2744535760648
[12, 9, 14] 2744535861576
```

Since id of C is different than that of A, append operation on A does not affect C as shown below.

```
A.append(-11)
print("A is:", A)
print("C is:", C)
```

```
A is: [12, 9, 14, -11]
C is: [12, 9, 14]
```

However, the shallow copy of list of lists is a special case and this is discussed in the following section, Copying list of lists.

For creating a true deep copy, we can use the deepcopy() function from the copy module, [https://docs.python.org/3/library/copy.html]

```
from copy import deepcopy
A = [12, 9, 14]
C = deepcopy(A)
print(id(A))
print(id(C))
```

```
1757391609480
1757392312584
```

Python**: Copying list of lists

Let us discuss the list of lists scenario in detail.

The list ml is a list containing a collection of lists. The shallow copy in the second line does not produce a brand-new object. Instead ml and ml_softcopy are both pointing to the same object that contains the list of lists. Thus, any operation performed on ml is performed on the corresponding object which in turn changes the value of ml_softcopy, even though ml_softcopy was not explicitly changed. As can be seen in the last print statement, the id of ml and ml_softcopy are the same, indicating that they point to the same object.

```
ml = [[1, 2, 3], [2, 3, 4], [3, 4, 5]]
ml_softcopy = ml
ml.append([4, 5, 6])
print(ml)
print(ml_softcopy)
print(id(ml), id(ml_softcopy))
```

```
[[1, 2, 3], [2, 3, 4], [3, 4, 5], [4, 5, 6]]
[[1, 2, 3], [2, 3, 4], [3, 4, 5], [4, 5, 6]]
1757392311944 1757392311944
```

Another way of creating a shallow copy can be performed by using the syntax in the code below. Since ml_scopy is a shallow copy with different ids, appending an element to ml does not automatically append it to the list ml_scopy. Also notice that value returned by id is different for ml and ml_scopy.

However, the last print statement that prints the id of the first element in both ml and ml_scopy indicates that the ids of the outer lists are different, the inner lists are pointing to the same object in both ml and ml_scopy.

```
ml = [[1, 2, 3], [2, 3, 4], [3, 4, 5]]
ml_scopy = ml[:]
ml.append([4, 5, 6])
print(ml)
print(ml_scopy)
print("ID of the 2 lists", id(ml), id(ml_scopy))
print("ID of the first element in the 2 lists", \
        id(ml[0]), id(ml_scopy[0]))
```

```
[[1, 2, 3], [2, 3, 4], [3, 4, 5], [4, 5, 6]]
[[1, 2, 3], [2, 3, 4], [3, 4, 5]]
ID of the 2 lists 1757391600520 1757391607240
ID of the first element in the 2 lists 1757391188808
1757391188808
```

Thus, the following code that changes the value of the element of inner list will result in updating the value of both lists. Hence the change of value from 2 to 10 affects both ml and ml_scopy.

```
ml[0][1] = 10
print(ml)
print(ml_scopy)
```

```
[[1, 10, 3], [2, 3, 4], [3, 4, 5]]
[[1, 10, 3], [2, 3, 4], [3, 4, 5]]
```

Deep copy of any list, can be made by using the deepcopy() function from the copy module as shown in the previous section. This can be easily handled by using the copy module [https://docs.python.org/3/library/copy.html]. In the example below, the change of value in the inner list from 2 to 10 only affected the list 'ml'. The list in ml_scopy is unaffected. Also notice that the id of the two outer lists and the id of the first element in the two lists are different, indicating that they are pointing to different objects.

Thus, the use of copy module allows copying of all types of Python object while [:] is useful only for a list.

```
from copy import deepcopy
ml = [[1, 2, 3], [2, 3, 4], [3, 4, 5]]
ml_deepcopy = deepcopy(ml)
ml[0][1] = 10
print(ml)

print(ml_deepcopy)
print("ID of the 2 lists", id(ml), id(ml_deepcopy))
```

174

```python
print("ID of the first element in the 2 lists", \
        id(ml[0]), id(ml_deepcopy[0]))
```

```
[[1, 10, 3], [2, 3, 4], [3, 4, 5]]
[[1, 2, 3], [2, 3, 4], [3, 4, 5]]
ID of the 2 lists 1757391664648 1757391664968
ID of the first element in the 2 lists 1757392285768
1757391189000
```

Truthiness in data structures

We have seen that the bool of all non-trivial basic datatypes such as int, float, string etc., is True. Similarly, the bool of non-trivial data structure is True as well. The bool of all trivial data structure evaluates to False. Thus, an empty list, empty tuple, empty dictionary or an empty set evaluates to False. In the examples below, we demonstrate that trivial data structures return False.

```python
list1 = []
print("Bool of list1:", bool(list1))
tuple1 = ()
print("Bool of tuple1:", bool(tuple1))
D = {}
print("Bool of D1:", bool(D1))
```

```
Bool of list1: False
Bool of tuple1: False
```

175

```
Bool of D1: False
```

In the examples below, we demonstrate that non-trivial data structures return True.

```python
list2 = [1]
print("Bool of list2:", bool(list2))
tuple2 = (2,)
print("Bool of tuple2:", bool(tuple2))
D2 = {1:'apple'}
print("Bool of D2:", bool(D2)
```

```
Bool of list2: True
Bool of tuple2: True
Bool of D2: True
```

9. Functions

Introduction

In a programming language, functions provide a mechanism to reuse code. So, if you have a code that is repeated more than once in your program, then it is better to place that code in a function. Subsequently calls can be made to the function in order to use it.

Additionally, functions provide an abstraction, so that the users of the function do not have to concern themselves with the details of the function. For example, a user of sine function (which is in the math module) do not have to concern themselves with the implementation of the sin function.

Functions make testing of blocks of code easy which are otherwise difficult if they are amidst a larger code block. We will discuss this in more details in a later chapter on unit testing.

In this chapter, we will discuss the syntax of a Python function followed by few examples. We will then discuss the difference between call-by-object and call-by-object-reference. We will also discuss the *args and **kwargs, a mechanism to specify parameters at run time. We will discuss functional programming using filter, map and reduce. Finally, we will conclude with advanced topics such as closures and decorators.

Syntax

The function definition starts with 'def' keyword followed by the name of the function. All the arguments to the function are enclosed inside a pair of parentheses. A colon (:) at the end of the function signature indicates the beginning of the code block containing the function definition. Code blocks belonging to the function are indicated by spaces or a tab in front of each line. The function ends with an optional return statement. If no return statement is specified in the function, then None will be returned.

The syntax for a function definition is:

def name_of_the_function(list of arguments):

    statements that need to be executed
    return some_value

Below we are defining a function called num_double that takes only one argument A. We multiply the input A with 2 and we store the value in B. Then we are using the formatted print statement to print the value stored in B. Finally, we exit the function when the return statement is executed. This is the function definition. These statements are not executed until a call is made to the function and the required arguments are passed.

To execute the statements, we make a call to the num_double function and pass a value 20. The variable A in the function definition is 20. Thus, B will contain a value of 40 as it is two times A. The print() function will be executed and the function returns the value 40 to the caller. In a function definition, a return statement is optional. But when a return statement is included, then it is the last statement that will be executed in the function.

```
def num_double(A):
    B = 2*A
    print("Double of A is: %d" %B)
    return B
```

```
print(num_double(20)) # call the function and pass the
required argument
```

```
Double of A is: 40
40
```

As shown above, the return statement allows the function to pass values back to the caller. We can assign the value returned by the function call to another variable for later use. In the below code, the return statement ships the value of B and this value is assigned to C.

```
def num_double(A):
    B = 2*A
    print("The double value is: %d" % B)
    return B
C = num_double(20) # calling the function and passing a
required argument.
print('Value of C is:', C
```

```
The double value is: 40
Value of C is: 40
```

Notice that in the below code, B is a local variable to the num_double function. That means its scope lies within the function. While we can print B inside the function, we will not be able to access it from outside the function. In the code below, when we try to print B from outside the function definition, Python will raise NameError, as B does not exist outside.

```python
def num_double(A):
    B = 2*A
    print('The double value is: %d' %B)
    return B
num_double(20) # call the function and pass a required
argument.
print(B)
```

```
The double value is 40
--------------------------------------------------------------
--------------
NameError                                 Traceback (most
recent call last)
<ipython-input-5-7eb78d4fe8ca> in <module>()
      7
      8 num_double(20) # call the function and pass a
required argument.
----> 9 print B
NameError: name 'B' is not defined
```

Positional Arguments

The arguments that are passed to a function call based on their position in the function definition are called positional arguments. In the below example, we show that the function can take multiple inputs. To the add_two function, we pass arguments A and B. When we make a call to the function, we pass values 3 and 10. Python will assign 3 to A since A is the first argument and 10 to B.

```python
# A function can take multiple inputs
def add_two(A, B):
    C = A + B
    print('The value of A is: %d' %A)
    print('The value of B is: %d' %B)
    return C
print(add_two(3, 10)) # calling the function and passing two required
# arguments.
# 3 will be assigned to A and
# 10 will be assigned to B. So, these are called
positional arguments.
```

```
The value of A is: 3
The value of B is: 10
13
```

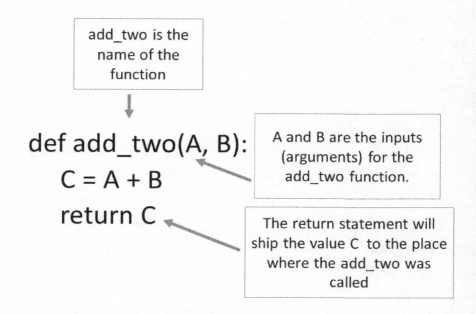

If we want to return more than one value, then we can put all of them in the return statement separated by comma. Since return statement can return only one value, Python will pack them and return them as a tuple.

```python
def add_two(A, B):
    C = A + B
    print('The value of A is: %d' %A)
    print('The value of B is: %d' %B)
    return C, A, B # these multiple values will be
returned as a tuple
print(add_two(10, 3))
```

```
The value of A is: 10
The value of B is: 3
(13, 10, 3)
```

In the below code, we are explicitly returning the values of C, A and B as a tuple instead of the implicit tuple conversion in the previous example.

```python
def add_two(A, B):
    C = A + B
    print('The value of A is: %d' %A)
    print('The value of B is: %d' %B)
    return (C, A, B) # returning multiple values as a tuple
print(add_two(10, 3))
```

```
The value of A is: 10
The value of B is: 3
(13, 10, 3)
```

Learning Activity 1: Define a function called pword that takes a string and prints one character at a time from the string.

Learning Activity 2: Define a function that converts Fahrenheit into Celsius. The formula is C = (F - 32)*(5.0/9). Get the F from the user.

Default Values

Default values for the arguments are specified at the time of function definition. Defaults values are supplied to ensure that when a value for one or more arguments is not supplied, Python will use the default value(s). Thus, it allows passing fewer arguments when a call to the function is made.

In the below code, we are assigning a default value of 11 to B. When we make a function call, we are only passing one value. Python will assign this value to A and use the default value B=11 to do the calculation inside the function.

```python
# Specifying default values
def add_two(A, B=11):
    C = A + B
    print('The value of A is: %d' %A)
    print('The value of B is: %d' %B)
    return C
print(add_two(10))
```

```
The value of A is: 10
The value of B is: 11
21
```

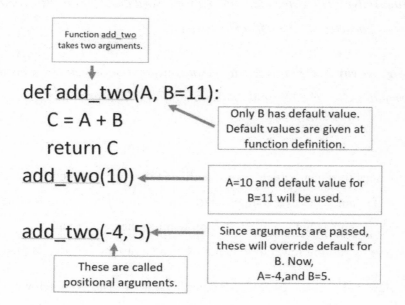

We can also choose to supply the value for both A and B. Below, in the function call we are passing two values, -4 and 5. Due to the position, A will be assigned -4 and 5 will overwrite the default value of B. The new value of B=5, will be used for computation and hence the output is 1.

```
print(add_two(-4, 5))
# here the B is assigned a value of 5 which
# overrides the default value
```

1

By using default values, we created two different function calls with a single function definition. In the first version, we supplied one value and in the second version, we supplied two values, thus overloading the meaning of the function.

In the code below, we have two default values for the arguments A and B so when we make a function call, we can choose not to pass any or all arguments and use default value for missing arguments inside the function.

```
def add_two(A=10, B=11):
    C = A + B
    print('The value of A is: %d' %A)
    print('The value of B is: %d' %B)
```

185

```
    return C
print(add_two())
```

```
The value of A is: 10
The value of B is: 11
21
```

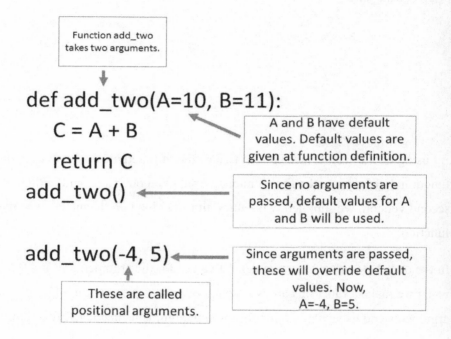

Keyword Based Arguments

Previously, we discussed arguments supplied to a function based on its position a.k.a. positional arguments. For a function with many arguments, it may be cumbersome to match the position of the argument with the correct value. To overcome this, Python provides keyword-based arguments, where at function call, the argument is specified by providing the variable name and then passing the value.

Below we assign default values for both A and B in the function definition. In the function call we are assigning new values for both A and B, while clearly indicating that the value -4 is for variable A while 5 is the value for variable B. The advantage is that we do not have to worry about the order in which we supply the arguments and their values. Also, the label ensures code readability. This requires extra keystrokes for typing the name of the variables but the code readability is sometimes worth the trouble, especially for functions with large number of inputs or complex natured inputs.

In this example the new values A=-4 and B=5 will overwrite the default values A=10 and B=11.

```python
def add_two(A=10, B=11):
    C = A + B
    print('The value of A is: %d' %A)
    print('The value of B is: %d' %B)
    return C
print(add_two(A=-4, B=5)) # two keyword-based arguments
```

```
The value of A is: -4
The value of B is: 5
1
```

Since values in keyword-based arguments are assigned based on the argument name, the order of arguments can be changed and Python will assign the value to the arguments correctly. Notice, below we are passing B=5 and A=-4 in that order, even though in the function definition, the order is A followed by B. Python will correctly assign A=-4 and B=5.

```
print(add_two(B=5, A=-4))
# Unlike positional arguments, order is not important
for keyword arguments.
```

```
The value of A is: -4
The value of B is: 5
1
```

Function add_two takes two arguments

↓

def add_two(A=10, B=11): ← A and B have default values.

C = A + B

return C

add_two(B=5, A=-4) ← With keyword based arguments, you can pass arguments in any order. **Order is not important.**

↑

These are called keyword based arguments, which are given at function call.

Positional arguments and keyword-based arguments can be combined in the same function call. The rule in such cases is that keyword-based arguments would come to the right of all the positional arguments. Below, in the call to the function we say 10, B=5, Python will match the value in the call to the first value in the function definition, so A will be 10 and B will be 5.

```
print(add_two(10, B=5)) # if you assign a value for a
keyword argument
# then other arguments to its right should also be
assigned values.
```

```
The value of A is: 10
The value of B is: 5
15
```

Below, we are passing the keyword-based argument before positional. This is incorrect, as positional arguments should never be passed after keyword-based arguments. When we try to execute this code, Python will raise a SyntaxError exception with a clear error message, "non-keyword arg after keyword arg."

```
print(add_two(A=10, 5)) # This will generate a Syntax
error
```

```
  File "<ipython-input-16-495757ba7941>", line 1
    print add_two(A=10, 5) # This will generate a Syntax
error

SyntaxError: positional argument follows keyword
argument
```

Function Objects

In Python, everything is a first-class object
[http://www.diveintopython.net/getting_to_know_python/everything_is_an_object.html]. This implies, that functions are also objects (i.e.,) a function thus has attributes and methods. Since function is an object, it can be passed to other functions as arguments. We will use this functionality later in decorators.

When we print the type of a function using type(add_two), Python will return that add_two is a function. Notice that there is no parenthesis after add_two.

If we print add_two, it will give details of the function object. It clearly specifies that add_two is a function object and has an id.

The dir() function clearly shows that the function has attributes such as __doc__ and methods such as __gt__ etc., indicating that the function is an object. We will learn about these methods later in object-oriented programming.

```
print(type(add_two))
print(add_two)
print(dir(add_two))
```

```
<class 'function'>

<function add_two at 0x116554598>

['__annotations__', '__call__', '__class__',
'__closure__', '__code__', '__defaults__',
'__delattr__', '__dict__', '__dir__', '__doc__',
```

```
'__eq__', '__format__', '__ge__', '__get__',
'__getattribute__', '__globals__', '__gt__', '__hash__',
'__init__', '__kwdefaults__', '__le__', '__lt__',
'__module__', '__name__', '__ne__', '__new__',
'__qualname__', '__reduce__', '__reduce_ex__',
'__repr__', '__setattr__', '__sizeof__', '__str__',
'__subclasshook__']
```

Python**: Call-by-object and call-by-object-reference

So far, we discussed functions that took integers which are immutable object as arguments. We can also pass mutable objects such as list, dictionary etc. However, passing the mutable values to a function may have an effect on the passed value itself based on two factors.

1. The mutability of the data and

2. The type of mutation on the data.

When we call an argument, we have to be mindful whether it is a call-by-object or a call-by-object-reference. Call-by-object-reference means that the arguments passed by the caller and the arguments in the callee are referring to the same object. So, depending on whether the object is mutable (list, dictionary) or immutable (integer, string, float, tuple), any changes to the object in the function will affect the caller argument as well. Call-by-object means that the argument passed by the caller is a copy of the object, so any changes to the copy of the object will not affect the caller argument.

In the below example, the caller is passing B, an integer object which is immutable. When Python goes to the function definition, A will be set to 2.

Since integers are immutable, any changes to A will not affect B. When we print A and B and notice that A = 4 while B which is outside the function definition remains at 2.

```
def my_fun(A):# A is an int
    A = A*2
    print("A = ", A)
    return A
B = 2
my_fun(B) # caller and we are passing 2, which is an
          #integer and immutable.
          # So, changes to A will not affect B
print("B = ", B)
```

```
A = 4
B = 2
```

In the below example, B is a tuple which is immutable. Even though B is passed to the function my_fun, any change to A within the function will not affect the variable B as shown in the output.

```
def my_fun(A):
    A = (4, 5, 6,)
    print("A = ", A)
    return A
B = (1,2,3)
```

192

```
my_fun(B)
print("B = ", B)
```

```
A = (4, 5, 6)
B = (1, 2, 3)
```

Let's look at an example with a mutable object such as list. In the below example, we are passing B, which is a list. Inside the function, we are assigning a new value to A within the function. So, any changes to A do not affect B.

```
def my_fun(A):
    A = [4,5,6] # we are giving a new value to A
    A.extend([-14])
    print("A = ", A)
    return A


B = [1,2,3]
my_fun(B)
print("B = ", B)
```

```
A = [4, 5, 6, -14]
B = [1, 2, 3]
```

Finally, we will look at an example where we pass a mutable object and mutate few elements in that object. In the example below, we pass a list as an input to the function. We mutate the list A within the function by appending

193

a value 4 and popping the element at the 0th index. Notice that the changes made to A affected B. This is because, B was passed as a call-by-object-reference.

```python
def my_fun(A):
    A.append(4)
    print("A = ", A)
    A.pop(0)
    print("A = ", A)
    return A
B = [1,2,3]
my_fun(B)
print("B = ", B)
```

```
A = [1, 2, 3, 4]
A = [2, 3, 4]
B = [2, 3, 4]
```

NOTE: The last example experienced a side-effect, a process that results in the change the values outside the function due to operations inside the function. This can be avoided by

1. Passing immutable values as in case 1 and 2.

2. Passing mutable values but not mutating them as in case 3.

3. Creating a deep copy of the mutable object prior to mutating as shown in the example below. This option would be costly on memory depending on the size of the object.

In this example, we are making a shallow copy of the mutable object within the function definition by using A[:] and assigning it to A. Now with this change, A is pointing to a new object in memory and hence any changes to A will not affect B and vice-versa as long as the list is not a list of list.

```python
from copy import deepcopy
def my_fun(A):
    A = deepcopy(A) # Creating a deep copy to solve the
    # problem of call by reference
    A.extend([4])
    print("A = ", A)
    return A


B = [1,2,3]
my_fun(B)
print("B = ", B)


A = [1, 2, 3, 4]
B = [1, 2, 3]
```

Let us consider another example with the list of lists and we will use the my_fun defined above. Below, C is a list of lists. We make a call to my_fun and pass C. Then in C, we change the second element in the first list. Notice that the first list in C has been updated but this change didn't affect A.

```python
C = [[2, 3], [4, 5]]
my_fun(C)
```

```
C[0][1] = 10
print("C = ", C)
```

```
A =  [[2, 3], [4, 5], 4]
C =  [[2, 10], [4, 5]]
```

Learning Activity 3: Create a function that takes list1 = [-11, -8, 4, 15, 20] and returns a list of even numbers from list1.

Learning Activity 4: Create a function called squared which takes mylist=[-6, -3, 2, 5, 8] and returns another list where the elements are square of mylist. Also write another function that takes mylist and returns a dictionary where the key is the input and the value is the square of the input. Use list comprehension and dictionary comprehension.

Python**: *args and **kwargs

So far, we have seen how to pass fixed number of inputs to a function. There might be situations, when we might need to send variable number of arguments. For such cases, use args and kwargs.

The words args and kwargs are not keywords, we could replace them with any other names. However, * and ** are mandatory syntax to indicate args and kwargs respectively. If we put one star, * in front of the argument name, then the argument is available as a tuple inside the function. If we put two stars, ** in front of the argument name, then the argument is available as a dictionary inside the function. The following examples will clearly demonstrate the use of *args and **kwargs.

196

Below we are defining a function each_word() that take *args as an argument. Inside the function, we print the tuple args and also the type(args). Then we iterate through the tuple and print one item at a time. We then call each_word() and supply one string, 'Summer'.

```
# inside the function, args is of type tuple.
def each_word(*args):
    print(args, type(args))
    for i in args:
        print(i)
each_word('Summer')
```

```
('Summer',) <class 'tuple'>
Summer
```

In the example below, we are calling the same function but instead of passing one value, we are passing two values.

```
each_word('Summer', 'Solistice')
```

```
('Summer', 'Solistice') <type 'tuple'>
Summer
Solistice
```

Thus, we overloaded the definition of the each_word() function by using *args by calling this function with zero or more arguments.

*kwargs creates a variable length dictionary, Below, we define a function called unlimited() and pass **kwargs. Inside the function, we print kwargs and the type(kwargs). Finally, we make a call to unlimited() function and pass one key-value pair. The name of the argument, 'e' is the key in the dictionary while the argument value is the corresponding value in the dictionary.

We then make another call to unlimited() and pass two key-value pairs. In the output notice that the type(kwargs) will return dict for both cases.

```
def unlimited(**kwargs):
    print(kwargs, type(kwargs))


unlimited(e='Earhart')
unlimited(e='Earhart', g='Lindbergh')
```

```
{'e': 'Earhart'} <type 'dict'>
{'e': 'Earhart', 'g': 'Lindbergh'} <type 'dict'>
```

Thus, we overloaded the definition of the unlimited() function by using **kwargs by calling this function with zero or more arguments.

The difference between the *args and **kwargs example is in the function call. In the case of *args, we list all the arguments. However, in the case of **kwargs, we list arguments as argument name = argument value. The argument name is the key in the dictionary while the argument value is the value in the dictionary. The argument name is stored as a string in the dictionary while the value retains the data type of the argument value.

*Learning Activity 5: Define a function that takes five integer values using *args and returns the sum of all the values in that args tuple.*

*Learning Activity 6: Define a function that takes a dictionary as **kwargs and prints each key and value as a tuple.*

Lambda functions

Lambda functions provide an easy and quick way to create functions. They are particularly useful for creating small functions that need to be used only once. The main advantage of lambda functions is that they are one liner.

To understand lambda functions, we begin with a regular function definition. In the function below, the input value A is squared and returned. To test the function, we supply an input of 4 and notice that the output value 16, the square of 4.

```
def square(A):
    return(A**2)
print(square(4))
```

16

The above function can be rewritten using lambda function as follows. The lambda function begins with the lambda keyword. The item(s) to the left of the ':' (colon) are the input to the lambda function and the item to the right of the colon are the value returned by the lambda function. The lambda function is then saved to the variable lambda_sq. We can now use the lambda_sq function in a manner similar to a function. We will test the function by passing an input of 4 and obtaining an output value 16, the square of 4.

```
lambda_sq = lambda x:x**2
print(lambda_sq(4))
```

```
16
```

If we print the type of the lambda function, you will notice that it indicates that it is type of function. Hence it can be used as a replacement for functions in appropriate places.

```
print(type(lambda_sq)
```

```
<class 'function'>
```

Due to the pithiness of the lambda function, it is generally used for creating small functions. For larger functions, it is still preferable to use a regular function.

Python**: Filter, map and reduce

We previously discussed list comprehension as a means to use the values in a list and create new ones. In this section, we will discuss a new technique for mutating lists and other iterable objects using filter, map and reduce.

A **filter** operation works like a water filter. It retains only the needed elements and removes all others. The programmer has to define the criteria for elements that are desirable using a regular or lambda function. Filter needs a function that returns True or False. Each element in the iterable (list, iterator etc.) is passed to the function. If the function returns a True, then that element is placed in the output iterable object. If the function returns a False, then the element is not placed in the output iterable object.

In the example below, we are going to filter all odd numbers from the iterable object returned by range function. The output of the range function is stored into the variable allnums. A function is_odd_only is defined with one input argument. The function checks if the input is odd or even using the modulo operator and returns True if the input is odd and False if input is even.

The filter function passes every element in the iterator, allnums and passes it to the is_odd_only function. The odd numbered elements will be placed in the output iterator and the even numbered elements are discarded. The first print statement clearly indicates that the output of the filter function is an iterable object. Finally, the print function call in the for-loop clearly demonstrates that the output only contains odd numbers.

```
def is_odd_only(x):
    return x % 2 != 0


allnums = range(2,10)
oddnums = filter(is_odd_only, allnums)
print(allnums, oddnums)
```

201

```
for nums in oddnums:
    print(nums)
```

```
range(2, 10) <filter object at 0x1047b2f28>
3
5
7
9
```

The function that we are passing to the filter function can replaced with a lambda function as in the example below. The code below also outputs an iterable object of odd numbers. Instead of defining a function is_odd_only, we define a lambda function inside the filter function. The lambda function takes x as argument and returns True if x is odd and False if x is even. The lambda function has made the code more succinct.

```
allnums = range(2,10)
oddnums = filter(lambda x:x%2!=0, allnums)
for nums in oddnums:
    print(nums)
```

```
3
5
7
9
```

The important things to remember are:

1. Filter needs a function that returns a boolean.

2. If the input iterable object has n-items, then the output will have n or fewer than n-items.

A map operation works like a map function in set theory that you would have learnt in high school. The map operation in mathematics, defines a one-to-one relationship between one set of values and another. In Python, the map operation takes an iterable object and creates another iterable object. For every element in the input iterable object, there will be a corresponding element in the output iterable object.

The programmer has to define the criteria for element mapping using a Python function. This function may return any Python data type. Each element in the iterable (list, iterator etc.) is passed to the function. The value returned by the function is stored in the output iterable object.

In the example below, we are going to map all numbers in the range 1 to 5 to another iterable object that will be the squares of the elements from the input iterable object. A function squared is defined with one input argument. The function returns the square of the input.

The map function takes the iterable object and passes it to the function. The squares of the individual element will appear in the output iterable object. The print function call in the for-loop clearly demonstrates that the output contains squares of the input.

The important things to remember are:

1. map needs a function that returns any Python data type.

2. If the input iterable object has n-items, then the output will have n-items.

```
def squared(x):
    return x*x

squares = map(squared, range(1, 5))
for items in squares:
    print(items)
```

```
1
4
9
16
```

We can also replace the squared function with a lambda function. In the example below, the lambda function takes the input x and returns the square of the input. The lambda function code is more succinct.

```
squares = map(lambda x:x*x, range(1, 5))
for items in squares:
    print(items)
```

```
1
4
9
16
```

The map function can also take more than one input iterable object. In the example below, we supply 3 iterable objects, mla, mlb and mlc and find the element by element sum of the three iterable objects. The add function takes three inputs and returns the sum of the three numbers. In the first iteration, the first value from the three iterable objects are passed to the function. The sum is then stored in the output iterable object. This process is repeated for each element until all the elements are exhausted.

```python
mla = [1, 2, 3]
mlb = [4, 5, 6]
mlc = [7, 8, 9]
def add(mla1, mlb1, mlc1):
    return mla1+mlb1+mlc1
sum_map = map(add, mla, mlb, mlc)
for s in sum_map:
    print(s)
```

```
12
15
18
```

If the iterable objects are of different length, you will receive a TypeError exception.

A reduce operation takes an iterable object and reduces it to one value. The programmer has to define the criteria for the reduction using a Python function. Each element in the iterable (list, iterator etc.) is passed to the function.

In the example below, we perform summation of all the numbers in the list, listnum. A running sum is maintained. When the first element is supplied to the reduce function, its value is added to the running sum value. This operation is repeated for each element in the iterable.

In the code below, the reduce function takes an iterator stored in listnum and passes it to the lambda function. The lambda function takes two inputs x and y and reduces it to one value which is a sum of x and y. In the first iteration, reduce will add the first two elements of listnum namely 1 and 3 and creates a running sum 4. In the next iteration, the value 6 will be added to the running sum to produce a new value for the running sum of 10. This process is repeated until all elements in listnum have been evaluated.

```
from functools import reduce

listnum = [1, 3, 6, 9]
print(reduce(lambda x, y: x+y, listnum))
```

19

The important things to remember are:

1. Reduce takes a function and an iterable.

2. Regardless of number of items in the iterable, the result will be only one item.

Python**: None as default values for functions

We previously discussed passing default arguments to functions. We also discussed the call-by-object and call-by-object-reference. In this section, we will combine the two concepts and understand why in some cases, it is preferable to use None as the default argument.

A default value can be specified to arguments in a function as shown in example below.

```python
def process_int(someint = 0):
    return someint*10
print(process_int())
print(process_int(2))
```

```
0
20
```

The function process_int takes an argument someint. If the value of the argument is not specified at run-time, a value of 0 is used by default. Hence in the first call to process_int, when no argument is supplied, someint is 0 and the function returns 0. In the second call, the value of someint is 2 and hence the function returns 20.

An int is an immutable data type in Python and we previously learnt that its value is passed by call-by-object.

If we apply default value of argument to mutable type such as a list or dictionary, an interesting behavior is observed as shown in example below.

```
def appendval_empty(alist = []):
    alist.append(4)
    return(alist)

print(appendval_empty())
print(appendval_empty())
print(appendval_empty([1, 2, 3]))
```

```
[4]
[4, 4]
[1, 2, 3, 4]
```

The "appendval_empty" function, has one argument namely a list called "alist". If the value of the argument is not specified at run-time, a value of [ ], an empty list is assumed. Hence, in the first function call when the value of alist is not specified, the value of alist is assumed to be [ ]. A value of 4 is appended to this empty list and the first print function confirms our understanding.

In the second call to the "appendval_empty" function, no argument is supplied. Hence, we may assume that the value of alist = [ ]. However, the output indicates that the value of the input alist = [4] and the function in turn appends another 4 to this list. This results in printing of a list with two values instead of the expected one value. This could lead to subtle and hard to debug defects in the code.

This is due to the fact, that in Python, default values are only set for the first function call for mutable types. All subsequent call will not set the default value.

In the third call, since the value of argument is specified, alist will be set to that value and the previous value will be overwritten which is an expected behavior.

One way we could overcome this problem, is by specifying an immutable default value to the argument, "alist". This immutable value could be 0 (say). However, assigning an int value to a list results in poor readability. A better option is to set it to None, an immutable type that stands for nothing.

```
def appendval_none(alist = None):
    if alist is None:
        alist = []
    alist.append(4)
    return(alist)
print(appendval_none())
print(appendval_none())
print(appendval_none([1, 2, 3]))
```

```
[4]
[4]
[1, 2, 3, 4]
```

However, setting the default value of alist to None, still requires resetting the value to an empty list before any list-based operation can be performed.

Hence in the function appendval_none above, in the first 2 lines of the function definition, we check if alist is None. This will be true only if the value was not specified. In such case, the value of alist is reset to an empty list. Now, new elements can be appended to the list.

In the first and the second call to the appendval_none function, the value of alist is set to [ ]. Subsequently, the value 4 is appended to the list. Hence, the output is predictably correct.

Python**: Nested functions and closures

A function defined inside another function is called a nested function. In such cases, the scope of the inner function is limited to the outer function.

In the example below, we define an "outer" function which in turn has a function called "squared" defined inside. The inner function takes an input and returns a square of that value. The outer function then calls the squared function and supplies a value stored in x and in turn returns the squared value. A call to the "outer" function returns the squared value which is stored in the variable "sq".

```
def outer(x):
    def squared(y):
        return y**2
    return squared(x)
sq = outer(5)
print(sq)
```

25

In the above example, the variable between the inner and outer function was not shared. Any input to be supplied to the inner squared function was explicitly passed by the outer function. **However, Python allows for sharing variables in the outer function scope in to the inner function without explicitly passing them as function arguments.**

In the next example, the outer function takes an input "x". An inner function called "multiple" is defined inside the outer function. It is important to notice that the inner function has access to the variable "x" whose scope is in the outer function. The outer function returns the value from the call to the inner multiple function.

```
def outer(x):
    def multiple(y):
        # Notice that the x whose scope is in the outer function
        # is accessible in the multiple function
        return x*y
    return multiple(3) # The input value to the multiple function call is hardcoded

o = outer(5)
print(o)
```

15

One of the problems with the existing outer function is the fact that the input value to the inner function call is hardcoded making the outer function less useful. We can convert this in to a more generic function by returning the inner function object instead of returning the call to the inner function as shown below.

The code below is same as the one above except for the return statement in the outer function. In this case, we return the function object 'multiple' instead of calling the function multiple and returning the output of the function call.

When the "outer" function is called with a value of 5, it returns the function object corresponding to the inner function multiple. The print function call clearly indicates that "o" is a function object. To call the function associated with the function object, "o", we pass a value 3 to the function. This is a more generic version of the previous example. The inner function is also referred as a closure.

The properties of a closure are:

1. It wraps one function inside another.

2. The scope of the variable is retained even if the program flow does not demonstrate it.

3. It returns a function object.

```python
def outer(x):
    def multiple(y):
        # Notice that the x whose scope is in the outer function
        # is accessible in the inner function
        return x*y
```

```
    return multiple # The code changed to return inner
function object


o = outer(5)
print(o)
print(o(3))
```

```
<function multiple at 0x0000000004521C88>
15
```

Python**: Decorators

The use of closure leads to another important feature of Python namely decorators, which is a function that takes another function as input and extends the behavior of the latter without explicitly modifying the code of the latter.

We will define an outer function call check_age. This function takes a function object as an argument. Inside the check_age function, an inner function called wrapper is defined. This function takes an int age as input. The wrapper function as it is a closure has access to the variables in the outer function including the variable func, which will be defined soon. A call is made to the as yet undefined function and the value returned by that call is compared with 18. If the returned value is greater than 18, True is returned, else False is returned. The outer function 'check_age' returns the function object 'wrapper'. We also define another function called process_data that returns an integer age.

The check_age function is called with the function object "process_data" as the input. The statement check_age(process_data) returns a function object

corresponding to the function wrapper. The call
"check_age(process_data)(23)" with input of 23 will be passed to the
wrapper function.

In essence, we have modified the behavior of the "process_data" function by
wrapping it around another function "check_age". Normally, the
"process_data" function returns an integer. However, the wrapped function
checks if that integer is greater than 18 and returns True if it is and False if it
is not. We can also refer to this process as decorating the function
"process_data" with the function "check_age" and hence the name decorator.

```
def check_age(func):
    def wrapper(age):
        if func(age) > 18:
            return True
        else:
            return False
    return wrapper

def process_data(age):
    return age

print(check_age(process_data)(23)
```

```
True
```

The syntax above for the call to the wrapper can be further improved by
using the notation below. The example below has the same function

definition for "check_age" as above. The difference is in the "process_data" function definition and also its call. The "process_data" function is decorated with the "check_age" function using the @.

The call to "process_data" function is also simplified, as we no longer have to refer to the "check_age" function in the call. When "process_data" is called, Python will automatically wrap that call with a call to the "check_age" function.

```python
def check_age(func):
    def wrapper(age):
        if func(age) > 18:
            return True
        else:
            return False
    return wrapper

@check_age # Added a decorator
def process_data(age):
    return age


print(process_data(12))
```

```
False
```

Even though the two techniques are equivalent, there are some advantage to using the latter compared to the former.

1. The programmer using the latter does not have to specify the decorator function. This simplifies the syntax and makes the code readable.

2. The programmer using the latter does not have to concern themselves with the details of the decorators that they need to call. They only have to concern themselves with the function that they are interested and that function in turn calls the decorator(s).

We will discuss a more realistic example of a decorator by creating one that determines the time to execute a function. Below, we want to compute the time taken to compute the cube of million values using the function pow3, which is decorated by the decorator named timer. The timer takes a function object as an input, in this case, pow3. The wrapper function takes an argument, in this case, 1000000. In the wrapper function, we check the clock time and store the value in t1. Then result=f(a) makes a call to the function pow3(1000000) which computes the cube of 1000000 using list comprehension. Then we check the time again and store the value in t2. We print the time taken as a difference of t2-t1. The wrapper function returns result pow3(1000000) and the timer function returns the wrapper function object. Since pow3 is decorated using @timer, a call to pow3 will result in execution of pow3 and also printing of the time to run the function call. If pow3 was not decorated by the timer function, then a call to pow3(1000000) will be made but the time to execute pow3 will not be printed.

```
import time
def timer(f):
    def wrapper(a):
        t1 = time.clock()
```

```
        result = f(a)
        t2 = time.clock()
        print("The time to run the function is %f
seconds" %(t2-t1))
        return result
    return wrapper
@timer
def pow3(n):
    a = [i*i*i for i in range(n)]
pow3(10000000)
```

```
The time to run the function is 1.596752 seconds
```

Python**: Reduce the number of function calls

Functions are convenient mechanism for storing instruction that are
repeatedly called from different portions of the code. It is recommended that
programmers use functions to make the code modular. However, every
function call has a performance penalty. If a function is called a few times,
the cost is small. However, if the function is called many times, say 1 million
times, then the cost will add up and show up as slow run time. The following
example illustrates the effect of function calls on computational time.

We will import the time module, so that we can measure the time to perform
an operation. If the code is run in Python 2+, we will create a list of 1 million
numbers and if we run the code in Python 3+, we will iterator that can
generate 1 million numbers on demand.

In the first method, we will use list comprehension to create a list with million items where each item is the cube of the items in 'nums'. In a particular run, the time taken to complete this list comprehension was 0.153 seconds. This is the fastest method among all the four methods.

In the second method, we define a function, 'cu_fn' which returns the cube of a given number. The function is called from inside the list comprehension. In a particular run, the time taken to complete this list comprehension was 0.191 seconds.

In the third method, we define a lambda function that returns the cube of a given number. This lambda function is assigned a name, 'lambda_func'. In a particular run, the time taken to complete this list comprehension was 0.196 seconds.

In the fourth method, we define a lambda function that returns the cube of a given number. However, unlike the third method, in this method the lambda function is anonymous. In a particular run, the time taken to complete this list comprehension was 1.303 seconds, which is approximately 4 times slower than method 3.

Observations

In method 2, a million-function call is being made. For every such calls, Python has to perform extra operations such as function initialization that are not needed if using method 1. Hence method 2 is slow.

In method 3, we are defining a lambda function and have given it a name. This is equivalent to method 2, where we defined a regular function. Thus, the time taken for method 2 and 3 are approximately the same. In method 2 and 3, there is only one copy of the function that is being created.

218

In method 4, the lambda function is defined inside the list comprehension. Thus, the lambda function needs to be created and destroyed a million times while in method 3, it needs to be created only once. Hence it is inefficient to create lambda function inside a comprehension or a loop. The bottom line is that one needs to reduce the number of function calls if performance is paramount and hence choose the appropriate approach.

```
import time
nums = range(1000000)

# METHOD 1
t0 = time.time()
sq_lc = [x*x*x for x in nums]
print('list comprehension {0}'.format(time.time()-t0))


# METHOD 2
def cu_fn(x):
    return x*x*x
t1 = time.time()
sq_fn = [cu_fn(x) for x in nums]
print('function with list comprehension
{0}'.format(time.time()-t1))


# METHOD 3
t2 = time.time()
lamda_func = lambda x:x*x*x
sq_lambda = [lamda_func(x) for x in nums]
```

```
print('non-anonymous lambda with list comprehension
{0}'.format(time.time()-t2))

# METHOD 4
t3 = time.time()
sq_lambda = [lambda x:x*x*x for x in nums]
print('anonymous lambda with list comprehension
{0}'.format(time.time()-t3))
```

```
list comprehension 0.1532330513
function with list comprehension 0.190538883209
non-anonymous lambda with list comprehension
0.196748971939
anonymous lambda with list comprehension 1.30340409279
```

Introduction

In object-oriented programming, a class is an extensible program-code-template for creating objects, providing initial values for state (member variables) and implementations of behavior (member functions or methods) according to Wikipedia
[https://en.wikipedia.org/wiki/Class_(computer_programming)].

In short, a class is an encapsulation of methods (functions) and data. It contains the definition of the functionality in the methods and the variables that the method will manipulate.

To keep syntax simple, unlike other languages, Python expects programmers to only implement functionality in a class that they need. This significantly reduces the boiler-plate code.

The class is a definition. An instance of class also called object needs to be created in order to use the functionality defined in the class. This process is referred to as instantiation. Unlike C++, programmers do not have to explicitly destroy the objects. The garbage collector and reference counter will delete the objects that are not referenced by any variable.

Python has support for many of the features of object-oriented programming systems (OOPS) such as single and multiple inheritance, method overloading, method overriding, operator overloading, abstract classes etc.

Since OOPS in Python has many important features that cannot be covered in a single chapter, we will be discussing all these features over many chapters. However, in this chapter, we will focus our attention to basic definition and create a single class.

Syntax

A Python class is defined with the "class" keyword which is followed by the name of the class. The convention for naming classes requires use of Pascal Case (i.e.,) first letter of words in the name must be capitalized. A function on the other hand is recommended to use all lowercase characters with words separated by _ (underscore). This convention is followed to distinguish between a function call and a class instantiation. All the methods and variables are placed in the code block under the class name.

In the code below, we define a class called Student that inherits from Python object (which we will discuss later). The Student class has __init__ (double underscore before and double underscore after init), tuition and payment methods. Note that double underscore is also known as dunder. All methods in the class (except for class methods and static methods that we will discuss later) should have self as the first argument. We will later use the self to assign values to instance variables. The use of name self is a convention. It can be replaced with a different name. However, for the sake of readability, stick to the convention.

The __init__ method is called a magic method. A regular method is called explicitly whereas magic methods are called when a specific condition is met. For example, __init__ method is called when the object is created. We do not have to invoke it explicitly. We will learn more about magic methods in a later chapter.

We can define a class without __init__ method. However, when it is defined, __init__ method is recommended to be the first method in the class. In the below example, __init__ method takes three arguments. The first argument is self, the second argument is name and the third argument is ssn.

In __init__ method, we assign the value from name to self.name and also assign the value from ssn to self.ssn. These two variables self.name and self.ssn are called instance variables as their values are for a specific instance or object. All methods in that instance will have access to the instance variable. If this mapping is not done with self (i.e.,) instance variable was not created, then the argument of the method will only be available to that particular method (i.e., local to that method) and not to other methods in the class. We assign the instance variable balance to 0.0, which is consistent with the fact that the student balance may start with zero in real life.

The tuition and payment are called bound methods as they are bound (i.e., called with) to an instance of the Student class. The tuition method, takes self and amount as arguments. Since the amount is only used locally within the tuition method, we do not assign it to an instance variable. This amount is added to the self.balance to indicate how much the student has to pay. The statement self.balance += amount is short for self.balance = self.balance + amount.

The payment method takes self and amount as arguments. If the student is paying a certain amount, then that amount has to be deducted from the self.balance. The statement self.balance -= amount is short for self.balance = self.balance - amount.

This completes the explanation for the definition of a class. However, a class with only definition that is not instantiated does not serve any purpose. The explanation about what comes after the class definition is as follows:

- In line b = Student("Leo", 123456789), we create the first instance of the Student class (a.k.a object) and call it b. Since we have name and ssn as arguments in the __init__ method, so when we create an instance of the class, we have to pass values of name and ssn. As soon as an instance is created by Python, the __init__ method will assign the values "Leo" to name and 123456789 to ssn. Hence self.name = "Leo" and self.ssn = 123456789 for that instance.

- In line print(b.tuition(2000)), we are calling the tuition method and passing the amount 2000. In the tuition method, the amount = 2000 and so self.balance will be updated to 0 + 2000 = 2000 for that instance.

- In line print(b.payment(500)), we are calling the payment method and passing the amount 500. Since student Leo has paid 500, amount = 500 should be deducted from self.balance. The self.balance = 2000 - 500 = 1500.

- In the line print("Student name %s and balance %0.2f "%(b.name, b.balance)), we have a formatted print statement where we print b.name and b.balance. Note that when we access arguments outside the class definition, we don't have to specify b.self.balance, we can just say b.balance.

```
'''

Variables such as self.name, self.balance and self.ssn
are usable by more than one method. Their values are
also specific to that instance. '''
class Student:
```

```python
    '''The attributes for this class are name, ssn and
balance'''

    # __init__ is a magic method
    def __init__(self, name, ssn):
        self.name = name
        self.ssn = ssn
        self.balance = 0.0

    # you must explicitly list self as the first
argument for each method
    # including in __init__ method
    # tuition is a method
    def tuition(self, amount):
        self.balance +=amount
        return self.balance

    # payment is a method
    def payment(self, amount):
        self.balance -=amount
        return self.balance

# creating an instance of the class named Student
b = Student("Leo", 123456789)
print(b.tuition(2000)) # calling tuition method and
passing a value
print(b.payment(500)) # calling payment method and
passing a value
```

```
print("Student name %s and balance %0.2f " %(b.name,
b.balance))
```

2000.0

1500.0

Student name Leo and balance 1500.00

Notice that unlike the tuition and payment method, the __init__ method was not explicitly called. However, we learnt that it was called when the instance was created. It is important to remember that magic methods do not have to be called explicitly. However, their calls are deterministic. Only a specific action will trigger them. The plumbing for these methods is defined by Python.

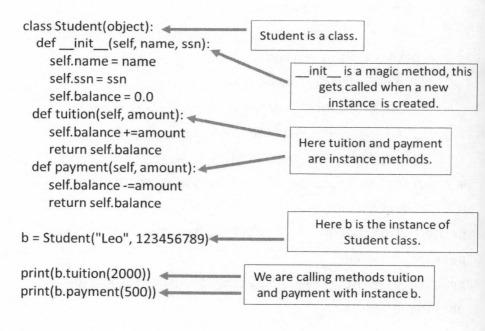

226

Method Overloading

Method overloading is process of assigning more than one behavior to a particular method. We discussed it in the chapter on functions where we defined functions with default arguments. If the function takes n arguments while in the function call we supply fewer than n arguments, then the function will assume default values for the missing arguments. This allows calling the function with variable number of arguments and hence produce different behavior for the same function definition. Since a method in a class is a function, we can overload them as well. In the below code, we will overload the __init__ method. The discussion however is applicable to any method.

Unlike the previous example, we will pass a fourth argument called balance to the __init__ method and set its default value to None. In the __init__ method, we have an if statement that checks if balance is None and if this condition returns True then the balance is set to 0.0. If the if-statement returns False, the value in the balance is not modified. The tuition and payment method are same as the previous example.

An instance of this class can be created by passing either the 2 values or 3 values. In the former the value of name and ssn are passed while in the latter, name, ssn and balance are passed. In the code below, the former is marked as "Overload 2" in the comment while the latter is marked as "Overload 1" in the comment.

In "Overload 1", the three values passed are Leo, 123456789, 10000 for name, ssn and balance to create an instance of Student called 'st'. We increase the balance in that instance by 500 by calling the tuition method.

We decrease the balance by 2000 by calling the payment method. Finally, we print the name and balance stored in the instance.

In "Overload 2", two values are passed namely Euler and 112345678 for name and ssn respectively. Since the balance is not supplied, a default of None is assigned. The if-statement is True and hence the value of the local variable balance is set to 0.0. Consequently, the self.balance is also set to 0.0.

```python
# A class with method overloading
class Student:
    def __init__(self, name, ssn, balance=None):
        self.name = name
        self.ssn = ssn
        if balance is None:
            balance = 0.0
        self.balance = balance

    def tuition(self, amount):
        self.balance +=amount
        return self.balance

    def payment(self, amount):
        self.balance -=amount
        return self.balance

# Overload 1
st = Student("Leo", 123456789, 10000)
st.tuition(500) # calling tuition method and passing a
```

```
value
st.payment(2000) # calling payment method and passing a
value
print("Student name %s and balance %0.2f "%(st.name,
st.balance))


# Overload 2
st = Student("Euler", 112345678)
print("Student name %s and balance %0.2f "%(st.name,
st.balance)
```

```
Student name Leo and balance 8500.00
Student name Euler and balance 0.00
```

Learning Activity 1: To the Student class, add a method called scholarship. Ask the user if they want to know about scholarships. Depending on their choice, show them the offer or print thank you.

Learning Activity 2: Create a class called Permission that takes name and age as input. Create a method called compage that checks if the person's age is greater than 18. Implement another method called printpermission to print the output of comparison. In that method, if the persons age is greater than 18, then you should print that they are eligible to create a login otherwise print that they can't create a login.

Private Variables

Private variables and methods are used to restrict the usage of a specific variable or a method outside the class definition. They can be created by prepending the instance variable name with __ (double underscore or dunder).

In the below example, we make the variable balance private by adding double underscore before balance. Now, self.__balance is a private variable that can be accessed within the class but not outside.

```python
class Student:
    def __init__(self, name, ssn):
        self.name = name
        self.ssn = ssn
        self.__balance = 0.0
        # __ (double underscore) before the instance variable will
        # make the variable private to the class

    def tuition(self, amount):
        self.__balance +=amount
        return self.__balance

    def payment(self, amount):
        self.__balance -=amount
        return self.__balance
```

```
    def balance_amount(self):
        return self.__balance


b = Student("Leo", 123456789)
print(b.tuition(2500))
print(b.payment(2000))
print(b.balance_amount())
```

500.0

When we try to print b.__balance outside the class definition, we get an AttributeError.

```
print(b.__balance)

# this will fail with an attribute error as the
# variable/attribute __balance is private to the class
```

```
---------------------------------------------------------
-----------
AttributeError                          Traceback (most recent
call last)
<ipython-input-2-37d8a5b036f4> in <module>()
----> 1 print(b.__balance)
      2 # this will fail with an attribute error as the
      3 # variable/attribute __balance is private to the
class
```

```
AttributeError: Student instance has no attribute
'__balance'
```

It is important to remember to add dunder as a prefix to the instance variable at all places in the class definition. If the dunder is missed, the variable is "self.balance" and not "self.__balance". The former is a public variable while the latter is a private variable and these are different variables.

Private Methods

Just like private variables, we can also create private methods and restrict access of a particular method outside the class.

In the code below, the class NewClass has two methods. The outer method is a public method, while __inner method is a private method because there are double underscores before the inner function name. The __inner method is accessible within the NewClass.

We create an instance of the NewClass and call the outer method for that instance. This will result in the execution of the print statement.

```
class NewClass:
    def outer(self):
        print("We are inside outer method")
    # To create a private method, prefix __ (double
underscore) to the
    # method name
    def __inner(self):
        print("We are inside inner method")
```

```
p = NewClass()
p.outer() # this will work
```

We are inside outer method

However, if we call the __inner method, we will receive AttributeError, because it is a private method and cannot be accessed from outside the class.

```
p.__inner()

# this will not work as we are calling a private method
```


```
AttributeError                    Traceback (most recent
call last)

<ipython-input-9-4bccaa994def> in <module>()
----> 1 p.__inner()
      2 # this will not work as we are calling a private
method

AttributeError: NewClass instance has no attribute
'__inner'
```

We can use private and public instance variables inside the private method just as you would for public methods. In the example below, we create an instance of the NewClass and assign it to the variable 'p'. We call the outer method for that instance. This sets the value of the public instance variable somevar to 10. We then print the value of somevar outside the class and notice that it returned the value 10.

```python
class NewClass(object):
    def outer(self):
        print("Inside outer  method")
        self.somevar = 10

    def __inner(self):
        self.somevar = 20
        print("Inside inner method")

p = NewClass()
p.outer()
print(p.somevar)
```

```
Inside outer  method
10
```

The private method __inner() is defined in the class but it is not used. If we cannot call the private method outside the class, how do we use it? Private methods have to be called in a public method inside a class definition. They could also be called by other private methods but at some level, they need to be called by a public method. For example, in the below code, we are calling __inner method inside public method outer().

We create an instance p of NewClass and call outer method. Python uses the definition of the outer method and sets self.somevar to 10. The __inner() is then called that changes the value of self.somevar to 20.

```python
class NewClass(object):
    def outer(self):
        print("Inside outer method")
        self.somevar = 10
        print("somevar value before calling the private
method, inner ",self.somevar)
        self.__inner()

    # To create a private method, prefix __ (double
underscore) to the
    # method name
    def __inner(self):
        print("Inside inner method")
        self.somevar = 20

p = NewClass()
p.outer()
print(p.somevar)
```

```
Inside outer method
somevar value before calling the private method, inner
```

```
10
Inside inner method
20
```

Learning Activity 3: Create a class called Roles that has a public method called, characters that takes three names and a private method called extras that takes two names. Both methods must print the name passed as input. Make a call to extras from characters. Create a instance of Roles and make a call to characters method.

Python uses 'name mangling' to protect variables and methods, so that it can be used as a private variable or method. The process of name mangling as the name suggests mangles the name of the variable with other inputs. In the case of private variables, the name mangling is achieved by combining the name of the class and the name of the private variable. To understand name mangling with an example, we will first begin our discussion using dir() function. Below, we are printing dir(b), which will return all the attributes of b, including user defined methods both private as well as public and other attributes that Python provides.

```
print(dir(b))
```

```
['_Student__balance', '__class__', '__delattr__',
'__dict__', '__dir__', '__doc__', '__eq__',
'__format__', '__ge__', '__getattribute__', '__gt__',
'__hash__', '__init__', '__le__', '__lt__',
'__module__', '__ne__', '__new__', '__reduce__',
'__reduce_ex__', '__repr__', '__setattr__',
```

```
'__sizeof__', '__str__', '__subclasshook__',
'__weakref__', 'balance_amount', 'name', 'payment',
'ssn', 'tuition']
```

The first one on the list _Student__balance (single underscore Student
followed by double underscore balance) will give us access to the private
variable __balance.

```
# Accessing the private variable by b._Student__balance
print(b._Student__balance)
```

```
500.0
```

Even though __balance is defined as private variable, it can still be accessed
by using the mangled name instead.

Class Variables

A class variable is a variable that is shared by all instances of a class. Class
variables are defined within a class and outside any of the class's methods.

In the below example, in Students class, student_count and class_name are
class variables. They are created outside of any of the methods. They do not
have the self-prefix, as they are shared by all instances.

In the __init__ method, we are incrementing the student_count by 1 using the
statement Students.student_count +=1. Notice that we refer to the variable by
using the name of the class and not the self-keyword. The Students class has
two methods- displayCount and displayStudent. In displayCount method, we

are printing the Students.student_count and in the displayStudent method, we are printing the students name and degree.

We create four instances of the Students class, s1, s2, s3 and s4. For every instance created, the student_count is incremented by 1 in the corresponding __init__ method call. Since we created four instances, the student_count is 4. Notice that when we call s2.displayCount(), we get Total Students 4. We will obtain the same value if we print Student.student_count. This is due to the fact that a class variable belongs to a class and not to an instance, and hence its value is the shared across all instances. Its value can either be obtained by using the instance or by using the class.

```python
class Students:
    student_count = 0 # Class variable. No self. prefix
    class_name = 'Students' # Class variable. No self. prefix
    def __init__(self, name, degree):
        self.name = name
        self.degree = degree
        Students.student_count +=1

    def display_count(self):
        print("Total Students %d"
%Students.student_count)
    def display_student(self):
        print("Name ", self.name, " : ", self.degree)

s1 = Students("Tamara", "Math")
```

```python
s2 = Students("Indu", "Chemistry")
s3 = Students("Jason", "Biology")
s4 = Students("Sean", "Math")
s2.display_student()
s2.display_count()

if(s2.class_name == 'Students'):
    print("We have a Students class")
```

Name: Indu: Chemistry

Total Students 4

We have a Students class

```python
class Students:
    student_count = 0 # Class variable. No self. Prefix ◄──────── Here student_count and
    class_name = 'Students' # Class variable. No self. Prefix ◄──── class_name are class
                                                                    variables

    def __init__(self, name, degree): ◄──────── Here name and degree are
        self.name = name                        instance variables. To use
        self.degree = degree                    them inside all the instance
        Students.student_count +=1              methods we have to map
                                                them to self.variable_name as
                                                shown.

    def display_count(self):                    Syntax to call a class variable is
        print("Total Students %d" %Students.student_count)◄── ClassName.class_variable_name.
                                                            So, we say
                                                            Students.student_count.

    def display_student(self):
        print("Name:  ", self.name, ", :  ", self.degree)
```

239

Python**: What happens if the name of the class variable is same as the name of the instance variable?

Compared to the example above, in the example below, the class variable name has been changed from 'class_name' to 'name'. An instance variable self.name is defined in the __init__ method. Thus, we have created instance and class variable with the same name. The question is what happens when we call instance.name? Would that return the value of instance variable or class variable (as in the previous example)?

The call to print value of name in the two instances cv1 and cv2 returns "Leo" and "Euler", the values stored in the instance variable name. The call to print value of name given the class prints "ClassVar", the value stored in the class variable.

Thus, Python keeps track of these two variables as independent entities. The value in the instance variable does not affect the value in the class variable. Yet, it is not a good idea to have the same name for class and instance variable for readability purpose.

```
class ClassVar(object):
    name = 'ClassVar'
    def __init__(self, name):
        self.name = name
cv1 = ClassVar('Leo')
cv2 = ClassVar('Euler')
print('The value of class variable from cv1 is
```

```
"{0}"'.format(cv1.name))
print('The value of class variable from cv2 is
"{0}"'.format(cv2.name))
print('The value of class variable from the class is
"{0}"'.format(ClassVar.name))
```

```
The value of class variable from cv1 is "Leo"
The value of class variable from cv1 is "Euler"
The value of class variable from the class is "ClassVar"
```

Learning Activity 4: Create a class that has a class variable that keeps count of number of instances of the class. The class must have an __init__ method that takes name and age as arguments. Create three instances of the class. Then print the value of the class variable.

Class Method

The methods we have learnt had self as the first argument. Using the self, the method had access to all the instance variables in the class. They are generally referred to as bound methods.

Sometimes, a class may have methods that do not need access to the instance variables in the class. However, they might still need to be part of the class. One such method is the class method. The class methods have access to the class and not the instance. Hence, they can create instances of itself or use class variables but cannot access any instance variables.

The method is defined using the @classmethod decorator. We have previously seen that a decorator is a function that takes another function and extends the behavior of the latter function without explicitly modifying it. The first argument is the cls, which is not a Python keyword. It can be replaced by a different name. However, it is recommended to use the convention.

In the example below, the class method decorator modifies print_radius method. In the example below, the print_radius method receives the class itself as an argument. It then returns the value of the class variable radius using cls.radius. We could also print using Cylinder.radius. The advantage of using cls over Cylinder becomes clear when we realize that any change to the name of the class does not require change to the code inside the class. Outside the class definition, to call the print_radius method, we refer to it by the class name "Cylinder" and not necessarily with an instance.

```python
class Cylinder(object):
    radius = 42
    @classmethod
    def print_radius(cls):
        print("The radius is: ", cls.radius)
b = Cylinder.print_radius()
```

```
The radius is:  42
```

Class methods are also useful when we need to create an instance of the class from within the class itself. In the below example, createvec is a classmethod and it returns a randomly created Vector object. The __init__ method sets a

242

and b to the corresponding instance variable. The class method createvec uses the random module to generate 2 random integers between 0 and 10 for a and b respectively. It then creates an instance of the Vector class using the cls and returns it. Finally, we print the value of a and b in the random vector.

```python
import random
class Vector:
    def __init__(self, a, b):
        self.a = a
        self.b = b
    @classmethod
    def createvec(cls):
        return cls(random.randint(1,10),
random.randint(1,10))
v1 = Vector.createvec()
print(v1.a, v1.b)
```

6 1

Static Method

Static method is a special method that does not know details of the instance of which it is a part or the class to which it belongs. It does not take either cls or self as arguments. Thus, it does not have access to any of the instance variables or class variables in the class. It is generally used to define functions that logically belong to the class and are accessible to all the instances of the class.

In the code below, the Cylinder class has a __init__ method and print_volume method. It also has a circle_area static method. The circle_area method as the name indicates calculates the area of a circle while the class in general is designed for dealing with cylinders. Since the method is not related to the class but since it needed to be part of this class, we made it static using the @staticmethod decorator. This method takes the radius as input and returns the area. To call this method, you can either use the name of the class or create an instance and calculate the area. The former is calculated using "Cylinder.circle_area(30)" while the latter is done using "cy.circle_area(30)" where cy is an instance of the Cylinder class. Note that both print statements return the same value.

```python
import math
class Cylinder:
    def __init__(self, radius, height):
        self.radius = radius
        self.height = height
    @staticmethod
    def circle_area(radius):
        area = math.pi * (radius ** 2)
        return area
    def print_volume(self):
        return self.compute_volume(self.height,
self.radius)
# Creating an instance and also calling the static
method
area_class = Cylinder.circle_area(30)
```

```python
print("The area when calling using the class is
%0.3f"%(area_class))
# Creating an instance and in the next line calling the
static method
cy = Cylinder(10, 20)
area_instance = cy.circle_area(30)
print("The area when calling using the class is
%0.3f"%(area_instance))
```

```
The area when calling using the class is 2827.433
The area when calling using the class is 2827.433
```

11. Magic methods

Introduction

In the previous chapter, we discussed the __init__ method one of the many magic methods in Python. We invoked non-magic methods by specifically calling them by name. However, the magic method __init__ was not called by name. It was called when an instance of the object was created.

The methods in a class that start with double underscore and end with double underscore are called magic methods [http://minhhh.github.io/posts/a-guide-to-pythons-magic-methods]. Although they are referred as magic methods, they are not necessarily called or created magically.

The following are the characteristics of these methods:

1. Their call is deterministic. Hence, there is a well-defined point of time when a given magic method is called. For example, __init__ method is called when an instance of a class is created. The programmer does not have to explicitly call the __init__ method.

2. They are often not explicitly called.. In most cases, the programmer using the class does not have to explicitly call the method with that signature. For example, the programmer does not have to call __str__ method explicitly. Instead it will be called as part of print function call.

3. A method does not become a magic method by prefixing and suffixing its name with __ (double underscore). There is mechanism built behind the magic method, so that Python can call the magic method at the appropriate time.

246

In this chapter, we will learn a few magic methods. In subsequent chapters, we will introduce few more methods as well.

Pretty printing objects

The __str__ is a magic method that is used to accomplish pretty printing of user defined objects. The statement that needs to be printed has to be given to the return statement. When the instance is printed, this method will be called and executed.

Before we discuss the effect of __str__, we will see the effect of not using __str__. In the example below, we created an instance of the class Class1 and store it in the variable obj1. The call to print the object, prints the module in which the class was found (namely __main__) followed by the name of the class and finally the id. The print function call for the second object obj2 returns a similar output. The two print functions do not help us distinguish the nature and content of the object. We will now modify this code using __str__ to add more context to the object.

```
class Class1:
    def __init__(self, name):
        self.name = name
    def listname(self):
        return self.name
obj1 = Class1('This is a brand-new instance.')
print(obj1)
obj2 = Class1('This is the second instance.')
print(obj2)
```

```
<__main__.Class1 object at 0x107af8da0>
<__main__.Class1 object at 0x107af8da0>
```

In the code below, after we create obj1 and print obj1. Since the __str__ method is defined, it will be called and executed. The __str__ method prints the content of self.name. The important rule to remember is that the __str__ method must return a string.

```
class Class1:
    def __init__(self, name):
        self.name = name
    def listname(self):
        return self.name
    # in the following method, a string is returned
whenever the print
    # is called with the instance as input
    def __str__(self):
        return "The name is - %s " %self.name

obj1 = Class1('This is a brand-new instance.')
# This will call __str__ method, thus enabling a pretty
printing of object
print(obj1)
obj2 = Class1('This is the second instance.')
print(obj2)
```

```
The name is - This is a brand-new instance
```

248

Learning Activity 1: *Create a class called YourWish that has an __init__ method, that takes two names. Define a __str__ method that prints the two names. Create an instance of the class and give two names. Use the __str__ method to print the names.*

The reproduction of an object using __repr__

In the previous section, we used __str__ to print a string representation of an object. The string representation is useful for the end user, as it gives insight in to the content of the object. Python provides another method __repr__ to print objects that is more useful for developers. The output of __repr__ is designed so that the object being printed can be recreated.

In the example below, we define __repr__ instead of __str__ method. The method returns a string which uses format to add the instance variable name to the string. The output of the method hence is Class1('This is a brand-new instance.'). The aim of defining __repr__ is to recreate the object if needed. So, we will pass it through the eval function and generate a new object obj2. To check if obj2 is a complete reproduction of obj1, we will compare the instance variable name in both obj1 and obj2. Since obj1 and obj2 contain the same information, the last print function returns a True.

We recommend the reader to obtain the id of obj1 and obj2 and notice that they are two different objects sharing the same content.

```
class Class1:
    def __init__(self, name):
        self.name = name
```

249

```
    def listname(self):
        return self.name
    def __repr__(self):
        return "Class1('{0}')".format(self.name)


obj1 = Class1('This is a brand-new instance.')
# This will call __repr__ method, as __str__ method is
not available
print(obj1)
obj2 = eval(repr(obj1))
print(obj2)
print(obj2.name == obj1.name
```

```
Class1('This is a brand-new instance.')
Class1('This is a brand-new instance.')
True
```

If __repr__ is defined and __str__ is not, then Python will use the output of __repr__ when the object is printed.

Operator Overloading

Mathematical operation

A Python expression a = 5+2, evaluates and stores the value 7 in the variable a. The evaluation is possible due to the fact that the + operator is defined for integers by Python. If we define classes and create objects as in the previous example, how could we evaluate the expression obj1 + obj2? Python does not have a default implementation for such user defined class. We can solve this problem by using operator overloading, a mechanism to assign functionality to an operator. For example, + means adding or concatenating two things. However, for any general class/object, Python allows you to define the behavior of choice.

To understand the example below, we need to learn about vectors. A 2-dimensional vector consists of 2 parts namely the x and y. The negative of a vector is calculated by taking the negative of each of the parts. Hence a vector (5, 8) will have a negative vector (-5, -8).

In the code below, we define a Vector class that contains __init__, __str__ method and a __neg__ method. The __neg__ method is called when the − (negation) operator is called with only one input. In the __neg__ method, we create a new Vector that contains the negative of the x and y values that were given in the input. We then create an instance v1 that contains x = 5 and y = 8. Since the __neg__ takes only one input, it is a type of a unary operator.

```python
class Vector:
    def __init__(self, x, y):
        self.x = x
        self.y = y
    def __str__(self):
        return 'Vector(%d, %d)' % (self.x, self.y)
    def __neg__(self):
        return Vector(-self.x, -self.y)
v1 = Vector(5,8)
```

```
v2 = -v1
print("The value of -v1 is", v2)
```

```
The value of -v1 is Vector(-5, -8)
```

A vector addition is calculated by summing the value of x from the two vectors and summing the value of y from the two vectors and forming a new vector that contains the sum of x and y respectively.

In the code below, we want to add two vectors of type Vector. This class has __init__ method, __str__ method and a __add__ method. In the __add__ method, we take two arguments, self and other. The self refers to the first value being added, in this case it is v1. The 'other' is the Vector v2. The sum of x values of self and other is found and is used for the x value of the new Vector while the sum of the y values of self and other is found and is used for the y value of the Vector instance. The add (+) operator in v1+v2 calls __add__ method and supplies self and other. Since __add__ takes two inputs, it is a type of binary operator.

```
class Vector:
    def __init__(self, x, y):
        self.x = x
        self.y = y
    def __str__(self):
        return 'Vector(%d, %d)' % (self.x, self.y)
    def __add__(self, other):
        return Vector(self.x + other.x, self.y +
other.y)
```

```
v1 = Vector(5,8)
v2 = Vector(5,-2)
v3 = v1+v2
print("The value of v1+v2 is", v3)
```

```
The value of v1+v2 is Vector(10, 6)
```

Comparison operator

We will now discuss implementing comparison operation on a user defined class. For integers, floats etc., Python defines the behavior for ==, !=, >= etc. However for user defined classes, it is the responsibility of the user to define the mechanism for comparison.

The first method we will discuss involves implementing six dunder methods: __eq__ for equality, __ne__ for not equal, __gt__ for greater than, __ge__ for greater than or equal to, __lt__ for less than and __le__ for less than or equal to.

In this example, we create a class called Person that contains two instance variables name and age. We define two instances of the Person class are same if the age in the two instances are same. Other dunder methods are defined by comparing the age of the two objects.

```
class Person:
    def __init__(self, name, age):
        self.name = name
        self.age = age
```

```
def __eq__(self, other):
    return self.age == other.age


def __ne__(self, other):
    return self.age != other.age


def __gt__(self, other):
    return self.age > other.age


def __lt__(self, other):
    return self.age < other.age


def __ge__(self, other):
    return self.age >= other.age


def __le__(self, other):
    return self.age <= other.age
```

We then create three instances of the Person class with age 10, 20 and 20 respectively. Then we print few comparisons.

1. In the first comparison, we check if p1 is equal to p1, which returns a True. This calls the __eq__ method where self is p1 and other is also p1.

2. In the second comparison, we check if p1 is not equal to p2, which returns a True. This calls the __ne__ method where self is p1 and other is also p2.

3. In the third comparison, we check if p1 is greater than p2, which returns a False. This calls the __gt__ method where self is p1 and other is also p2.

4. In the fourth comparison, we check if p2 is greater than or equal to p3, which returns a True. This calls the __ge__ method where self is p2 and other is also p3.

```
p1 = Person("Leo", 10)
p2 = Person("Euler", 20)
p3 = Person("Newton", 20)

print("Is p1 == p1? ", p1 == p1)
print("Is p1 != p2? ", p1 != p2)
print("Is p1 >  p2? ", p1 > p2)
print("Is p2 >= p3? ", p2 >= p3)
```

```
Is p1 == p1?  True
Is p1 != p2?  True
Is p1 >  p2?  False
Is p2 >= p3?  True
```

The one drawback of this mechanism is the need to type six dunder methods for comparison. This can be alleviated by the following observations:

1. If we have __eq__ we can derive __ne__ which is the negation of the former.

2. If we have one of the four other methods, we can derive all the other three. For example, if we define __gt__ only, __ge__ can derived as __gt__ "boolean or" with __eq__.

The following rules can be implemented using the functools module as shown in the example below. The functools module is imported and then class PersonNew is decorated with the functools.total_ordering decorator. We then implement only the __eq__ and __gt__ method.

```python
import functools

@functools.total_ordering
class PersonNew:
    def __init__(self, name, age):
        self.name = name
        self.age = age

    def __eq__(self, other):
        return self.age == other.age

    def __gt__(self, other):
        return self.age > other.age
```

We then create three instances of the class with age 10, 20 and 20 respectively. The four comparison are then computed based on the two dunder methods.

```
p1 = PersonNew("Leo", 10)
p2 = PersonNew("Euler", 20)
p3 = PersonNew("Newton", 20)

print("Is p1 == p1? ", p1 == p1)
print("Is p1 != p2? ", p1 != p2)
print("Is p1 >  p2? ", p1 > p2)
print("Is p2 >= p3? ", p2 >= p3)
```

```
Is p1 == p1?   True
Is p1 != p2?   True
Is p1 >  p2?   False
Is p2 >= p3?   True
```

It is important to define these comparison dunders for all classes, so that you can perform operations such as sorting. Recall that Python's sort is a comparison sort. It needs to compare two objects and determine the lowest and highest value. In the example below, we create three instances of the PersonNew class with age 10, 20 and 30. We then create a list where the elements are not sorted and the corresponding age are 30, 10 and 20. We then perform a sort on this list, which will use the comparison operator to arrange the items in an increasing order. When the items are printed in the for-loop, the ages are printed in increasing order.

```
p1 = PersonNew("Leo", 10)
p2 = PersonNew("Euler", 20)
p3 = PersonNew("Newton", 30)
```

```
lst = [p3, p1, p2] # Create a list that contains p1, p2
and p3 in a random order
lst.sort() # perform inline sort
for items in lst:
    print(items.name, items.age)
```

```
Leo 10
Euler 20
Newton 30
```

You can find the complete list at
https://docs.python.org/3/reference/datamodel.html. A few operators that
emulate numeric objects is given below. The readers are advised to read the
documentation for the return type of each of these methods.

Method and Syntax	Description
object.__add__(self, other)	Addition.
object.__sub__(self, other)	Subtraction.
object.__mul__(self, other)	Multiplication.
object.__truediv__(self, other)	Floating point division.
object.__mod__(self, other)	Returns the remainder.

object.__floordiv__(self, other)	Returns the largest integer for the quotient.
object.__pow__(self, other)	Exponent.
object.__lt__(self, other)	Less than (<)
object.__le__(self, other)	Less than or equal to (<=)
object.__eq__(self, other)	Equal to (==)
object.__ne__(self, other)	Not equal to (!=)
object.__gt__(self, other)	Greater than (>)
object.__ge__(self, other)	Greater than or equal to (>=)
object.__getitem__(self, index)	Index operator []
object.__contains__(self, value)	Check membership
object.__len__(self)	The number of elements returned by len()

NOTE: The addition of two integers return an integer, the addition of two tuples return a tuple. In other words, addition of two items of a certain type must return an item of the same type. Thus, the __add__ method must return item of the same type as self and other.

Magic attributes

In addition to the magic methods that we have seen so far, Python also provides some magic attributes that can provide useful information about a class or object.

The first one we will discuss is __doc__. This returns the documentation of the class provided right below the class name and before any of the methods are defined. The documentation must be enclosed between a pair of triple single quotes or between a pair of triple double quotes.

In the below example, we have """This is a documentation of Savewater""" serves as the documentation for the SaverWater class. Documentation is included for guidance and readability of the code

```python
# Example of documentation in a class
class SaveWater:
    """ This is a documentation of SaveWater"""
    def __init__(self,statename):
        self.statename = statename
        if self.statename.lower() == "california":
            print("Use less water!")
        else:
            print("Still use less water!")


statename = input("Please enter name of your state ")
s = SaveWater(statename)
```

```
Please enter name of your state texas
Still use less water!
```

The documentation for a class can be obtained by using

instance_name.__doc__

or

class_name. .__doc__

In the following print statements using s.__doc___ or *SaveWater.__doc__*,
we are printing the documentation of the class based on the object or the
class respectively.

```
print(s.__doc__)
print(SaveWater.__doc__)
```

```
This is a documentation of SaveWater
This is a documentation of SaveWater
```

The other magic attributes are:

__dict__: Dictionary containing the class's namespace.

__name__ : Class name.

__module__: Module name in which the class is defined. This attribute is
"__main__" in interactive mode.

__bases__ : A possibly empty tuple containing the base or parent classes, in
the order of their occurrence in the base class list.

261

```python
class Class1:
    def __init__(self, name):
        self.name = name
    def list_name(self):
        return self.name
    def set_name(self,name):
        self.name = name


obj1 = Class1('Rob')
print("object dictionary: ", obj1.__dict__)
print("Class documentation: ", Class1.__doc__)
print("Class1.__name: ", Class1.__name__)
print("Class module: ", Class1.__module__)
print("Base classes: ", Class1.__bases__)
```

```
Object dictionary:  {'name': 'Rob'}
Class documentation:  None
Class1.__name:  Class1
Class module:  __main__
Base classes:  (<class 'object'>,)
```

In the above example, we define Class1 with __init__, list_name and set_name methods. The __init__ method has name as the only argument.

In obj1 = Class1('Rob'), we create an instance of Class1 and pass value 'Rob' for name.

The attribute obj1.__dict__ returns a dictionary of attributes and their values for obj1. Since the class contains only one attribute, the __dict__ contains only one element.

Class1 doesn't have any documentation, hence Class1.__doc__ returns None.

Class1.__name__ returns class name which is Class1.

Since Class1 is in the main namespace, Class1.__module__ returns __main__.

Since Class1 doesn't have any parent class, Class1.__bases__ returns empty tuple. We will learn about base (parent) classes in the next chapter.

Context manager

Context managers are one of the most important yet least understood concepts in Python. In examples found online and in books, it is primarily used to open files and close them upon ending the block. The example below illustrates the functioning of the context manager. The file 'somefile.txt' is opened for writing. One line of text is written to the file. The print function call for fo.closed inside the context manager indicates that file is not yet closed.

However, outside the with-block, the print function indicates that the file is closed, even though an explicit call to file close was not made. This mechanism ensures that the programmer does not have to explicitly call file close and yet close it safely.

```
# Proof that file is closed even if there is an
exception if we use the
# with keyword
with open('somefile.txt', 'w+') as fo:
    fo.writelines('Test')
    print('File is closed? : {0}'.format(fo.closed))
print('File is closed? : {0}'.format(fo.closed))
```

The example below goes a step further. An ZeroDivisionError exception is thrown inside the with block simulating a situation that could be found in a code. Before the exception was raised, the print function indicates that the file is still open.

```
with open('somefile.txt', 'w+') as fo:
    fo.writelines('Test')
    print('File is closed? : {0}'.format(fo.closed))
    raise ZeroDivisionError # Throwing or Raising an
exception
```

```
File is closed? : False
-------------------------------------------------------------
--------------------
ZeroDivisionError                          Traceback
(most recent call last)

<ipython-input-15-d118e8a6f7b1> in <module>()
      2     fo.writelines('Test')
      3     print('File is closed? :
{0}'.format(fo.closed))
```

```
----> 4      raise ZeroDivisionError # Throwing or
Raising an exception

ZeroDivisionError:
```

However, in the print call shown below, the function is closed. **Thus, even if Python process dies due to an exception, the context manager closed the file.** This is the main advantage of using a context manager.

```
print('File is closed? : {0}'.format(fo.closed))

# The with keyword closed the file
```

Examples found online or in books use context manager as a way to open and close file even in the midst of an exception. However, the context manager has to be viewed as a resource manager. We personally would prefer the name, 'resource manager' over 'context manager' as it clearly highlights its purpose.

A file is a resource. Similarly, a thread or a socket or a ssh connection are also resources. The context manager can be used to manage these resources. Any finite resource that needs to be opened and closed even under error can use context manager.

Since context managers are so vital for good programming, Python has multiple mechanisms for creating one.

1.   Using __enter__ and __exit__ methods in a class.
2.   Using contextmanager decorator found in contextlib module [https://pymotw.com/3/contextlib/].

Python**: Store any resources using context manager

Imagine that an object of type 'FileData' holds a large data (say) 100MB. If the data needs to be held only for a short time and needs to be cleared before destroying the object, a context manager can be used to handle the clearing of data without explicit call.

The class, 'FileData' contains an initializer that initializes the instance variable 'list_of_data' with a None. This variable will eventually contain a large amount of data. The second function, 'get_last_value' gets the last value in the list. There can also be more functions that will operate on the data.

The function 'resourcemanager' is decorated by the contextlib's contextmanager. This function creates an instance of the 'FileData' class and yields it to the caller. Hence, in the with statement, the variable fd will contain the instance created inside the 'resourcemanager' function. Inside the with block, the list is assigned value and its last value is retrieved. Further operation on the list can be performed either inside the with block or using the methods in the class.

When we exit the 'with' block, the control is returned back to the function after the yield statement. This will set the instance variable fd.list_of_data to None, thus marking the content of fd.list_of_data for garbage collection. Using this mechanism, any resource can be created and destroyed using a context manager.

Note that the last two print function calls, clearly demonstrate that the object fd is not destroyed but only the value fd.list_of_data is set to None.

```python
import contextlib

class FileData:
    def __init__(self):
        self.list_of_data = None

    def set_data(self, list_of_data):
        self.list_of_data = list_of_data

    def get_last_value(self):
        return self.list_of_data[-1]

@contextlib.contextmanager
def resourcemanager():
    fd = FileData()
    yield fd
    print("Setting the list value to None.")
    fd.list_of_data = None

with resourcemanager() as fd:
    # Using list(range()), so that this code is
    # compatible with both Python 2 and 3
    fd.set_data(list(range(100000)))
    print(fd.get_last_value())
    # Perform other complex calculation using the data

# The value in data will be automatically cleared
```

```
# on the exit of the context manager
print(fd)
print(fd.list_of_data)
```

```
99999
Setting the list value to None
<__main__.FileData object at 0x10e11f208>
None
```

In a scenario where more than one class such as, 'FileData' needs to be managed, a more generic version will help. The code below is a generalized version. The code is almost the same as the previous one, except for the fact that the 'resourcemanager' function can take a class as an input. Thus, the function is not hard-coded to a specific class. The function creates the instance of the supplied class and upon exit, it clears that instance.

```
import contextlib

class FileData(object):
    def __init__(self):
        self.list_of_data = None

    def set_data(self, list_of_data):
        self.list_of_data = list_of_data

    def get_last_value(self):
        return self.list_of_data[-1]
```

```python
@contextlib.contextmanager
def resourcemanager(MyClass):
    mc = MyClass()
    yield mc
    print("Setting the list value to None.")
    mc.list_of_data = None

with resourcemanager(FileData) as fd:
    # Using list(range()), so that this code is
    # compatible with both Python 2 and 3
    fd.set_data(list(range(100000)))
    print(fd.get_last_value())
    # Perform other complex calculation using the data

# The value in data will be automatically cleared
# on the exit of the context manager
```

```
99999
Setting the list value to None
```

Previously, we used a function with yield keyword to define a context manager. The example below uses the __enter__ and __exit__ methods to achieve the same result. The number of lines of code is higher but the code is more readable as the enter and exit portions of the context manager are separated.

The class, 'FileData' is same as the previous example. The second class, ResourceManager's initializer takes a class definition as an input and assigns it to the instance variable self.MyClass, which contains a class definition as well.

The __enter__ method creates an instance of self.MyClass and returns it. This instance is then assigned to the variable fd in the with statement. The __exit__ method sets the self.mc.list_of_data to None.

```python
class FileData(object):
    def __init__(self):
        self.list_of_data = None

    def set_data(self, list_of_data):
        self.list_of_data = list_of_data

    def get_last_value(self):
        return self.list_of_data[-1]

    def __del__(self):
        print("Inside the __del__ method in FileData ")

class ResourceManager(object):
    def __init__(self, MyClass):
        self.MyClass = MyClass
        self.mc = None

    def __enter__(self):
```

```python
        self.mc = self.MyClass()
        return self.mc

    def __exit__(self, *args):
        print("Setting the list value to None.")
        self.mc.list_of_data = None

with ResourceManager(FileData) as fd:
    # Using list(range()), so that this code is
    # compatible with both Python 2 and 3
    fd.set_data(list(range(100000)))
    print(fd.get_last_value())
    # Perform other complex calculation using the data
if fd == None:
    print("End of code")
```

```
99999
Setting the list value to None.
```

We recommend that you read the following links:
https://rszalski.github.io/magicmethods/, https://dbader.org/blog/python-dunder-methods and https://www.python-course.eu/python3_magic_methods.php

12. Inheritance

Introduction

In the previous chapter, we learnt about creating a class and its attributes. In this chapter, we will learn about creating one or more classes where the classes can inherit properties from each other. This is called inheritance, a process of expanding the functionalities of a parent class to child classes that inherit it.

The main advantage of inheritance is the ability to program a system, where characteristics such as variables and methods can be added to a class in stages by creating parent, grand-parent class etc. In a largescale application, these parents and grand-parents can be written by one team and other teams can use them.

We will discuss single and multiple inheritance, diamond problem and finally scope of variables during inheritance.

Single inheritance

The code below has three classes: Agency, FBI and CIA. The FBI and CIA class both have a common parent namely Agency indicated by the name of the Agency class in the class definition. In other words, FBI and CIA inherits Agency class.

The Agency class has one method, 'what_type'. The two child classes also have the same method signature. However, the string returned by the parent and the child are different.

When an instance of the Agency class is created and a call to what_type method is made, the string, "We are an agency!" is printed as indicated by the first print function call. When an instance of FBI class is created and a call to what_type method is made, the string, "Internal Affairs" is printed as indicated by the second print function call. Finally, when an instance of CIA class is created and a call to what_type method is made, the string, "External Affairs" is printed as indicated by the third print function call.

```python
# example of an inherited class
class Agency:
    def what_type(self):
        return "We are an agency!"

# child class or derived class
# FBI is the child class that is inheriting from the
parent class called
# Agency. In the child class, what_type method overrides
the behavior
# of what_type of the parent class. This is called
method overriding.

class FBI(Agency):
    def what_type(self):
        return "Internal Affairs"

class CIA(Agency):
    def what_type(self):
        return "External Affairs"
```

```
a = Agency()
print(a.what_type())
d = FBI()
print(d.what_type())
c = CIA()
print(c.what_type())
```

```
We are an agency!
Internal Affairs
External Affairs
```

The image below has labelled few of the details.

To find a list of the parents (also called base class) for a given class, you print the attribute __bases__ for that class. For example, in the code below, we print the list of parent classes for the class FBI. The attribute returns a tuple of parent classes.

```
print(FBI.__bases__) # Prints the list of base or parent
classes
```

```
(<class '__main__.Agency'>,)
```

The corresponding output for the Agency class is the Python's object class, which is a parent to all classes that otherwise do not have an explicit parent.

```
print(Agency.__bases__)
```

```
(<class ' object'>,)
```

```
class Agency(object):
    def what_type(self):
        return "We are an agency!"
```
> Agency is the parent class.

```
class FBI(Agency):
    def what_type(self):
        return "Internal Affairs"

class CIA(Agency):
    def what_type(self):
        return "External Affairs"
```
> FBI and CIA are child classes or subclasses that are inheriting from Agency.

```
a = Agency()
print(a.what_type())
d = FBI()
print(d.what_type())
c = CIA()
print(c.what_type())
```
> We are creating one instance each of Agency, FBI and CIA and we are calling the what_type for each one.

Super() function

In the above example, we overrode the method in the parent class with a corresponding method in the child class. However, in some cases you will have to call both the child class method and also the parent class (also called super class) method. You can do so by using super function as shown in the example below. This code is very similar to the previous one except for the call to super() function inside the 'what_types' method in the child class and the subsequent concatenation of the string.

When an instance of FBI class is created and then a call is made to the what_types method, the super() function is called. This function will determine the parent of the FBI class which is Agency in this case and call the what_types method of Agency. The value returned by that call is then concatenated with the "For Internal Affairs" and returned.

```python
class Agency(object):
    def what_types(self):
        return "We are an agency!"


#child class or derived class
class FBI(Agency):
    def what_types(self):
        # super().methodname()
        # here methodname() should be the method that
        # you want to call from the parent class
        s = super().what_types()
        return "%s - %s" %(s, "For Internal Affairs")


class CIA(Agency):
    def what_types(self):
        s = super().what_types()
        return "%s - %s" %(s, "For External Affairs")
c = FBI()
print(c.what_types())
```

```
d = CIA()
print(d.what_types())
```

```
We are an agency! - For Internal Affairs
We are an agency! - For External Affairs
```

You can learn more about super() function and its use case from

https://rhettinger.wordpress.com/2011/05/26/super-considered-super/

Method overriding between child and parent class

In the two examples we have seen so far, the child class have the same method signature as the parent class. A better use of inheritance is in defining methods in parent but not in child. If an instance of child is created and the method is called, Python in turn will call the parent's method. This process is called method overriding.

In the below code, the parent Agency has both hiring and firing methods and the child CIA has only the hiring method. We create an instance of CIA using d = CIA(). When the d.hiring() is called, Python executes the hiring method in the child class CIA. However, when the d.firing() is called, and since CIA does not have a firing method, Agency's firing method will be called. In general, if a child does not have an attribute, Python will check if the parent has the attribute. If the attribute exists in the parent, it will be executed. If the attribute does not exist, Python will check the parent's parent until it reaches the Python object. If in the chain of calls, the attribute does not exist, Python returns an AttributeError. If the attribute is found in the child or one of the parent class, it will be executed.

```python
# Method overriding between child and parent class.
class Agency:
    name = 'Agency'
    def hiring(self):
        print("Agency can hire.")
    def firing(self):
        print('Agency can fire.')


class CIA(Agency):
    name = 'CIA' # class variable
    def hiring(self):
        print("CIA is hiring!")


d = CIA()
d.hiring()
print(d.name)
d.firing()
```

```
CIA is hiring!
CIA
Agency can fire.
```

Let's look at another example to cement our understanding of the chain of
calls. In the below example, parent class Agency has hiring and firing
methods. While child class CIA has two methods namely hiring and
firing_exclusive. We create an instance of CIA using d = CIA(). When the
d.hiring() is called, Python executes the hiring method in the child class CIA.

When a call is made to print d.name, the content of the class variable 'name' in the CIA class will be printed. However, when the d.firing() is called, and since CIA does not have a firing method, Agency's firing method will be called. When d.firing_exclusive() method is called, CIA's firing_exclusive method will be executed.

```python
class Agency:
    name = 'Agency'
    def hiring(self):
        print("Agency can hire.")
    def firing(self):
        print('Agency can fire.')


class CIA(Agency):
    name = 'CIA' # class variable
    def hiring(self):
        print("CIA is hiring!")

    def firing_exclusive(self):
        print('CIA can fire too.')


d = CIA()
d.hiring()
print(d.name)
d.firing()
d.firing_exclusive()
```

```
CIA is hiring!
CIA
Agency can fire.
CIA can fire too.
```

Multiple inheritance

So far, we have considered examples with single inheritance where the child class is inheriting from one parent. Below is an example of multiple inheritance. There are two parent classes Federal and Agency. CIA is a child class that is inheriting from both Federal and Agency in that order. If a child class is inheriting from more than one parent then the hierarchy of the parent is based on its position and the order is from left to right. Since CIA is inheriting first from Federal and then from Agency, parent Federal class has hierarchy over Agency.

We create an instance of CIA using d = CIA(). When d.hiring() is called, and since CIA doesn't have hiring method, Python will check if this method is defined in parent class Federal and since it is, Federal's hiring method will be executed. When a call is made to print d.name, the content of the class variable 'name' in the CIA class will be printed. However, when the d.firing() is called, and since CIA doesn't have firing method, Python will check if this method is defined in parent class Federal. Since it is not defined in Federal, Python will then check if the method is in the parent Agency, and since it is, Agency's firing method will be executed.

```
# multiple inheritance. A child can have multiple
parents.
class Federal:
```

```
    name = 'Federal'
    def hiring(self):
        print("Yes Federal is hiring")
class Agency:
    name = 'Agency'
    def hiring(self):
        print("Agency can hire.")
    def firing(self):
        print('Agency can fire.')
class CIA(Federal, Agency):
    name = 'CIA' # class variable
d = CIA()
d.hiring()
print(d.name)
d.firing()
```

```
Yes Federal is hiring
CIA
Agency can fire.
```

As we have seen in case of method overriding, if the methods are defined in the child class then the child class methods will be executed. Below, since child class CIA has both hiring and firing methods defined, for d.hiring() and d.firing(), CIA hiring and firing methods will be executed.

```
# multiple inheritance
'''
```

```python
When two parents have same method(s) then the method in the left most
parent of the child class will be executed.
'''

class Federal:
    name = 'Federal'
    def hiring(self):
        print("Yes Federal is hiring")

class Agency:
    name = 'Agency'
    def hiring(self):
        print("Agency can hire.")
    def firing(self):
        print('Agency can fire.')

class CIA(Agency, Federal):
    name = 'CIA' # class variable
    def hiring(self):
        print("CIA is hiring!")

    def firing(self):
        print('CIA can fire too.')

d = CIA()
d.hiring()
```

```
print(d.name)
d.firing()
```

```
CIA is hiring!
CIA
CIA can fire too.
```

Diamond Problem

Let us say that we have a three-level inheritance. There is a grandparent, two parents that inherit from the grandparent and a child that inherits from both the parents.

If we are calling a method that is not in the child class, then Python will check if it is defined in the first parent. If it is not defined in the first parent, then Python will check if it is defined in the child's second parent. If this is not the case, then Python will check in the grandparent. This is known as the diamond problem [http://en.wikipedia.org/wiki/Multiple_inheritance#The_diamond_problem]. In multiple inheritance, Python does breadth first search of parents.

In the following example, grandparent class Domestic has two methods. Both Federal and Agency inherit from Domestic. The class CIA inherits from Federal and Agency in that order.

We create an instance of CIA using d = CIA(). When d.reason() is called and since CIA does not have reason method defined, Python first goes to class Federal as it is the first parent of CIA. But reason method is not defined in class Federal. Python then checks whether Agency has the method. However, reason method is not defined in Agency as well. Python then goes to

283

Federal's parent, Domestic. Since reason method is defined in Domestic, it will be executed.

When d.firing() is called and since CIA has the method firing, it will be called. But in the firing method, we have a super call. Python checks in Federal for firing method and doesn't find it, it then checks Agency class. Since Agency class has it, the firing method in the agency will be executed.

When d.affordable() is called and since neither CIA nor its parents have the method affordable, Python will look for the method in the grandparent class, Domestic. Since Domestic has the affordable method it will be executed.

```python
class Domestic:
    name = "Domestic"
    def reason(self):
        print("There are several reasons for anything,
we are in domestic.")
    def affordable(self):
        print("Domestic should be able to afford it.")


class Federal(Domestic):
    name = 'Federal'
    def hiring(self):
        print("Yes Federal is hiring.")
class Agency(Domestic):
    name = 'Agency'
    def hiring(self):
        print("Agency can hire.")
    def firing(self):
```

```python
        print('Agency can fire.')

class CIA(Federal, Agency):
    name = 'CIA' # class variable
    def hiring(self):
        print("CIA is hiring!")
    def firing(self):
        super(CIA, self).firing()
        print('CIA is firing.')

d = CIA()

d.reason()

d.firing()

d.affordable()
```

There are several reasons for anything, we are in domestic.
Agency can fire.
CIA is firing.
Domestic should be able to afford it.

You can learn more about multiple inheritance from the following link

http://stackoverflow.com/questions/3277367/how-does-pythons-super-work-with
-multiple-inheritance

Magic methods in inheritance

So far, we discussed inheritance from a single or multiple parent class for a non-magic method. However, the call order is still the same for magic method. We will discuss it with an example.

In the below example, the Person class has an __init__ method. AccountHolderV1 class inherits from the Person class but does not have its own __init__ method but has three other methods.

An instance of AccountHolderV1 class is created with name 'JJ' and ssn '102-321-4512'. When the setbalance method is called on the instance a1, the setbalance method from the AccountHolderV1 class will be executed. Finally, the print statement will use the __str__ method from AccountHolderV1 to pretty print the balance.

```
class Person:
    def __init__(self, name, ssn):
        self.name = name
        self.ssn = ssn


class AccountHolderV1 (Person):
    def setbalance(self, balance):
        self.balance = balance


    def deposit(self, amount):
        self.balance += amount
```

```
    def __str__(self):
        return "This is your current balance: %0.2f"
%self.balance


a1 = AccountHolderV1('JJ', '102-321-4512')
a1.setbalance(2000)
print(a1)
```

```
This is your current balance: 2000.00
```

In the code below, Person class has an __init__ but the AccountHolderV2 which inherits from the Person class also has its own __init__ method. But the assignment of the instance variables is spread across the both the inits using the super function call. The __init__ in Person initializes the instance variables name and ssn while the AccountHolderV2's __init__ initializes the instance variable balance. Thus, self.name, self.balance and self.ssn will be available across all the methods in the child class.

```
'''
Here the Person class as well as its child class,
AccountHolderv2 have their own
init methods.
'''

class Person(object):
    def __init__(self, name, ssn):
        self.name = name
        self.ssn = ssn
```

```python
class AccountHolderV2(Person):
    def __init__(self, name, ssn, balance):
        self.balance = balance
        super().__init__(name, ssn)

    def deposit(self, amount):
        self.balance += amount

    def __str__(self):
        return "The current balance for %s is: %0.2f"
%(self.name, self.balance)

a1 = AccountHolderV2('JJ', '102-321-4512',2000)
print(a1)
```

```
The current balance for JJ is: 2000.00
```

The process of inheriting is sometime referred as **is-a relation**. In the example above, the AccountHolderV2 inherits Person or alternately it can be said that AccountHolderV2 is-a Person.

Delegation

An alternate method to connect two classes is called delegation [https://programmingideaswithjake.wordpress.com/2015/05/23/python-decorator-for-simplifying-delegate-pattern/] where we create an instance of one class inside another. Thus, delegation can also be characterized as **has-a relation**.

In the example below, we will use delegation instead of inheritance. The Person class is same as the previous example. However, unlike in the inheritance examples, in the AccountHolder class, we do not inherit the Person class. Instead we create an instance of the Person class in the AccountHolder's __init__ method and store it in the instance variable person.

The name is accessible only by calling the name on the instance variable person as can be seen in the __str__ method.

```python
# Using Delegation which is "HAS-A" relationship
class Person:
    def __init__(self,name,ssn):
        self.name = name
        self.ssn = ssn


class AccountHolder:
    def __init__(self, name, ssn, balance):
        self.person = Person(name, ssn)
        self.balance = balance


    def deposit(self,amount):
        self.balance += amount


    def __str__(self):
```

```
        return "The current balance for %s is: %0.2f" %\
                        (self.person.name, self.balance)


a1 = AccountHolder('JJ', '102-321-4512', 2000)
print(a1)
```

```
The current balance for JJ is: 2000.00
```

Learning Activity 1: *Define a parent class called Employee with info_data as a method that takes employee name and major. Define a child class called Student that inherits from Employee with student_data as a method that takes student name and a course name. Create an instance of Student and then access student_data and info_data.*

Learning Activity 2: *Create a class, Travel with a method, croute that will randomly choose a city from ['Sao Paulo', 'Hyderabad', 'Lisbon', "Madrid] and print it. Create another class called uName that inherits Travel. uName should have a method, cyour that takes a name and prints it. Create an instance of uName and pass a name. Call cyour and croute.*

Python**: Using *args and **kwargs in OOPS inheritance

The *args and **kwargs are useful for passing values to a function via variable number of arguments. We previously discussed their use in functions. Since methods are functions inside a class, they can also accept *args and **kwargs.

One of the questions that students frequently ask is: Give me an example of a clever use of *args and **kwargs?

The following example uses *args and **kwargs, to handle variable number of arguments. The parent class, 'Parent' has an initializer that is overloaded with the ability to take zero or more arguments by the use of *args and **kwargs. The child class, 'Child' inherits the 'Parent' class. In the 'Child' class initializer, a call is made to the parent class's initializer using the 'super' function call. This call uses *args and **kwargs passed as input to the child class initializer. If *args and **kwargs was not used, then every input to the child's initializer needs to be retyped in the super call as well.

```python
class Parent:
    def __init__(self, *args, **kwargs):
        self.name = args[0]
        print("Inside parent's initializer
{0}".format(self.name))


class Child(Parent):
    def __init__(self, *args, **kwargs):
        super().__init__(*args, **kwargs)
        self.name = args[0]
        print("Inside child's initializer
{0}".format(self.name))


c = Child('Leo', 'Euler', age=81, area='Math')
```

```
Inside parent's initializer Leo
Inside child's initializer Leo
```

What happens to private variables in parent class when it is inherited?

It is quite simple. Private variables are not inherited by the child. In the example below, the child class, 'Child' inherits from the parent class, 'Parent'. The parent class has one private instance variable and one publicly accessible method called set_name. In the child class, 'Child', calling the set_name method with the string, 'I. Curie' will result in setting the __name defined in the parent class. However, the child still does not have direct access to __name by calling self.__name. Hence the last print call in the child's initializer will fail with AttributeError.

The rules that apply to private variables also apply to private methods.

```
class Parent:
    def __init__(self, name):
        self.__name = name

    def set_name(self, name):
        self.__name = name

class Child(Parent):
    def __init__(self, name):
        self.child_name = name
        self.set_name('I. Curie')
        print("The parent's name is %s" %(self.__name))
```

```
c = Child('Irene Curie')
```

```
------------------------------------------------------------
--------------------
AttributeError                              Traceback
(most recent call last)
<ipython-input-29-094c60009b7b> in <module>()
    15             print("The parent's name is %s"
%(self.__name))
    16
---> 17 c = Child('Irene Curie')

<ipython-input-29-094c60009b7b> in __init__(self, name)
    13             self.child_name = name
    14             self.set_name('I. Curie')
---> 15             print("The parent's name is %s"
%(self.__name))
    16
    17 c = Child('Irene Curie')

AttributeError: 'Child' object has no attribute
'_Child__name'
```

Does Python have protected variable?

Protected variables in most language refer to variables in the parent class that are available to the child class but not available outside the class definition. There are no true protected variables in Python. A convention of using a single underscore has been developed to identify a protected variable using Python.

In the example below, the variable _name needs to be treated as a protected variable (as it is identified with a single underscore) and must only be accessed in the parent and child class definition. The programmers must not access the variable _name outside the class definition as shown in the last print function call. The call will not fail, as Python does not have real protected variable.

```python
class Parent:
    def __init__(self, name):
        self._name = name

    def setname(self, name):
        self._name = name

class Child(Parent):
    def __init__(self, name):
        self.childname = name
        self.setname('I. Curie')
        print("The parent's name is %s"%(self._name))
```

```
c = Child('Irene Curie')
print("The parent's name outside class definition is
'{0}'".format(c._name))
```

The parent's name is I. Curie
The parent's name outside class definition is 'I. Curie'

NOTE: The instance variables __name, _name or name refer to different variables. It is imperative that you are careful with the names as mistakes can result in hard to fix bugs.

Python**: Default arguments for mutables

In the functions chapter, we discussed the effect of using mutable values as default arguments to functions. In the example below, we will study the effect of using mutable values as default arguments to methods.

In the example below, we have a method called setlist, that takes one argument alist and whose default value is an empty list, a mutable type. Inside the method, we assign alist to an instance variable alist. We then proceed to append 4 to this list. We then create two instances lp1 and lp2 and call the setlist method for both without any argument. The first print function call prints the value of lp1's alist while the second one prints the value of lp2's alist. The first print returns [4], while the second print returns [4, 4].

It is important to observe that even though the lp2 is a different object compared to lp1, the value of alist in lp2 does not default to an empty list but instead to the value in lp1's alist. This becomes obvious by adding a print function call inside the setlist.

```
class ListProcessor:
    def setlist(self, alist=[]):
        self.alist = alist
        print(self.alist)
        self.alist.append(4)
        return self.alist

lp1 = ListProcessor()
lp1.setlist()
print("Value of alist in lp1 is {0}".format(lp1.alist))

lp2 = ListProcessor()
lp2.setlist()
print("Value of alist in lp2 is {0}".format(lp2.alist))
```

```
[]
Value of alist in lp1 is [4]
[4]
Value of alist in lp2 is [4, 4]
```

However, if we supply a non-empty list (as in the example below), the previous value from lp1 and lp2's alist does not affect lp3's alist.

```
lp3 = ListProcessor()
lp3.setlist([1, 2, 3])
print("Value of alist in lp3 is {0}".format(lp3.alist))
```

```
[1, 2, 3]
Value of alist in lp3 is [1, 2, 3, 4]
```

This seems paradoxical. However, it becomes clear when you realize that Python does not keep three copies of the function object, as we are creating three objects. Instead there is only one. This becomes obvious when we print the id for each function call, as shown below. For lp1 and lp2, the id is the same, indicating that they are modifying the same variable while the id for lp3 is different.

Hence the default value is shared between the instances, even though the function calls belong to different instances.

```
print(id(lp1.setlist()))
print(id(lp2.setlist()))
print(id(lp3.setlist([1, 2, 3])))
```

```
[4, 4]
4491649824
[4, 4, 4]
4491649824
[1, 2, 3]
4491650976
```

You can overcome this by replacing the empty list with None, as in the code below. Since alist is None by default, its value has to be reset to a list before append operation can be performed. This is accomplished by using the if statement check for alist is None.

In the corresponding output, we notice a consistent behavior. The lp1, lp2 and lp3 do not share the same id and hence are pointing to different objects and hence the call to lp1 does not affect lp2.

```python
class ListProcessor:
    def setlist(self, alist=None):
        if alist is None:
            alist = []
        self.alist = alist
        print(self.alist)
        self.alist.append(4)
        return self.alist


lp1 = ListProcessor()
lp1.setlist()
print("Value of alist in lp1 is {0}".format(lp1.alist))


lp2 = ListProcessor()
lp2.setlist()
print("Value of alist in lp2 is {0}".format(lp2.alist))


print("Printing the id of setlist in lp1 and lp2")
print(id(lp1.setlist()))
print(id(lp2.setlist()))
print(id(lp3.setlist([1, 2, 3])))
```

```
[]
Value of alist in lp1 is [4]
[]
Value of alist in lp2 is [4]
Printing the id of setlist in lp1 and lp2
[]
4483336096
[]
4483383592
[1, 2, 3]
4491627984
```

Introduction

Design Patterns is a general repeatable solution to a commonly occurring problem in software design. It is a description or template for how to solve a problem that can be used in many different situations according to https://sourcemaking.com/design_patterns

It defines the template of commonly occurring software patterns which in turn allows faster development that is repeatable, standardized and modularized. There are many design patterns and they are generally classified in to the following categories.

1. Creational pattern

2. Structural pattern

3. Behavioral pattern

4. Concurrency pattern

The creational pattern allows creation of instances of class (objects). The structural pattern provides mechanism to simplify the relationship between objects. The behavioral pattern allows communication between objects and finally the concurrency pattern allows multi-threaded programming. The most famous book to describe the design pattern is Design Patterns: Elements of Reusable Object-Oriented Software written by Erich Gamma, Richard Helm, Ralph Johnson and John Vlissides which is available at https://www.barnesandnoble.com/w/design-patterns-erich-gamma/1100886879. The authors are sometimes referred as the Gang of Four.

There are many design patterns under these four categories. In this chapter, we will discuss three of them.

1. Proxy pattern

2. Factory pattern

3. Prototype pattern

Before we begin discussing design patterns, we will discuss getting, setting and checking attributes that we will later use in our design patterns.

Get, Set and Has attributes

Let us consider the following class to demonstrates get and set. The class GetSetExample has __init__, listname and setname methods. As the name indicates, the listname() method returns the value of self.name. The method setname() is used to set self.name.

We create an instance obj1 and set the name to 'Leo'. In the next line, we change the name to 'Euler'. Finally, we print the value in obj1.name.

```python
class GetSetExample:
    def __init__(self, name):
        self.name = name
    def listname(self):
        return self.name
    def setname(self,name):
        self.name = name

obj1 = GetSetExample ('Leo')
```

```
obj1.name = 'Euler'
print(obj1.name)
```

Euler

The line obj1.name = 'Euler' is setting the value while line obj1.name is getting the value of the instance variable self.name.

The process of getting an attribute instead be achieved using getattr() function. The syntax is getattr(instance_name, attribute_name).

In the code below, we find the value of instance attribute name for instance obj1. The string, 'Euler' is returned. The getattr() function returns the same value as obj1.name. It is important to notice that in the getattr function, the second argument is a string.

```
print(getattr(obj1, 'name')) # Returns value of 'name'
attribute
print(obj1.name) # this will yield the same result as
getattr.
```

Euler
Euler

The process of setting the value of an attribute can be achieved using setattr() function. The syntax is setattr(instance_name, attribute_name, new_data).

In the code below, we are assigning new string, 'Leo Euler' to the obj1's attribute name. We can instead assign a new value by saying obj1.name = 'Leo Euler'. It is important to notice that in the setattr function, the second argument is a string.

```
setattr(obj1, 'name', 'Leo Euler') # Set attribute
'name' to Leo Euler
obj1.name = 'Leo Euler' # another way to assign new data
print(obj1.name)
```

```
Leo Euler
```

The hasattr() function is used to find if a particular instance has an attribute. Its syntax is hasattr(instance_name, attribute_name).

In the below code, we are checking if obj1 has attribute name. Notice that as in getattr and setattr, we are supplying the attribute name as a string.

```
print(hasattr(obj1, 'name'))      # Returns true if 'name'
attribute exists
```

```
True
```

The hasattr() function can be used to check if an attribute exists before we access the attribute.

We will use the getattr() function in creating our first design pattern, Proxy pattern.

Proxy pattern

This pattern is used when we want to shield access to an object from other objects. For proxy to work, in addition to the class that you want to shield, you also have to create a proxy class, which will internally create an instance of the shielded class when a certain requirement is satisfied or a request is made.

In the example below, class Maintenance and class NonMaintenance each have visitpage method. The Proxy class has __init__ and __getattr__ method.

First, we set the variable MAINTENANCE to True. Then we create an instance of proxy by passing MAINTENANCE is True. The __init__ method of the Proxy class will be called and an instance of the Maintenance class will be created and stored in self.__maintenance.

Note that the Proxy class does not have a visit page method. So, when a call is made to visitpage(), Python will check if __getattr__ method is defined in Proxy class. Since it is, the lines in __getattr__ method will be executed. The value for attribute name = visitpage and its type is string. The __getattr__ method returns the value associated with the attribute name in the self.__implementation class. That means it will call the visitpage method that is defined in Maintenance class.

Proxy Pattern is used when an object has to be
shielded from its clients.

304

```python
class Maintenance:
    def visitpage(self):
        print("Our site is under maintenance, please
visit us later.")


class NonMaintenance:
    def visitpage(self):
        print("Welcome to the site")


class Proxy:
    def __init__(self, maintenanceBool):
        if maintenanceBool:
            self.__implementation = Maintenance()
        else:
            self.__implementation = NonMaintenance()
    def __getattr__(self, name):
        print(name, type(name))
        return getattr(self.__implementation, name)


MAINTENANCE = True
p = Proxy(MAINTENANCE)
p.visitpage()
```

```
visitpage <class 'str'>
Our site is under maintenance, please visit us later.
```

Factory pattern

Factory pattern is used when an instance of the class has to be created on a fly. In all the example we have created, we created an instance of the class immediately after defining the class. However, in the real-world applications, objects are created at run-time and only on demand. The pattern that can produce objects is the factory pattern.

In the example below, we have three classes namely Menu, Burger and Fries. The Burger and Fries class inherit the Menu class.

The Menu class has one static method called factory which give an integer will produce an object. For example, when objtype is 1, the factory method produces a Burger object. The Burger and Fries both have a method called listitem() that prints the label for that object.

In the output below, we made a choice of 1. Hence the factory method will create and return an instance of the Burger object. Thus, the variable f will be of type Burger. Hence the call to f.listitem() prints "Burger".

If instead we chose 2, then the factory method will create and return an instance of the Fries object. Thus, the variable f will be of type Fries. Hence the call to f.listitem() prints "Fries".

```
# Factory pattern
class Menu(object):
    @staticmethod
    def factory(objtype):
        if objtype == 1:
            return Burger()
```

```
        elif objtype == 2:
            return Fries()


class Burger(Menu):
    def listitem(self):
        print("Burger")


class Fries(Menu):
    def listitem(self):
        print("Fries")


print("Choose a menu item")
print("1: Burger, 2: Fries")
choice = int(input('Enter your choice number :'))
f = Menu.factory(choice)
f.listitem()
print(type(f))
```

```
Choose a menu item
1: Burger, 2: Fries
Enter your choice number :1
Burger
<class '__main__.Burger'>
```

I have a really expensive object and I need to make copies. What should I do?

You can use a **Prototype pattern**, a creational pattern. The pattern is used to create clones of objects. This is especially needed for cases where creating an object is prohibitively expensive. An example of expensive object would be the following. Imagine that we need to parse a website or call a web API to create an object. Let's say that this process consumes 1 second for each call. If 100 such calls need to be made to build a single instance of a class, we will consume 100 seconds. Also, let's assume that the data from these 100 calls are stored in an object. If a copy of the object needs to be made, the previous steps can be retraced. However, this process not only takes 100 seconds but also requires that making 100 web or API calls. This can be easily avoided by using prototype pattern.

In the example below, we will demonstrate the use of prototype pattern with a simple example of storing large data. We will simulate the time taken to store or read data by using the sleep function.

The FileData class's initializer initializes the instance variable fileval to an empty list. The 'setval' function stores the content of variable 'fileval' in the instance variable. A sleep is added to simulate the expensiveness of the process. The clone function creates copy of itself using the copy module.

An instance of the FileData class is created and a list containing values is stored in the instance variable 'fileval'. A copy (fd1) of the original object (fd) is created by using the clone function. The output of the id function call for fd and fd1 indicates that these are two different copies even though they contain the same content. A subsequent call to append for fd1.fileval demonstrates that only fd1's content has changed but not fd. Thus, a deep copy of an object was created without recreating the object from scratch.

```python
import copy
import time

class FileData(object):
    def __init__(self):
        self.fileval = []

    def setval(self, fileval):
        self.fileval = fileval
        # A sleep of 10 seconds to simulate the
expensiveness of the process
        time.sleep(10)

    def clone(self):
        return copy.deepcopy(self)

fd = FileData()
fd.setval(list(range(20)))
fd1 = fd.clone()
print(id(fd), id(fd1))
print(fd.fileval)
print(fd1.fileval)
fd1.fileval.append(499)
```

```
print(fd.fileval)
print(fd1.fileval
```

```
(4354440144, 4357807568)
[0, 1, 2, 3, 4, 5, 6, 7, 8, 9, 10, 11, 12, 13, 14, 15,
16, 17, 18, 19]
[0, 1, 2, 3, 4, 5, 6, 7, 8, 9, 10, 11, 12, 13, 14, 15,
16, 17, 18, 19]
[0, 1, 2, 3, 4, 5, 6, 7, 8, 9, 10, 11, 12, 13, 14, 15,
16, 17, 18, 19]
[0, 1, 2, 3, 4, 5, 6, 7, 8, 9, 10, 11, 12, 13, 14, 15,
16, 17, 18, 19, 499]
```

There are many other design patterns. Interested readers are recommended to check the following GitHub link and books for more details.

1. https://github.com/faif/python-patterns

2. http://kennison.name/files/zopestore/uploads/python/DesignPatternsInPython_ver0.1.pdf

3. https://www.barnesandnoble.com/w/design-patterns-erich-gamma/1100886879

Introduction

In the last few chapters we discussed the various aspects of classes and object-oriented programming in Python. In this chapter, we strive to answer some of the questions that did not naturally fall into the previous chapters. The questions in this chapter are advanced. So, new programmers may wish to skip this chapter and read at a later time.

Python**: Are private variables really private?

In Python, there is no true concept of private variables. Python implements private variables and methods using name mangling (i.e.,) a user cannot access the private method such as __inner (in the code below) from outside the class but can access it by a mangled name _NewClass__inner. Hence a determined person can still access private method outside the class definition. By putting a __ in front of the attributes, you are informing your team that the variable's access is restricted and they should honor your code.

The dir method gives a list of all the methods in a class including private methods. When we print dir(NewClass) below, the output is a list where the first element is _NewClass__inner, the mangled name of the private method in the class. Using this _NewClass__inner, we can still call the private method inner from outside the class. The fourth element is the outer method which is the public method in the class.

```
class NewClass(object):
    def outer(self):
        print("Inside outer method")
```

```
        self.somevar = 10
        print("somevar value before calling the private
method, inner ",self.somevar)
        self.__inner()

    # To create a private method, prefix __ (double
underscore) to the
    # method name
    def __inner(self):
        print("Inside inner method")
        self.somevar = 20

p = NewClass()
p.outer()
print(p.somevar)
print(dir(NewClass))
```

```
['_NewClass__inner', '__doc__', '__module__', 'outer']
```

Thus, the following construct will allow us to call a private method outside the class.

```
p._NewClass__inner()
```

```
We are inside inner method
```

312

Python**: Can I create variables that are automatically updated?

Yes. You can by using the property decorator. We will first discuss the property decorator and later we will see how derived variables can be created.

In the example below, a Customer class is defined with one instance variable __name, a private instance variable. In the initializer, __name is set to an empty string. Since the private variable cannot be accessed outside the class definition (excluding the name mangling method), a function that can fetch (or get) the value and a function that can set the value needs to be provided. The method get_name gets that value corresponding to the __name and method set_name sets the value.

In the call to set the value, the string, "Leo" is supplied to the method set_name. Similarly, the name is obtained by calling get_name method. This construct works but it is not Pythonic.

```python
class Customer(object):
    def __init__(self):
        self.__name = ""

    def get_name(self):
        return self.__name

    def set_name(self, name):
        self.__name = name
c = Customer()
```

```
c.set_name("Leo")
print(c.get_name())
```

Leo

A Pythonic way to set the name would be to assign the variable name (and not the private variable __name) to the required value using . (dot) notation. Similarly, the name must be accessed by using the . (dot) notation.

The class definition below is same as the one above with one change: the call to property object. The property object [https://docs.python.org/3/library/functions.html#property, https://www.programiz.com/python-programming/property], takes 4 parameters. They are: getter, setter, deleter and a doc string. The new publicly accessible variable is the object created by the property class. The first three parameters to the property class are function objects. When the value of a variable is requested, then the getter is called, when the value is set, the setter is called and when the variable is deleted, delete is called.

In the example below, the getter is get_name which returns the value stored in __name and the setter is set_name assigns the parameter of the function to __name. The call to the property class creates the object, 'name'. With this change, the call to set the value to __name involves using c.name, the name of the object that was created with property class. Similarly, accessing the value is as simple as c.name. Thus, the call is Pythonic with only one extra line of code. This version is functional but the class definition is peppered with a line that on a first glance is not connected to the class.

```
class Customer(object):
    def __init__(self):
        self.__name = ""

    def get_name(self):
        return self.__name

    def set_name(self, name):
        self.__name = name

    name = property(get_name, set_name)
c = Customer()
c.name =  "Leo"
print(c.name)
```

Leo

The version below is Pythonic both in terms of class definition and object creation. In this version, the property decorator is used to get the value of __name. The getter is also renamed to 'name' instead of the previous, 'get_name'. The setter is decorated with name.setter, where 'name' refers to the name of the getter. Even though the getter and setter are methods, the variable is still 'name' with no parentheses.

```
class Customer(object):
    def __init__(self):
```

```python
        self.__name = ""

    @property
    def name(self):
        return self.__name

    @name.setter
    def name(self, name):
        self.__name = name
c = Customer()
c.name = "Leo"
print(c.name)
```

Leo

With the following background, we will create a dependent or calculated variable. A dependent variable is one which is not assigned via a getter call but rather calculated. The code below is similar to the one above except for a new calculated property, 'salutation_name'. The property converts the first letter in the name to capital case using capitalize() function and then prefixes it with the string, 'Dr. '. The method is decorated with the decorator property. The call to get the value of salutation_name is as simple as using the dot notation, as shown in the print function call. Even though the property is defined as a method, it can be accessed without using parentheses.

```python
class Customer(object):
    def __init__(self):
```

```python
        self.__name = ""

    @property
    def name(self):
        return self.__name

    @name.setter
    def name(self, name):
        self.__name = name

    @property
    def salutation_name(self):
        return "Dr.
{0}".format(self.__name.capitalize())
c = Customer()
c.name = "leo"
print(c.name)
print(c.salutation_name) # The variable is the name of
the function
```

```
leo
Dr. Leo
```

Since the property is calculated, its value cannot be set from outside the class
definition and hence the assignment statement below fails.

```
c.salutation_name = 'Dr. Euler'
```

```
AttributeError                          Traceback
(most recent call last)
<ipython-input-9-e5f7c659a136> in <module>()
----> 1 c.salutation_name = 'Dr. Euler' # This will
throw an error.
AttributeError: can't set attribute
```

Python**: Can I create nested classes?

Nested classes are defined as classes defined inside another class. In Python, you can define such classes. They are useful for keeping classes that are logically together, encapsulating functionality within the outer class and also makes the code easy to maintain.

In the example below, the class Outer has one initializer and a nested class called Inner. In the initializer of the Outer class, an instance of the inner class is created. When an instance of Outer class is created, a corresponding instance of the Inner class is also created.

```
class Outer(object):
    def __init__(self):
        print("Initialized Outer class")
        self.inner = self.Inner()

    class Inner(object):
```

```
        def __init__(self):
            print("Initialized Inner class")


outer = Outer() # Create an instance of Outer class.
Outer in turn contains an # instance of Inner
```

```
Initialized Outer class
Initialized Inner class
```

Since we defined the nested class Inner as a public class, an instance of Inner can be created outside the class definition as well as shown below.

```
i = outer.Inner() # We can create more instances of
Inner
```

```
Initialized Inner class
```

If we do not need an instance of the Inner class, we can make it private by using __ (double underscore or dunder). In this case, outer.__Inner() will fail with AttributeError. Thus, only the Outer class can create instances making this approach safest if you need to use nested classes. In fact, we recommend making the Inner class private always with __ in the class name.

```
class Outer(object):
    def __init__(self):
        print("Initialized Outer class")
        self.inner = self.__Inner()
```

```python
    class __Inner(object):
        def __init__(self):
            print("Initialized Inner class")

outer = Outer()
i = outer.__Inner() # This will fail as __Inner is a
private class
```

```
Initialized Outer class
Initialized Inner class
-----------------------------------------------------------
--------------
AttributeError                          Traceback (most
recent call last)
<ipython-input-21-a818bfaef49f> in <module>()
     10 outer = Outer()
     11
---> 12 i = outer.__Inner() # This will fail as __Inner
is a private class


AttributeError: 'Outer' object has no attribute
'__Inner'
```

What is the scope of variables in the Outer and Inner class?

The Outer class has access to all the public variables in the Inner class. However, the Outer class does not have access to private variables in the Inner class as is normally the case with private variables. Thus, in the example below, the public instance variable, 'a' in the Inner class is accessible to the Outer class. The public class variable 'classvar' in the Inner class is also accessible to the Outer class. However, the private variable, '__b' is not accessible in the Outer class. Hence the last print call in the Outer's initializer will fail due to AttributeError.

```python
class Outer(object):
    def __init__(self):
        print("Initialized Outer class")
        self.inner = self.__Inner()
        print("The value of a in the Inner class is
{0}".format(self.inner.a))
        print("Class variable, 'classvar' in the Inner
class via class name is
'{0}'".format(self.__Inner.classvar))
        print("Class variable, 'classvar' in the Inner
class via instance is
'{0}'".format(self.inner.classvar))
        print("The value of a in the Inner class is
'{0}'".format(\
                            self.inner.__b))

    class __Inner(object):
```

```
        classvar = "MyInnerClass"
        def __init__(self):
            print("Initialized Inner class")
            self.a = 10
            self.__b = 20


outer = Outer()
```

```
Initialized Outer class
Initialized Inner class
The value of a in the Inner class is 10
Class variable, 'classvar' in the Inner class via class
name is 'MyInnerClass'
Class variable, 'classvar' in the Inner class via
instance is 'MyInnerClass'
------------------------------------------------------------
--------------
AttributeError                         Traceback (most
recent call last)
<ipython-input-22-71e038349c23> in <module>()
    15              self.__b = 20
    16
---> 17 outer = Outer()
<ipython-input-22-71e038349c23> in __init__(self)
     6          print("Class variable, 'classvar' in the
Inner class via class name is '{0}'"
.format(self.__Inner.classvar))
```

```
    7            print("Class variable, 'classvar' in the
Inner class via instance is '{0}'"
.format(self.inner.classvar))
----> 8            print("The value of a in the Inner class
is {0}".format(self.inner.__b))
    9
   10     class __Inner(object):
AttributeError: '__Inner' object has no attribute
'_Outer__b'
```

__Inner class can access the class variables in Outer using the traditional mechanism of using class name. Thus, the last print function call in the __Inner's initializer will succeed in the example below.

However, __Inner does not have an instance of Outer. Hence it cannot access any of Outer's instance variables. This can be overcome by creating an instance of Outer and passing it to __Inner. However, this will result in circular reference. (i.e., Outer has an instance of __Inner and __Inner in turn has an instance of Outer)

```
class Outer(object):
    outerclassvar = 'OuterClass'
    def __init__(self):
        print("Initialized Outer class")
        self.outera = 30
        self.inner = self.__Inner()

    class __Inner(object):
```

```
      def __init__(self):
          print("Initialized Inner class")
          print("The value of 'outerclassvar' called
in the Inner class is
'{0}'".format(Outer.outerclassvar))


outer = Outer()
```

```
Initialized Outer class
Initialized Inner class
The value of 'outerclassvar' called in the Inner class
is 'OuterClass'
```

Would I really need it?

One of the main reason nested classes are useful is in the process of keeping code clean.

Imagine a scenario that Outer and Inner classes are not nested but instead are two different classes. However, if the Inner class is only used by Outer and no one else and if a need arises to keep the scope of accessing an instance of Inner restricted only to Outer, then nesting provides a convenient mechanism.

Another scenario for using nested classes is to keep all the code belonging to a certain functionality together. Imagine that Outer and Inner classes are two different classes and are not nested. However, the Inner and Outer class are strongly dependent on each other. So, during code rewrite, it becomes important to keep the two classes together. This can be achieved by using nesting.

15. Exceptions

Introduction

A Python program may contain errors. When Python encounters some of these errors, it stops the execution, which can result in poor user experience. Such errors can be classified in two categories: errors generated during code interpretation and errors generated during code execution. The errors such as SyntaxError are generated when Python interpreter cannot understand the code while errors such as ZeroDivisionError, IndexError etc. are generated during code execution (run-time). These errors are also called exceptions.

Python provides the ability to handle these exceptions. However it is the responsibility of the programmer to handle them as Python cannot make assumptions on the correct logic of the code.

To understand this better let's consider an example, consider a list with only two items and the user requests the third item. Python cannot complete this request as there are only two items in the list. This type of error is called an IndexError and the failure (if not handled by the code) is catastrophic and will terminate the Python process. It is the responsibility of the programmer to ensure that the third element is not accessed during program execution. If the error happens at runtime, the programmer has to handle these errors, so that the process does not terminate.

In this chapter, we will discuss handling both categories of exceptions. We will also discuss few of these exceptions and the mechanism to handle them.

Syntax Error

Syntax or parsing errors appear at interpretation time. In the code below, we get a SyntaxError as we did not include a colon at the end of the for-loop statement. Apart from the line number where the error occurred, the small arrow shows the exact location as well. This error message helps us to address the syntax error. If the program was run at least once, the error would be caught.

```
my_list = range(10)
for i in my_list
    print(i)
```

```
File "<ipython-input-1-6b76606b8b72>", line 2
    for i in my_list
SyntaxError: invalid syntax
```

The syntax error will appear even in the places where the code is not executed. In the code below, we define a function f that iterates through elements in range(10) and prints them. Notice that the function f is never called. However, when the code is executed, the Python interpreter identifies the SyntaxError.

```
def f():
    for i in range(10)
        print(i)
```

```
File "<ipython-input-1-83f9cc44ef4b>", line 2
```

```
    for i in range(10)
SyntaxError: invalid syntax
```

Exception

Errors generated during the run-time are called exceptions. In the following code, we try to convert a string into an integer. At the time of execution, the typecasting (a fancy word for convert) fails because the string contains a non-digit and the Python's built-in ValueError exception is raised. The traceback message points to the line where the error occurred.

```
A = int('345g')
print(A)
```

```
--------------------------------------------------------------
---------------
ValueError                                Traceback (most
recent call last)
<ipython-input-2-601db17d2a3e> in <module>()
----> 1 A = int('345g')
      2 print(A)

ValueError: invalid literal for int() with base 10:
'345g'
```

A few Python built-in exceptions are listed in the below table.

Exception Type	Description
IndexError	Raised when a index in a collection or sequence is out of range.
KeyError	Raised when a key is not found in a dictionary.
FileNotFoundError	Raised when an input or output operation fails.
NameError	Raised when a variable name is not found.
ValueError	Raised when a built-in operation or function receives an argument that has the right type but an inappropriate value. For example, the int function receives a string but the string contains a non-digit character.
ZeroDivisionError	Raised when the second argument of a division or modulo operation is zero.

You can find a list of all built-in exceptions at
https://docs.python.org/3/library/exceptions.html#bltin-exceptions. Some
modules may have their own list of exceptions.

Try-Except

Python provides a programmatic mechanism to handle these exceptions using try-except clauses, so that the program continues to run instead of terminating. If an exception is raised in the try block, the except block can handle it by printing the error message or by performing any other valid operation.

Let us reconsider the previous example for ValueError and handle the error using a try-except construct. In the try block, we try to typecast 345g to an integer. Since we know what type of exceptions could possibly be raised (based on experience and reading documentation), we create an except block with that particular exception type. In this example, since we typecast a string, we know the possible exception we could get is ValueError. So, we handle ValueError exception in the except block and assign a new value to A. If A can be successfully typecast, then no exceptions would be raised. If the exception raised is a ValueError, then the statements in the except block will be executed.

```
try:
    A = int("345g")
except ValueError:
    A = 100
print(A)
```

```
100
```

ValueError exception also carries a message that can be printed. Below, we say except ValueError as v and print v in the exception block, thus adding additional detail to the error message.

```python
try:
    A = int("345g")
except ValueError as v:
    print("The message is: ", v)
    A = 100
print(A)
```

```
The message is:  invalid literal for int() with base 10:
'345g'
100
```

In the example below, we typecast B = '345' to integer. Since this can be achieved without any problem; no exception will be raised and B will not be reassigned to 10.

```python
try:
    B = int('345')
except ValueError:
    B = 10
print(B)
```

```
345
```

It is always a good idea to use one try block to perform only one operation. Below, we perform typecasting and division in two separate try blocks and have an exception block for each try block. Since A can't be type casted, ValueError exception is raised. We enter the ValueError's except block where we print the error message and assign a new value to A. Then in the next try block we perform division. Since B is zero, ZeroDivisionError exception is raised and we enter the except block with the name ZeroDivisionError. In this except block, we print the error message and assign A to C.

```python
try:
    A = int('345g')
except ValueError as v:
    print("The error message is: ", v)
    A = 100
print("The value of A is: ", A)
B = 0
try:
    C = A/B
except ZeroDivisionError as z:
    print("The error message is: ", z)
    C = A
print("The value of C is: ", C)
```

```
The error message is:  invalid literal for int() with
base 10: '345g'
The value of A is:  100
```

The error message is: division by zero

The value of C is: 100

Try-Except-Else-Finally

The try-except clause has variations like try-except-else or try-except-else-finally. The else block is called only when there are no exceptions. The finally block is executed regardless of whether there was an exception or not. Below we have a try-except-else-finally construct. In the try block, we typecast a string to an integer. In the except block, we print the error message and reassign a new value to A. In the else block, we have a print statement indicating that there are no exceptions. In the finally block we print the value of A. For the specific value of A in this example, the type casting will fail and the ValueError exception is raised. So, the statements in the except block are executed and then the statement in the finally block is executed.

```
try:
    A = int('345g')
except ValueError as v:
    print("The error message is: ", v)
    A = 100
else:
    print("There were no exceptions!")
finally:
    print("The value of A is: ", A)
```

The error message is: invalid literal for int() with base 10: '345g'

```
The value of A is:   100
```

Instead if A is '345' as in the example below, then the typecast will succeed. So, the statements in the else clause will be executed and then the statements in the finally clause will be executed.

```python
try:
    A = int('345')
except ValueError as v:
    print("The error message is: ", v)
    A = 100
else:
    print("There were no exceptions!")
finally:
    print("The value of A is: ", A)
```

```
There are no exceptions!
The value of A is:   345
```

Custom Exceptions

When building large applications or libraries, there might be need for creating custom exceptions. In this section, we will learn how to create custom exceptions with just few lines of code.

All custom exceptions have to be derived from Python's Exception class or derived from other class that is also of type Exception. It may or may not contain any methods. However, it's a good practice to add a __init__ method that takes a descriptive message which can be returned when the exception is raised. The convention is to add the word "Error" as suffix to the exception name.

Below is an example of the custom exception class named FirstLetterError that is raised if the first letter of a string is not 'z'. We show two ways of defining this class. First, without any methods. Since no methods or attributes are defined, the FirstLetterError exception will inherit all methods from the Exception class.

```python
class FirstLetterError(Exception):
    pass
```

Another way of creating a custom exception is to define a __init__ method.

```python
class FirstLetterError(Exception):
    def __init__(self, *args, **kwargs):
        super().__init__(*args, **kwargs)
```

We will use the FirstLetterError exception defined above and perform an exception check in the code below. The checkstringforz function converts the string to lowercase and checks if the first element is 'z'. If so, it returns True or else it raises the FirstLetterError exception with the message, "The first letter is not z!".

Now let us obtain an input from the user and check and see if the first letter in the input is 'z' using the function, check_string_for_z. The try block calls the check_string_for_z function and passes the input supplied by the user.

335

The except block prints the error message. When we run this code, the user is prompted to input a string.

Let us take an example input where the user enters 'cute'. Since cute does not start with z, the FirstLetterError exception is raised and the print statement in the except block is executed.

```
class FirstLetterError(Exception):
    def __init__(self, *args, **kwargs):
        super().__init__(*args, **kwargs)
def check_string_for_z(ustring):
    if ustring.lower().startswith('z'):
        return True
    else:
        raise FirstLetterError("The first letter is not
z!")
ustring = input("Please enter a string that starts with
z: ")
try:
    check_string_for_z(ustring)
except FirstLetterError as f:
    print("The error message is:", f)
```

```
Please enter a string that starts with z: cute
The error message is:  The first letter is not z!
```

Learning Activity 1: A quadratic expression is of the form ax^2+bx+c where a, b and c are called the coefficients and $a \neq 0$. Assume that a, b and c for this

336

question to be an integer. Ask user to input the three coefficients of a quadratic expression. Create an exception class called *CoeffZeroError* that is flagged when the first coefficient of the user input is zero.

Learning Activity 2: *Ask user to input an integer greater than or equal to 30. Create an exception class called RangeError that gets flagged if the number is outside the specified range. If the number falls within the range, then compute 3^(the number).*

Learning Activity 3: *What exception would Python raise when you try to open a file that doesn't exist? After you have determined the potential Python exception, write a try-except block to handle this.*

As always prevention is better than cure. For example, a KeyError will be raised when we fetch an element that does not have a specific key in the dictionary. One approach would be use try-except and catch the KeyError exception. The other elegant approach is to check if the key exists in the dictionary using the "in" keyword before accessing it.

16. Modules and packages

Introduction

The important feature of any programming language is to provide ability to reuse code. We have already discussed features such as functions and classes that enable code reusability. However, if there are multiples functions and classes that need to be reused, a module or package can be created and share with others.

In Python, modules are files that contain functions, classes and variables that can be reused. A package on the other hand is directory that contains one or more files or directories that in turn contain Python functions, classes and other statements. Sometimes these two terms are used interchangeably.

Since Python is an open source software, hundreds and hundreds of developers have open sourced their modules and packages to the community. As of May 2018, there are more than 100,000 packages in https://pypi.org/. Python has a simplified import mechanism. For example, if we have to use sine function we can import the math module where the sine function is defined and use it.

Python also provides ways to create custom modules and share them with others.

Built-in Modules

Let us look at some built-in Python modules. Since there are 1000s of these modules, we will focus on only modules that are in core Python. This discussion will provide enough background that will then allow you to understand importing other modules.

math

The math module [https://docs.python.org/3/library/math.html] can be imported by using the following line:

import math

it is generally recommended that the import statements are at the top of the file even though Python allows importing modules in the middle of the code as well.

A few functions from math module are listed in the following table.

Function	Description
ceil(x)	Returns the smallest integer greater than or equal to x.
log(x, [base])	Returns the logarithm of x to the specified base. If no base is given then natural logarithm of x is returned.
pow(x,y)	Returns x raised to the power y, if x and y are finite. The pow(1.0, y) and pow(x, 0.0) is 1.0, even when x is a zero or a NaN. If both x and y are not integers, then pow(x,y) is undefined and raises ValueError.
sqrt(x)	Returns the square root of x.

cos(x)	Returns the cosine of x in radians
sin(x)	Returns the sine of x in radians.
tan(x)	Returns the tangent of x in radians.

There are two constants in the math module –

pi – The mathematical constant pi

e – The mathematical constant e

Let us consider some examples for math module. First let us import math module. Below, we print the first ten digits after decimal point in the constant pi. Since the value of pi is defined in the math module, we fetched the value of pi using math.pi and not just pi.

```
import math
print("Pi with first 10 digits after decimal point:
%0.10f" %math.pi)
```

```
Pi with first 10 digits after decimal point:
3.1415926536
```

To determine the value of sin(pi/2), we will use the sin() function and the constant value pi.

```
c = math.sin(math.pi/2)
print(c)
```

```
1.0
```

We use the pow() function to find the value of 5^7, here 5 is the base and 7 is the exponent.

```
z = math.pow(5, 7)
print(z)
```

```
78125.0
```

Below, we find the logarithm of 10 base 2.

```
b1 = math.log(10, 2)
print(b1)
```

```
3.3219280948873626
```

If we don't specify base in the log() function, then the natural log will be computed as shown below.

```
b2 = math.log(10)
print(b2)
```

2.302585092994046

The math module has other functions as well. We will leave it as an exercise to the readers to explore.

sys

The sys module [https://docs.python.org/3/library/sys.html] provides variables and functions that allows interaction with the Python interpreter. Hence, if you wish to interact with the interpreter from the command line or to fetch interpreter details, you would need the sys module.

Here is a list of a few sys attributes and functions.

Attribute	Description
sys.argv	Returns a list of command line arguments that were passed to a Python script. The first element is the file name.
sys.version	Returns a string containing the version number of the Python interpreter.
sys.winver	Returns the version number from the registry keys on Windows platforms.

One of the most common use of sys module is to fetch the parameters sent to the Python interpreter from the operating system command line.

Let us create a file called average.py, where the average of two values is computed. The file must contain the following code. In the code, the list of arguments supplied by the user is printed using sys.argv. The value in index 1 and 2 are extracted from the list sys.argv, converted to integers and the average is calculated.

```python
# save the content of this cell to average.py
# and run it from the OS command line using the syntax
# python average.py 12 19
import sys
print(sys.argv)
x = float(sys.argv[1])
y = float(sys.argv[2])
average = (x + y)/2
print("The average of the two values is: %0.2f"%average)
```

To run this file, we have to use command line or the terminal on your computer. Then we have to change directory (using the cd command) to the folder where the average.py file is located. In the folder containing this file, we have to type the following command and provide the file name along with the two values next to the file name.

```
> python average.py 12 19
```

The following output will be shown in the command line or the terminal

```
['average.py', '12', '19']
The average of the two values is: 15.50
```

To get the Python interpreter version number, we can use sys.version as in the example below. As the output indicates, we obtain the version number, 3.6.0, the details of the distribution such as Anaconda, the compiler used to build the version etc.

```
>>> import sys

>>> sys.version
```

```
'3.6.0 |Anaconda 4.3.1 (64-bit)| (default, Dec 23 2016,
11:57:41) [MSC v.1900 64 bit (AMD64)]'
```

os

The os module [https://docs.python.org/3/library/os.html] allows a portable way to access operating system functionality.

A few os functions are listed below.

Function	Description
os.walk(path)	Returns a tuple with (root path, directories, files names).

os.listdir(path)	Returns all the files in the path.
os.getcwd()	Returns the name of the current working directory.
os.mkdir(directory name)	Creates a new directory if no directory by that name exists. However, if a directory exists, then 'FileExistsError' is raised.
os.chdir(path)	Changes the current working directory to the given path.
os.remove(filename)	Remove a file.
os.rmdir()	Remove an empty directory.

Let us consider some examples.

Below, we import os and then use getcwd() function to obtain the information about the current working directory.

```
import os
print(os.getcwd())
```

```
C:\Users\username\notebooks
```

We create a new directory called New D using mkdir() function.

```
os.mkdir('New D')
```

Now we if want to create another directory by the name New D will raise 'FileExistsError' because the directory already exists.

```
os.mkdir('New D')
```

```
-----------------------------------------------------------
--------------------
FileExistsError                         Traceback
(most recent call last)
<ipython-input-9-95c030c51868> in <module>()
----> 1 os.mkdir('New D')

FileExistsError: [WinError 183] Cannot create a file
when that file already exists: 'New D'
```

glob

The glob module [https://docs.python.org/3/library/glob.html] returns all the pathnames that match a specified pattern as done in Unix shell. To use glob functions and attributes, we have to import glob module. In the example below, the glob() function in the glob module will return a Python list with the names of all the files that have py extension in the current working directory. However, a path can also be provided by having glob.glob(path, '*,py'). If there are no files or directories that match the criterion, glob() returns an empty list.

```
import glob
print(glob.glob('*.py'))
```

```
average.py
```

If you would rather use a memory efficient iterator version, then use iglob()
function instead of glob.

random

The random module [https://docs.python.org/3/library/random.html] can be
used to generate pseudo random numbers. A few mostly used random
functions along with their description are listed below.

Function	Description
random.seed(seedvalue)	Initializes the random number generator with the provided seedvalue. If seedvalue is not given or is None, then the current system time is used. If seedvalue is an int, the value is used. If seedvalue is not an int, it is converted to an int.

	You can also supply an optional version number. The default value is 2.
random.randrange(a)	Returns a randomly selected integer from the range [0, a). Notice that a is not included.
random.randrange(a, b, [step])	Returns a randomly selected integer from the range of values [a, b) with the specified step size. If step size is not specified, then a random integer from range [a, b) is returned. The value b is not included.
randint(a, b)	Returns a random integer between range [a, b] including b.
random.choice(sequence)	Returns a random element from the non-empty sequence. If sequence is empty then 'IndexError' is raised.
random.sample(sequence, k)	Returns k randomly selected values form the sequence without replacement.
random.random()	Returns a floating-point number in the range $[0.0, 1.0]$.

Let us consider a few examples. Below, we use random() function to obtain a floating-point number in the range $[0.0, 1.0]$.

```
import random
print(random.random())
```

```
0.1004721389464337
```

We will see a few examples for randrange. In the first example, we provide only the stopping value, 11 to randrange() function. An integer between [0, 11) is returned. In this case, the output is 5.

```
print(random.randrange(11))
```

```
5
```

We provide both the starting value, 2 and the stopping values, 11 to randrange() function. An integer in range [2, 11) is returned. In this case, the output is 3.

```
print(random.randrange(2, 11))
```

```
3
```

Below, to the randrange() function, we provide, the starting value, 10, the stopping value, 21 and also the step size, 2. An integer in range [10, 21) with step size 2 will be returned. The possible integers would be 10, 12, 14, 16, 18 and 20 (i.e.,) even numbers only. In this case, the output is 20.

```
print(random.randrange(10, 21, 2))
```

20

If we want to include the stopping value, then we should use randint().
Below, we find a random integer between 12 and 22 including 12 and 22
using randint() function. In this case, the output is 19.

```
print(random.randint(12, 22))
```

19

Here, we randomly choose a value from a list using the choice() function.
The output in this case is 14.

```
list1 = [13, 14, 19, 21, 23]
print(random.choice(list1))
```

14

Below, from range(11, 21) and we select 5 numbers without replacement
using the sample() function. In this case, the output is [12, 20, 11, 18, 14].

```
print(random.sample(range(11, 21), 5))
```

```
[12, 20, 11, 18, 14]
```

The time module [https://docs.python.org/3/library/time.html] provides functions that allow manipulation of time.

A few mostly used time module functions are listed below.

Function	Description
time.asctime([t])	If t is provided, then a string representing time is returned. If t is not provided, then localtime is returned.
time.clock()	In Unix, the current processor time is returned. In Windows, the wall-clock time elapsed, since the first call to this function will be returned.
time.struct_time	It is a data type similar to a named tuple that is returned by gmtime(), localtime() and strptime(). The elements in a tuple are explained below.
time.time()	Returns the time in seconds since the epoch as a floating-point number. The epoch time for most computers is Jan 1, 1970 00:00:00 (UTC).

time.gmtime([seconds])	If seconds from epoch time is provided then, struct_time is returned. Otherwise, the current Greenwich meantime is returned.
time.localtime([seconds])	If seconds from epoch time is provided then, struct_time is returned. Otherwise, the current local time is returned.
time.sleep(seconds)	Suspends execution of the calling thread for the given number of seconds.
time.strftime(format, [t])	Converts a tuple or a struct_time to string format. If t is not provided, the current local time is returned as a string. For various formatting options please check the documentation.
time.strptime()	Converts a string representing date and time into a struct_time data type. This is reverse of strftime().

To use time module, we have to import time as shown below. We then print the formatted local time using asctime() function.

```
import time
time1 = time.localtime()
print(time.asctime(time1))
```

```
Sun May 28 21:14:12 2018
```

Below, the clock() function will return the seconds lapsed from the first time a call was made to this function.

```
print(time.clock())
```

```
3.526170177204156e-07
```

Here, the time() function returns the seconds lapsed from the epoch time.

```
print(time.time())
```

```
1496032010.2932568
```

time.struct_time returns a tuple that contains the date, time and few other attributes. The below table explains the value in each of the indices in the tuple. The values can be accessed by using the index or the attribute name.

Index	Attribute	Values
0	tm_year	Represents year in 4 digits.
1	tm_mon	Represents month in the range [1, 12].

2	tm_mday	Represents the day of the month in the range [1, 31].
3	tm_hour	Represents hours in the range [0, 23].
4	tm_min	Represents minutes in the range [0, 59].
5	tm_sec	Represents seconds in range [0, 61]. The value 60 is considered for leap year and value 61 for historical reasons.
6	tm_wday	Represents days of the week as digits in the range [0, 6], Monday is 0, Tuesday is 1 etc.
7	tm_yday	Represents the day from the range [1, 366].
8	tm_isdst	Returns 1 if the daylight savings are in effect and 0 when it is not.

When a function is expecting struct_time but instead a tuple of incorrect length is passed, TypeError will be raised.

If you need to convert the time in seconds since the epoch to time.struct_time object, then you can use the gmtime() function as shown below.

```
print(time.gmtime())
```

```
time.struct_time(tm_year=2018, tm_mon=5, tm_mday=29,
tm_hour=18, tm_min=47, tm_sec=38, tm_wday=0,
tm_yday=149, tm_isdst=0)
```

The strftime function can be used to convert a datetime object to a string, so that it can be shown to a user or transmitted to another application. The various format arguments for time.strftime() function can be found in the documentation at https://docs.python.org/3/library/time.html#time.strftime. We will discuss a few examples here.

Below, we use the strftime to convert the current local time to a string and we specify format type. Here %a is for abbreviated weekday name, %d is for day of the month as a decimal number [0, 31], %b is for abbreviated month name, %Y is for year with century as a decimal number, %H is for hours as 24-hour clock as a decimal number [0, 23], %M is for month as a decimal number [01, 12], and %S is for seconds as a decimal number [00, 61].

```
print(time.strftime("%a, %d %b %Y %H:%M:%S",
time.localtime()))
```

```
Tue, 29 May 2017 11:49:49 +0000
```

The inverse of strftime is the strptime function, which takes a string as an input and returns a struct_time object. This function is useful when the date time string was read from a file and has to be converted to a struct_time object for further manipulation.

In the example below, we supply the stirng, '29 May 2017 ' to the strptime() function. The function also needs to be informed about the formatting of the string, so that it can interpret the string correctly. In this example, the format arguments %d stands for the day of the month, %b for abbreviated month and %Y for year with century. The output contains the struct_time object. The values not specified are filled with default values.

```
print(time.strptime("1 Jan 2017", "%d %b %Y"))
```

```
time.struct_time(tm_year=2017, tm_mon=1, tm_mday=1,
tm_hour=0, tm_min=0, tm_sec=0, tm_wday=6, tm_yday=1,
tm_isdst=-1)
```

datetime

The datetime module [https://docs.python.org/3/library/datetime.html] provides functions and classes for manipulating dates and times in multiple ways. A few datetime functions are listed below.

Function	Description
datetime.time(hour, minutes, second)	Returns formatted time with hours:minutes:seconds

datetime.date.today()	Returns today's date with four-digit year-month-day of the month.
datetime.timedelta()	Time difference in terms of day, hours, minutes, seconds or microseconds can be specified.

Below, to the datetime.time() function we provide 1, 2, 4, where 1 represents the hour, 2 represents the minutes and 4 represents the seconds.

```
import datetime
print(datetime.time(1, 2, 4))
```

```
01:02:04
```

To get today's date, we can use datetime.date.today() function as shown below.

```
print(datetime.date.today())
```

```
2018-05-20
```

If we want to add one day to today's date, we could use the datetime.date.today and datetime.timedelta to achieve this as shown below.

```
td = datetime.date.today()  # Today's date
tomd = datetime.date.today()+datetime.timedelta(days=1)
print(td, tomd)
```

2018-05-20 2018-05-21

Learning Activity 1: For the first ten million positive integers, find the sin(x) for each value with list comprehension and without list comprehension. Using the time module, compute the time taken for both.

Learning Activity 2: Take five numbers from the user and make it into a list. Randomly select a number from the list. Write a function to compute 2 power that number. And show the result to the user.

Learning Activity 3: Power ball machine creator. A power ball needs a list of 6 numbers. The first 5 numbers have value between 1 and 59. The last number also called power ball number will be between 1 and 35. Before generating the numbers, seed the process with an integer. Then run the code multiple times.

Learning Activity 4: In the code that you wrote for learning activity #3, seed the random number generator with today's date and then with today's date and time. What do you observe?

Creating custom modules

So far, we have seen how to use Python built-in modules. Now let us consider writing our own modules. Let us first define a function called fun_list in file1.py. The function takes a list and return a randomly chosen item from the list.

```python
# We are in file1.py
import random


def fun_list(list1):
    choice = random.choice(list1)
    return choice
```

Now let us import file1 into another file called file2.py and let us make a call to the fun_list. Note that in this case file1.py and file2.py are in the same directory. When we make a call to fun_list() we have to prefix this function with file1. The output of the function call is an item randomly returned from list1. Since an item was chosen randomly, your output might be different.

```python
'''
We are in file2.py. We are importing file1 that is
in the same directory as file2.py
'''

import file1
list1 = ["Apple", "Koala", "Giraffe"]
# since fun_list() is a function in file1, we have to
```

```
                    prefix the
# fun_list with file1
print(file1.fun_list(A))
```

Koala

You can also add other variables, functions and classes to this file and import them as needed in other files. As you can see, creating a Python module is easy. Just remember to appropriately document your code.

Creating custom packages

As we discussed earlier a package is a folder that contains one or more Python files or folders. In this section, we will discuss creating a custom package.

We will create a folder called folder1 and place the file1.py from the previous example in to this folder. To make folder1 Python importable as a package, it should contain a file named __init__.py. The __init__.py can be an empty, zero-byte file but the file has to exist. The file1.py contains definition of the function fun_list(). Let file2.py be in the same level as folder1. To use fun_list() from file1.py in file2.py, we should first import folder1 into file2.py and then make a call to fun_list() as shown in the code below. Notice that the call to fun_list in file2.py is folder1.file1.fun_list.

```
'''

We are in file2.py. The file2.py is in the same level as
folder1.
```

```
We are importing folder1 that is in the same directory
as file2.
'''

import folder1

list1 = ["Apple", "Koala", "Giraffe"]
# since fun_list() is a function in file1 which is in
the folder folder1,
# we have to prefix the fun_list with folder1.file1
print(folder1.file1.fun_list(list1))


Apple
```

If your package contains folders, sub-folders etc., then each of the folders
and sub-folders must also contain the __init__.py file. As you can see,
creating a Python package is also easy.

In the example above, file2.py that imports the package and the package are
in the same directory. This however is not necessarily the common method
for importing packages. How do we import a package that is anywhere on
your computer? How can Python find this particular folder? We can do so by
adding the folder containing Python package to PYTHONPATH.

NOTE: When Python needs to import a particular module, it will first check
the local directory from which the file was run, then it will search in the
folders in PYTHONPATH, and finally it will check the site-packages folder
[https://docs.python.org/3/install/] for the specific Python installation. If
Python fails to find the module, then it will throw an error. You can read

more details at https://docs.python.org/3/tutorial/modules.html#the-module-search-path.

Setting up PYTHONPATH

PYTHONPATH is an environment variable similar to the environment variable PATH. It contains a list of directories separated by : (colon) in the case of Linux or Mac or separated by ; (semi-colon) in the case of Windows. If it does not exist, it can be added using the following instruction. In the explanation below, we term 'folder' refer to the folder where the Python modules are located.

On Windows: Open systems environment variables, which opens a new window called System Properties. Select Environment Variables, which opens a new window. In the System Variables check if PYTHONPATH is already there. If not, then click New and this will open a new window called New System Variable. Type Variable name: PYTHONPATH and for the Variable value: the whole path where your folder is located. You can also browse and select.

If PYTHONPATH already exists, then add the path where your folder is located to the existing list of folders. Apply and press ok.

On Mac: Check if PYTHONPATH is already there by typing

```
echo $PYTHONPATH
```

in your terminal. If you get a blank screen then type the following. Make sure to replace the folder_path with the folder containing packages.

362

```
export PYTHONPATH=$PYTHONPATH:folder_path
```

This will setup the environment variable for only the current session.

To ensure that the PYTHONPATH is available permanently, you should put the PYTHONPATH in the bashrc or bash_profile file and source it. Then, whenever you open a new session, OS will check the bash file and setup the environment. You should type

```
export PYTHONPATH=$PYTHONPATH:folder_path >> ~/.bashrc

# or bash_profile

source ~/.bashrc # or bash_profile
```

Use bashrc for OS less than OS X 10.10 Yosemite. For others, use bash_profile.

On Linux: To add PYTHONPATH permanently

```
echo 'export PYTHONPATH=$PYTHONPATH:folder_path' >> .bashrc

source ~/.bashrc
```

Once you have the Python importable folder in the PYTHONPATH, then you can import the folder and start using it. For example, if folder1 was on your Desktop and you have included path to your Desktop in

PYTHONPATH, then you can just import folder1 in any Python file or Jupyter notebook and use it.

17. File Input Output

Introduction

In this chapter, we will learn about the various options available in reading and writing text files. We will then follow it with reading and writing various file types such as comma separated value (CSV) format, pickle and shelve.

Text and binary files

To read a file or to write to a file, we need to open the file and when we no longer need the file, we close it. We need to create a file object also known as file handler to perform any operations on the file. The open() function takes two arguments: filename and mode, both are provided as strings. It returns a file object.

Different modes for reading a file are described in the table below.

Mode	Description
For all the read modes, the file pointer is placed at the beginning of the file.	
r	Reading only.
rb	Reading in binary.
r+	Reading and writing.

| rb+ | Reading and writing in binary. |

Different modes for writing to a file are described below:

Mode	Description
All the writing modes overwrite an existing file or create a new file if the file does not exist.	
w	Writing only.
wb	Writing in binary format.
w+	Writing and reading.
wb+	Writing and reading in binary format.

Different modes for appending to an existing file are described below.

Mode	Description
All the appending modes append to an existing file or create a new file if the file does not exist.	
a	Appending only.
ab	Appending in binary format.

a+		Appending and reading.
ab+		Appending and reading in binary format.

A few methods to read and write, opening and closing text files are described below.

Method/ Function	Syntax	Description
open	open(filename, mode)	Opens the file in the specified mode. If no mode is provided, then the default mode is read.
close	filehandler.close()	Closes the file object.
read	filehandler.read(size)	Reads file's content as per the size. If no size is given or is negative, then entire contents of the file will be read and returned as string in the text mode and as byte object in binary mode.
readline	filehandler.readline()	Reads a single line from the file.

readlines	filehandler.readlines( )	Returns a list with all the lines in a file as elements of the list.
write	filehandler.write(string)	Writes the string to the file.
writelines	filehandler.writelines (sequence)	Writes strings from the sequence. Will not add newline character.
tell	filehandler.tell()	Returns file object's current position as number of bytes from the beginning of the file.
seek()	filehandler.seek(offset, from_postition)	Considers the offset and from_position and changes the file object's position, from_position where 0 means beginning of the file, 1 means current location, 2 means end of the file.

We will apply some of these methods to read and write files.

Reading files

Let us first read a file named python_list.txt file. The file contains the following information

Today

is a

sunny day

make sure to

wear a   hat!

We open this file in the read mode and use a file object, readfile to handle the file. The readline() function returns a list with every line as an element in the list. We loop through the lines in the file using readlines() method. We strip leading and trailing newline, tab, carriage return and whitespace using strip() function.

```python
readfile = open("python_list.txt","r")
for lines in readfile.readlines():
    print(lines.strip())
```

Today

is a

sunny day

make sure to

wear a   hat!

Now let us only print the lines that are not empty. In the code below, apart from opening the file and looping through each line, we strip the lines and for each iteration, it is stored in cleaned. Only the lines that have a non-empty string will be printed.

```python
readfile = open("python_list.txt","r")
for lines in readfile.readlines():
    cleaned = lines.strip()
    if cleaned:
        print(cleaned)
```

```
Today
is a
sunny day
make sure to
wear a    hat!
```

In the above examples, we did not close the file and this is a bad habit. Before we close the file, let us use tell() function to know the file object's current position.

```python
readfile = open("python_list.txt","r")
for lines in readfile.readlines():
    print(lines.strip())

print("The current position is: ", readfile.tell())
```

```
Today
```

```
is a

sunny  day

make  sure  to

wear  a        hat!
The  current  position  is:   76
```

Once the file is read the file object is at the end of the file. To read again, we have to reopen the file or use seek() method to move the file object's position. Now let us use the seek() method to move the file object's position from the current position which is the end of the file to the beginning of the file with offset 25. We read using read() method. Since the offset is 25, the read() method prints all the remaining lines in the file after the first 25 bytes.

```
readfile.seek(25, 0)
print(readfile.read())
```

```
        make  sure  to

        wear  a        hat!
```

Writing files

Below, we write into a new file called new_list.txt. This file will be created in the same folder where the py file resides if it does not exist. Since writelines() does not automatically insert a newline character we exclusively include it.

```python
fh = open('new_list.txt', 'w+')
fh.writelines('Too much')
fh.writelines('\n')
fh.writelines('jelly')
fh.writelines('\n')
fh.writelines('is not good.')
```

Since our mode is 'w+', we use seek(0,0) to move the file object's position to the beginning of the file and then we start reading the file.

```python
fh.seek(0,0)
print(fh.read())
```

```
Too much
jelly
is not good.
```

We will finally close the file object using close() method. If we try to open a closed file, then Python will give a ValueError.

```python
fh.close()
```

```
print(fh.read())
```

```
--------------------------------------------------------------
--------------
ValueError                              Traceback
(most recent call last)
<ipython-input-16-150f5b3dc47d> in <module>()
      1 fh.close()
----> 2 print(fh.read())

ValueError: I/O operation on closed file.
```

Now, we open the new_list.txt again and append a couple of lines using the 'a+' mode. We then use seek to move the file object's location and then read the lines in the file. Note that 'Is it' is added to the line before because the previous line 'is not good' did not end with a newline and writelines() doesn't automatically add newline character.

```
fh = open('new_list.txt', 'a+')
fh.writelines('Is it')
fh.writelines('\n')
fh.writelines('true?')
fh.seek(0,0)
print(fh.read())
fh.close()
```

```
Too much
```

```
jelly
is not good.Is it
true?
```

Context Manager

In one of the previous chapters, we discussed context managers. For completeness sake, here we will use it to open and write to a file using the context manager.

Below, we open a file named, 'chances.txt' in w+ mode. We provide strings to write. Then we seek to the beginning of the file and then read the file. Notice that the output of the read method call results in printing the file content. After the with block, a call to read the file again, results in Python generating a ValueError: I/O operation as the file is closed and cannot be read until opened again.

```python
with open('chances.txt', 'w+') as fh:
    fh.writelines('I can')
    fh.writelines('\n')
    fh.writelines('code')
    fh.writelines('\n')
    fh.writelines('all night long.')
    fh.seek(0, 0)
    print(fh.read())
print(fh.read())
```

```
I can
code
all night long.
------------------------------------------------------------
--------------
ValueError                              Traceback
(most recent call last)
<ipython-input-29-f6705f06d0e2> in <module>()
      7       fh.seek(0, 0)
      8       print(fh.read())
----> 9 print(fh.read())
ValueError: I/O operation on closed file.
```

CSV Files

Comma separated value (CSV) [https://en.wikipedia.org/wiki/Comma-separated_values] is one of the most popular spreadsheet formats. It is text-based format with a simple and clear definition. Unlike Microsoft Excel file, csv files can be viewed using any text editor or any spreadsheet software. It also has very little overhead and it can be used to read and write data fast. To read from a csv file or write to a csv file in Python, we have to import the csv module.

The table below describes the two csv functions that are mostly used.

Function	Syntax	Description
csv.reader	csv.reader(filename, [dialect], [format_parameters])	Returns a reader object. The dialect and format_parameters are optional.

csv.write	csv.writer(filename, [dialect], [format_parameters])	Returns a writer object. Dialect and format_parameters are optional.
A dialect specifies all of the parameters used for parsing a file or writing to a file.		
The arguments in the format_parameters override the parameters given in the dialect.		

In the below example, we open the csv file in the read mode and store the file handler in fh. We then pass fh to the csv.reader function along with the optional parameters. The csv.reader returns an iterator that can be used in a for-loop to obtain each line in the csv file separately. The print function demonstrates that each line in the csv file is returned as a list. Also notice that the individual elements in the list are strings and not integers. For further processing, you can typecast these strings to integers.

```
import csv
with open("class_grades.csv", "r") as fh:
    alllines = csv.reader(fh, delimiter=',')
    for lines in alllines:
        print(lines)
```

```
['14', '3', '12', '1']
['21', '6', '23', '0']
```

```
['32', '7', '15', '7']
```

We use csv.writer to write into a new file called, animals.csv. The variable lines, which is a list of lists will be written to the file using the writerows() function.

```python
with open('animals.csv', 'w') as fo:
    wo = csv.writer(fo)
    lines = [['Zebra', 10], ['Giraffe', 17]]
    wo.writerows(lines)
```

To check if the file write was successful, we will use the code below to read the animals.csv file and print its content.

```python
with open("animals.csv", "r", newline='') as fh:
    alllines = csv.reader(fh, delimiter=',')
    for lines in alllines:
        print(lines)
```

```
['Zebra', '10']
['Giraffe', '17']
```

The default delimiter is comma. If the file needs an alternate delimiter, they can be specified using the register_dialect() function. Below, we call ';' (semi-colon) as the delimiter and we register the new dialect and name it as semicon. Then we give the semicon to the writer, so that the new delimiter can be used.

```
csv.register_dialect('semicon', delimiter=';',
quoting=csv.QUOTE_NONE)
with open("fruits.csv", "w", newline='') as fo:
    wo = csv.writer(fo, 'semicon')
    lines = [['Strawberries', 90], ['Kiwi', 100]]
    wo.writerows(lines)
```

To check if the file write was successful, we will use the code below to read the fruits.csv file and print its content. The output of the print function looks similar to the output from the previous examples. The one difference between this code and all the previous reader call is the delimiter ; (semicolon).

```
with open("fruits.csv", "r", newline='') as fh:
    alllines = csv.reader(fh, delimiter=';')
    for lines in alllines:
        print(lines)
```

```
['Strawberries', '90']
['Kiwi', '100']
```

However, when we open the csv file in a text editor, we notice the semicolon between the strings in the same row, as shown below.

```
Strawberries;90
Kiwi;100
```

Learning Activity 1: *To a text file called state_capitals.txt, write the following in to individual lines: Indonesia – Jakarta, Malaysia - Kuala Lumpur, Thailand – Bangkok. Then open the file and print the lines.*

Learning Activity 2: *To a csv file called name_grade.csv, write the following four lines using the csv module: AK 23, Bobby 24, Indu 27, Pink 22. Then open the file and print its content.*

Storing Python Objects

So far, we have seen how to save textual information and retrieve them. When storing the content in to a text file or csv file, we need a serializer and de-serializer. A serializer is a program that can convert data structures in to a format that can be stored or transmitted. A de-serializer is a program that convert textual data to data structures. The csv module is the serializer and de-serializer for csv format.

Python provides two different modules namely pickle and shelve that can be used to store Python objects and data structures directly.

Pickle

The pickle module implements serializer and de-serializer for Python object structure. During serialization, Python objects are converted into a byte stream that can be stored or transmitted. During serialization, the byte streams are converted to Python objects.

In a pickle file, the order of data retrieval data is the order of data write. The two most commonly used functions in pickle are dump() and load(). They are explained the following table.

379

Function	Description
pickle.dump(obj, file, protocol=None, fix_imports=True)	Pickles the Python object obj in to the file. Protocol and fix_imports are optional arguments.
pickle.load(file, fix_imports=True, encoding="ASCII", errors = "strict")	Unpickles the byte stream into a Python object. Arguments fix_imports, encoding, errors are all optional arguments.

To learn more about the optional arguments, please visit the documentation page at https://docs.python.org/3/library/pickle.html

Below, we have a list t1, a dictionary t2. We open a pickle file called pickle.ck. A new file will be created if a file by that name does not exist. The extension of a pickle file is not mandated by the pickle module. We should of course avoid the usual file extensions to avoid confusion. In this case we use ck as the file extension. We then use the dump() function to store Python objects to the pickle file.

```python
import pickle
t1 = ['Abe', 'Franklin', 'Johnson']
t2 = {'Cartons': 12, 'Shoes': 20 }
f = open('pickle.ck','wb')
pickle.dump(t1,f) # this command dumps d1 into the file
pickle.ck
```

```
pickle.dump(t2,f) # this command dumps d2 into the file
pickle.ck
f.close()
```

To read the contents in the pickle.ck file, we re-open the file. We use the
load() function to read and unpickle one item at a time. We assign the first
value to nt1 and the second value to nt2. We then close the file and print the
values.

```
f = open('pickle.ck','rb')
nt1 = pickle.load(f)
nt2 = pickle.load(f)
f.close()
print('Read values are:')
print(nt1)
print(nt2)
```

```
Read values are:
['Abe', 'Franklin', 'Johnson']
{'Cartons': 12, 'Shoes': 20}
```

Notice that we loaded the values in the same order in which they were
written.

Shelve

Shelve module can be used to store and retrieve Python objects similar to pickle except that the items can be retrieved in any order. It is a persistent data store for dictionary-like object. The keys in a shelf have to be strings and unlike in a database the values can be any Python objects. The values can be class instances, recursive data types and objects containing lots of shared sub-objects.

To use the shelve module, we have to import it by using

```
import shelve
```

To handle a shelve file we use shelve.open() function that is described in the below table.

Function	Description
shelve.open(filename, [flag], [protocol = None], [writeback= False])	Returns a shelve file object. Except for the filename, other arguments are optional. If writeback = True, then the objects that need to be stored in a shelve file will be in the memory and will be written into the file only when the file is closed.

To learn more about the optional arguments, please visit, https://docs.python.org/3.1/library/shelve.html.

As in a database, in a shelve file, Python objects can be stored in any order and can be retrieved in any order. This is the major difference between a pickle file and a shelve file.

Below, we have d1 and list1 which are dictionary and list respectively. We then open the file using shelve.open() function. The s is the shelve file object. To store any object, we use the dictionary syntax and assign values to the keys 'first' and 'second'. We print s, the shelve file object and finally close s. This will create a file called, 'fruits.db' in the local directory.

```python
import shelve
d1 = {'apple':'12', 'banana':20, 'cantaloupe': 35}
list1 = ['apricot', 'orange', 'pineapple']
s = shelve.open('fruit') # opens the shelve
try:
    s['first'] = d1
    s['second'] = list1
finally:
    print(s)
    s.close()
```

```
<shelve.DbfilenameShelf object at 0x00000224C0786DD8>
```

To check if the file write was successful, we open the shelve file in the read mode and assign the value in the key 'first' to newd. We close the file and print newd. Notice that unlike in the case of pickle, we read only the items that are of interest to us and not all items in the file.

```
import shelve
s = shelve.open('fruit','r')
try:
    newd = s['first']
finally:
    s.close()
print(newd)
```

```
{'apple': '12', 'banana': 20, 'cantaloupe': 35}
```

If you need to mutate the elements in a shelve file, then it is convenient to keep shelve dictionary in memory. This can be achieved by using the option writeback = True. The object(s) will be written only when the shelve file is closed or when the sync() function is called.

```
d3 = [{'a':'1', 'b':2, 'c':3}]
s = shelve.open('fruit',writeback=True)
try:
    s['firstdict'] = d3
finally:
    s.close()
```

If the key does not exist in the shelve dictionary, then Python generates a 'KeyError' as shown in the example below.

```
s = shelve.open('fruit')
print(s['notexist'])
```


```
KeyError                                Traceback
(most recent call last)
//anaconda/envs/tf-test2/lib/python3.5/shelve.py in
__getitem__(self, key)
    110         try:
--> 111             value = self.cache[key]
    112         except KeyError:


KeyError: 'notexist'


During handling of the above exception, another
exception occurred:

KeyError                                Traceback
(most recent call last)
<ipython-input-7-f81537058d0e> in <module>()
      1 s = shelve.open('fruit')
----> 2 print(s['notexist'])


//anaconda/envs/tf-test2/lib/python3.5/shelve.py in
__getitem__(self, key)
    111             value = self.cache[key]
```

```
112            except KeyError:
--> 113              f =
BytesIO(self.dict[key.encode(self.keyencoding)])
114                value = Unpickler(f).load()
115                if self.writeback:
```

```
KeyError: b'notexist'
```

To prevent this error, it is imperative to check if the key exists in the shelve dictionary using the 'in' keyword before accessing it. In the example below, we open the file and check whether 'firstdict' is in the shelve file object. If it is there, we print its value.

```
s = shelve.open('fruit')
if 'firstdict' in s: # we are checking if the key
firstdict exists
    print(s['firstdict'])
```

```
[{'a': '1', 'b': 2, 'c': 3}]
```

NOTE: Python has modules to write and read Excel files. The module xlrd is used to read xls files and module xlwt is used to write to an xls file. Alternately to write and read xlsx files, we can just use one module, openpyxl. Check documentation to learn more http://www.python-

386

excel.org/. We will not discuss this module but rather leave it as an exercise for the readers.

Learning Activity 3: *Create a class called StudentCourse. The class has to take the information: student name, year in college (freshman, sophomore, junior or senior) and two courses. Now store the information in a pickle file. The open the pickle file and print the contents.*

Learning Activity 4: *Create a class called StudentCourse. The class has to take the information: student name, year in college (freshman, sophomore, junior or senior) and two courses. Now store the information in a shelve file. The open the shelve file and print the contents.*

18. Regular Expression

Introduction

A regular expression is a text matching pattern that is described in a specialized syntax. The pattern has instructions, which are executed with a string as an input to produce a matching subset. The Python module to perform regular expression is re. Typically, re is used to match or find sub-strings in strings similar to searching for a word in a web page. They can also be used to extract information for text files, log files, etc. Some time, the term regular expression is abbreviated to regex, regexp or re.

To use regular expression module, we have to import re

```
import re
```

Raw String

Before we begin our discussion on regular expression, it is important to learn about raw strings with an example given below. We create a variable t1 that contains a string enclosed in single-quotes. The string also has a single quote between t and s to indicate an apostrophe. However, adding an apostrophe to the string results in a SyntaxError as the string is now the word "It" and everything else outside that word cause the error.

```
t1 = 'It's a red flower!\n'
print(t1)
```

```
File "<ipython-input-1-9be34b343cf4>", line 1
    t1 = 'It's a red flower!\n'
            ^
SyntaxError: invalid syntax
```

One way to overcome this problem is escaping the single quotes used for apostrophe by using backslash as in the example below. Even though, the backslash is present in the string t1, but it does not appear in the output. This is due to the fact that Python during the print function call evaluates the string and removes the backslash character as it is designed to be used as an escape character and not part of the string. The '\n' at the end of the string is interpreted by Python and the corresponding output is a newline in the output.

```
t1 = 'It\'s a red flower!\n'
print(t1)
```

```
It's a red flower!
```

Finally, we will learn about raw string. A raw string is identified by adding the character "r" in front of the string as shown in the example below. The backslash is present in the string t1 and also in the output. This is due to the fact that Python during the print function call does not evaluate raw string and retains the backslash character and also '\n'.

```
t1 = r'It\'s a red flower!\n'
print(t1)
```

```
r'It\'s a red flower!\n
```

As you will be learning soon, in regex we will be using many of the symbols including backslash. If we do not use raw strings, then Python will evaluate the string in a manner that we did not program. To prevent this side effect, we will use raw strings in regular expressions.

Regex functions

A few re functions are described in the table below.

Function	Description
re.search(substring, string)	Returns match object if the pattern is found in the text. Otherwise it will return None.
re.compile(substring, string)	Returns a Regex object. Using regex object is memory efficient. This regex object is then fed to another function to find the substring. This is a faster way to search through large text files.
re.findall(substring, string)	Finds all the substrings in the string and returns them as a list.

re.match(substring, string)	Checks if re matches at the beginning of the string.
re.finditer(substring, string)	Finds all the substrings in the string and returns them as an iterator.
re.sub(s1, s2, text)	Replaces s1 with s2 in text.

Below, we use **search() function** to see if 'and' occurs in the text. Since there is one 'and' in the text, an re object is returned. Then we use if-else condition to print whether we found a match or not. Since the search() returns a non-trivial value, the if condition becomes True and the print statement in the if block gets executed.

```
patterns = 'and'
text = 'Python is a dynamically typed language and also
has a simple syntax'
print(re.search(patterns, text))
if re.search(patterns, text):
    print('There is a match')
else:
    print('Found no match')
```

```
<_sre.SRE_Match object; span=(39, 42), match='and'>
There is a match!
```

However, for the same text if we are looking for 'or' in the text, the search() will return None, which is a trivial value. So, the if condition fails and so the statements in the else block will be executed.

```python
patterns = 'or'
text = 'Python is a dynamically typed language and also
has a simple syntax'
print(re.search(patterns, text))
if re.search(patterns, text):
    print('There is a match!')
else:
    print('Found no match.')
```

```
None
Found no match.
```

If we want to find multiple substrings in a text, we can provide the substring in a list and iterate through the list. In the below example, we have substrings: 'and', 'or' in a list. And iterate through the items in the list and search the text for a match.

```python
patterns = ['and', 'or']
text = 'Python is a dynamically typed language and also
has a simple syntax'
for pattern in patterns:
    print('Trying to find a match for "%s" in "%s" - '
%(pattern,text))
```

```
if re.search(pattern, text):
    print('There is a match!')
else:
    print('Found no match.')
```

Trying to find a match for "and" in "Python is a dynamically typed language and also has a simple syntax" - There is a match!
Trying to find a match for "or" in "Python is a dynamically typed language and also has a simple syntax" - Found no match.

We can use the start() and end() methods to determine at which position the match occurs. In the code below, we store the result of the search() function in compare and use start() and end() on compare to know the position of the match. The match 'and' starts at position 39 and ends at position 42-1 which is 41.

```
pattern = 'and'
text = 'Python is a dynamically typed language and also has a simple syntax'
compare = re.search(pattern, text)
s = compare.start() # start() returns the starting position of the match
e = compare.end() # end() returns the ending position of the match
```

```
print('Found "%s" in "%s"  from %d to %d '
%(pattern,text,s,e))
```

Found "and" in "Python is a dynamically typed language and also has a simple syntax" from 39 to 42

The **match() function** determines if there is match or not at the beginning of the string. Below, we check for whether 'ap' occurs at the beginning of 'apple'. Since 'ap' does occur in 'apple', match() will return a match object.

```
print(re.match('ap', 'apple'))
```

```
<_sre.SRE_Match object; span=(0, 2), match='ap'>
```

However, since 'le' does not occur at the beginning of 'apple', match() returns None as shown below.

```
print(re.match('le', 'apple'))
```

```
None
```

The **findall() function** gives a list of all occurrences of the substring in the string. Below, we want to find the occurrence of pattern = 10 in mynumber. Since regular expression works on strings only, we typecast pattern and mynumber to strings. Since there are 3 occurrences of '10' in mynumber_str, findall() returns a list of three '10'. To find the number of occurrences, we can use the len() function.

```
mynumber = 10345678103378103
pattern = 10
mynumber_str = str(mynumber)
pattern_str = str(pattern)
# findall() function finds all the substrings of the
input that match # the pattern without overlapping
syntax re.findall(pattern, string)
print(re.findall(pattern_str,mynumber_str))
count = len(re.findall(pattern_str,mynumber_str))
print('In the given text, %d occurred   %d times'
%(pattern, count)
```

```
['10', '10', '10']
In the given text, 10 occurred 3 times
```

The **finditer() function** returns an iterator that produces match instances instead of the list of strings returned by findall(). Below, we want to find occurrence of '78' in text. Since there are matches, the finditer() returns an object. We iterate through this object and print where the match starts and end. We use the count variable to find the number of occurrences of the match.

```
text = '10345678103378103'
pattern = '78'
```

```
count = 0
print(re.finditer(pattern,text))
for match in re.finditer(pattern,text):
    s = match.start()
    e = match.end()
    count = count + 1
    print('The pattern "%s" starts at %d and ends at %d
' %(pattern, s, e))
print('In the given text, "%s" occurred %d times'
%(pattern, count))
```

```
<callable_iterator object at 0x00000232E4C171D0>
The pattern "78" starts at 6 and ends at 8
The pattern "78" starts at 11 and ends at 13
In the given text, "78" occurred 2 times
```

The **compile() function** is used to compile pattern into pattern objects, which have methods for various operations such as searching for pattern matches or performing string substitutions. Python internally performs this step before regular expression search. If we have few patterns, then Python will cache the compiled version of the pattern even if the program does not specifically request it. However, if there are many patterns in the program, then it is more efficient to programmatically compile before searching. Since the additional cost to programming is minimal, we recommend it to programmers working with regular expressions.

Syntax

re.compile(pattern)

Below, we use compile() function and create a re object for the pattern 'San'. Then we use the re object along with the findall() function to determine the occurrences of 'San' in strval.

```
strval = 'San Francisco, San Jose, San Carlos,
Sunnyvale, Cupertino'
rec = re.compile('San')
print(re.findall(rec, strval))
```

```
['San', 'San', 'San']
```

The **sub() function** can be used to find and replace substrings

Syntax

re.sub(pattern,replacement,string)

In the below code, we replace 'San' with 'S.' in strval.

```
strval = 'San Francisco, San Jose, San Carlos,
Sunnyvale, Cupertino'
strval1 = re.sub('San','S.',strval)
print(strval1)
```

```
S. Francisco, S. Jose, S. Carlos, Sunnyvale, Cupertino
```

We could also use the string method replace() to find and replace using the following syntax

String.replace(s1, s2)

Below, we replace, 'San' with 'S.' using the replace() method. We print both the original string and the modified string.

```
strval = 'San Francisco, San Jose, San Carlos,
Sunnyvale, Cupertino'
a = strval.replace('San','S.')
print(strval)
print(a)
```

```
San Francisco, San Jose, San Carlos, Sunnyvale,
Cupertino
S. Francisco, S. Jose, S. Carlos, Sunnyvale, Cupertino
```

The **group() function** returns the substring that was matched by the re. Adding groups to a pattern lets you isolate parts of the matching text, expanding those capabilities to create a parser.

Below, we have strval and we want to determine if there is a match for (.*)Robinson Obama in strval. Since there is, we get group(0) which will return the entire string that matches with the substring. The group(1) will return everything before Robinson Obama.

```
strval = 'Michelle LaVaughn Robinson Obama'
sm = re.match(r'(.*)Robinson Obama', strval)
```

```
print(sm.group(0))
print(sm.group(1))
```

```
Michelle LaVaughn Robinson Obama
Michelle LaVaughn
```

In the below example, we split the string at ',' and get a list, strval_list. We go through individual item and check to see if there is a match for 'San(.*)' in each item. If there is a match, we add that item's group(1) which will give everything after San in the item, to a list called b. We use another strip() after the match so that there won't be any extra space before item's group(1) . At the end, we print b.

```
strval = 'San Francisco, San Jose, San Carlos,
Sunnyvale, Cupertino'
strval_list = strval.strip().split(',') #converting
strval into a list
b = []
for items in strval_list:
    allnames = re.match(r'San(.*)', items.strip())
    # returns a subset of the list which starts with San
    if allnames:
        b.append(allnames.group(1).strip())
print(b)
```

```
['Francisco', 'Jose', 'Carlos']
```

A few special characters are listed in the table below.

Special regex characters	Description
'.'	Dot matches everything except a newline.
'$'	Dollar matches the end of the string.
'*'	Matches 0 or more occurrences. AB* will match A, AB, A followed by any number of 'B's.
'+'	Matches 1 or more occurrences. AB+ will match 'AB', 'A' followed by one or more occurrences of 'B's.
'?'	Will match 0 or 1 repetitions of the preceding re. AB? Will match either 'A' or 'AB'.
{t,s}	Will match the resulting re to match from t to s repetitions. A{2,4} will match 2 to 4 occurrences of 'A'.
{t,s}?	Will match the resulting re to match few repetitions as possible. A{2,4}? Will match only two occurrences of 'A'. This is the non-greedy version of the preceding re.
'\'	Either escapes special characters pertaining to match characters like '*' and '?' or signals a special sequence or sequences discussed below.

	If raw string is not used to express the pattern, '\' is used to escape sequence in string literals.
[ ]	Is used to indicated a set of characters. Characters 'a', 'c' and 'w' can be put as [acw]. If we want all characters from 'a' through 'z', then we say [a-z]. Likewise, 0-9 can be represented as [0-9].
'|'	A|B will match either A or B, not both. If a match is found for A then match stops. '|' is not a greedy operator.
(?P<label>...)	Substring matched by the group is accessible via the symbolic group name label. The symbolic group is also a numbered group.
\b	Is used to specify a word boundary. To find only 'the' in a text and not 'the' from 'there' or 'they', we can use \b around the as r'\bthe\b'.
\s	Matches whitespace characters like tab, newline, carriage return and space.
\S	Matches everything except Unicode whitespace characters.
\d	Matches digits that are [0-9].
\D	Matches everything except digits.

\w	Matches Unicode word characters [a-zA-Z0-9_].
\W	Matches everything except Unicode word characters.
\Z	Matches only at the end of the string.

Below, we compile a match for email address that has word characters occurring at least once then there should be @ followed by one or more-word characters followed by a '.', the email address should only contain 'com' or 'edu'. We keep accepting the input from the user until we find a match for our compile re object. If there is a match, then we print 'You entered a valid email' and break. Otherwise we keep continuing to ask the user as we are in an infinite while-loop.

```
import re
email_pattern = re.compile(r'(\w+@\w+\.(com|edu))')
while True:
    email = input ("Please enter an email address: ")
    if email_pattern.search(email):
        print("You entered a valid email address.")
        break
    else:
        print("You entered an invalid email address.")
```

If we enter bob@somemail, an email address that does not satisfy the email_check requirement, the program will keep asking for email address until a valid email address is provided. When we enter bob@somemail.com, a valid email address that matches the re pattern, the if condition is satisfied and we get a print message and also break out of the while loop.

```
Please enter an email address: bob@somemail
You entered an invalid email address.
Please enter an email address: bob@somemail.com
You entered a valid email address.
```

Since, we know the re special characters, let's use them with search and group. Below, we parse the string 'Roosovelt, Eleanor'. We use (\w+), (\w+) to obtain different groups: group(0) will return the original string, group(1) will return the string to the left of ',' and group(2) will return the string to the right of ','. Here ',' acts like a pattern matching character. Hence, we have group(0), group(1) and group(2).

```
# The re.search() method takes a regular expression
pattern and a
# string and searches for that pattern within the
string.
# The syntax is re.search(pattern, string)
import re
name = 'Roosovelt, Eleanor'
a = re.search(r'(\w+), (\w+)',name)
# (\w+) matches multiple occurrences of A-Za-z0-9_
print(a.group(0))
```

```
print(a.group(1))
print(a.group(2))
```

Roosovelt, Eleanor

Roosovelt

Eleanor

Instead of using numbers for the group, we can use '?P<label>' to parse the information from the group. ?P stands for in place. Below, we use lastname and firstname labels in the search() function. Then we use the label to obtain information about the group.

```
name = 'Roosovelt, Eleanor'
a = re.search('(?P<lastname>\w+),
(?P<firstname>\w+)',name)
# ?P<lastname>\w+ finds pattern that has characters A-
Za-z0-9_ and assigns it to
# lastname
print(a.group(0))
print(a.group('lastname'))
print(a.group('firstname'))
```

Roosovelt, Eleanor

Roosovelt

Eleanor

Now, let us try to extract years in a text file, 'years.txt'. The file has the following content:

The Chandra X-ray Observatory was launched in 1999.

This line has year 25.

In 1998, International Space Station was launched.

Since the year has to have at least one digit we use '\d+' special sequence in the compile function. Then we enumerate through the file and check for pattern. The line with the year will be group(0) we extract year by group(1).

```
pattern = re.compile("(\d+)")
for i, line in enumerate(open('years.txt')):
    for m in re.finditer(pattern, line):
        year = m.group(1)
        print('The year is', year)
```

```
The year is 1999
The year is 25
The year is 1998
```

By using \d+, we captured years with 4 digits as well as 2 digits. If we wish to make the re pattern search more specific, we can use '\d{4}'. This will only extract numbers that have four digits and others are ignored.

```
pattern = re.compile("(\d{4})")
for i, line in enumerate(open('years.txt')):
```

```
for m in re.finditer(pattern, line):
    year = m.group(1)
    print ('The year is ', year)
```

```
The year is 1999
The year is 1998
```

In the code below, we use word boundary, \b to find whether a substring, 'poss' occurs at the beginning of a word in a string called mstring.

```
mstring = "Endless possibilities"
print(re.findall(r'\bposs', mstring))
print("'poss' occurred these many times: ",
len(re.findall(r'\bposs', mstring)))
```

```
['poss']
'poss' occurred these many times:   1
```

Now, let's consider another example where we want to find all occurrences of the word, 'the' in a string. To achieve this, we specify the word boundary by using \b around 'the' in the findall method, Python found two occurrences of the word 'the' in m1.

```
m1 = '''Trying out the new version of Python in there by
typing the program. '''
print(re.findall(r'\bthe\b', m1))
```

```
print(" 'the' occurred these many times: ",
len(re.findall(r'\bthe\b', m1)))


['the', 'the']
'the' occurred these many times:  2
```

Parsing a log file

Finally, we will consider using regular expression in a larger example where we extract information from a log file obtained from ----------------------------
------. The new_access.txt is a log file that has 21 records pertaining to requests received from the user. Here are the first 4 rows:

99.45.50.171 - - [23/Feb/2014:09:37:56 -0800] "GET /svds.com/rockandroll/
HTTP/1.1" 200 8507 "http://visual.ly/history-rock-100-
songs?view=truehttp://visual.ly/history-rock-100-songs?view=true"
"Mozilla/5.0 (Macintosh; Intel Mac OS X 10_9_1) AppleWebKit/537.73.11
(KHTML, like Gecko) Version/7.0.1 Safari/537.73.11"

99.45.50.171 - - [23/Feb/2014:09:37:49 -0800] "GET /svds.com/rockandroll
HTTP/1.1" 301 241 "http://visual.ly/history-rock-100-
songs?view=truehttp://visual.ly/history-rock-100-songs?view=true"
"Mozilla/5.0 (Macintosh; Intel Mac OS X 10_9_1) AppleWebKit/537.73.11
(KHTML, like Gecko) Version/7.0.1 Safari/537.73.11"

99.38.248.134 - - [31/Mar/2014:20:18:24 -0700] "GET
/svds.com/rockandroll/img/31.jpg HTTP/1.1" 200 18970
"http://www.svds.com/rockandroll/" "Mozilla/5.0 (Macintosh; Intel Mac OS
X 10_9_2) AppleWebKit/537.36 (KHTML, like Gecko)
Chrome/33.0.1750.152 Safari/537.36"

```
```

99.38.248.134 - - [31/Mar/2014:20:12:36 -0700] "GET
/svds.com/rockandroll/fonts/icons/entypo.ttf HTTP/1.1" 404 3847
"http://www.svds.com/rockandroll/" "Mozilla/5.0 (Macintosh; Intel Mac OS
X 10_9_2) AppleWebKit/537.36 (KHTML, like Gecko)
Chrome/33.0.1750.152 Safari/537.36"

In the above data, the first value is the host, the second value is user identity (which is empty in this case), the third value is user (which is empty in this case), the fourth value is date and time including the UTC offset enclosed in the [ ], the fifth value is the type of request and page information enclosed in double quotes " ", the sixth value is status that is in all digits, the seventh value is byte size of the rendered page, the eighth value is referrer that is pages that are linked to this url and the ninth value is user-agent, browser identification string . We create a pattern called parts to capture the different sections in each line. We use the groupdict to create a dictionary for each line and we print it. The status1 is a list that consists of all the request status.

The host is indicated with \S+ and hence will match all characters excepts space like characters. The status is indicated with [0-9]+ and hence will match one or more digits. To build the complete pattern, we use the string method join with the joiner of \s+. Thus, in our pattern we are indicating that one column of data in the log file is separated from the next column with one or more space like characters. As can be seen in the output, the group dictionary is populated with the values from the log file.

```
parts = [
    r'(?P<host>\S+)',                    # host %h
    r'\S+',                              # user identity
    r'(?P<user>\S+)',                    # user %u
```

```
    r'\[(?P<time>.+)\]',                    # time %t
    r'"(?P<request>.+)"',                   # request "%r"
    r'(?P<status>[0-9]+)',                  # status %>s
    r'(?P<size>\S+)',                       # size %b
(careful, can be '-')
    r'"(?P<referer>\S+)"',                  # referer is the
page that is linked to this URL
    r'"(?P<useragent>.+)"'                  # User-agent is
the browser identification string.
]
pattern = re.compile(r'\s+'.join(parts)+r'\s*\Z')
statuses = []
fo = open("new_access.txt")
for line in fo.readlines():
    m = pattern.match(line)
    res = m.groupdict()
    print(res)
    statuses.append(res['status'])
print(statuses
```

The output of the first four lines is shown below.

```
{'host': '99.45.50.171', 'user': '-', 'time':
'23/Feb/2014:09:37:56 -0800', 'request': 'GET
/svds.com/rockandroll/ HTTP/1.1', 'status': '200',
'size': '8507', 'referer': 'http://visual.ly/history-
rock-100-songs?view=truehttp://visual.ly/history-rock-
100-songs?view=true', 'useragent': 'Mozilla/5.0
```

(Macintosh; Intel Mac OS X 10_9_1) AppleWebKit/537.73.11
(KHTML, like Gecko) Version/7.0.1 Safari/537.73.11'}
{'host': '99.45.50.171', 'user': '-', 'time':
'23/Feb/2014:09:37:49 -0800', 'request': 'GET
/svds.com/rockandroll HTTP/1.1', 'status': '301',
'size': '241', 'referer': 'http://visual.ly/history-
rock-100-songs?view=truehttp://visual.ly/history-rock-
100-songs?view=true', 'useragent': 'Mozilla/5.0
(Macintosh; Intel Mac OS X 10_9_1) AppleWebKit/537.73.11
(KHTML, like Gecko) Version/7.0.1 Safari/537.73.11'}
{'host': '99.38.248.134', 'user': '-', 'time':
'31/Mar/2014:20:18:24 -0700', 'request': 'GET
/svds.com/rockandroll/img/31.jpg HTTP/1.1', 'status':
'200', 'size': '18970', 'referer':
'http://www.svds.com/rockandroll/', 'useragent':
'Mozilla/5.0 (Macintosh; Intel Mac OS X 10_9_2)
AppleWebKit/537.36 (KHTML, like Gecko)
Chrome/33.0.1750.152 Safari/537.36'}
{'host': '99.38.248.134', 'user': '-', 'time':
'31/Mar/2014:20:12:36 -0700', 'request': 'GET
/svds.com/rockandroll/fonts/icons/entypo.ttf HTTP/1.1',
'status': '404', 'size': '3847', 'referer':
'http://www.svds.com/rockandroll/', 'useragent':
'Mozilla/5.0 (Macintosh; Intel Mac OS X 10_9_2)
AppleWebKit/537.36 (KHTML, like Gecko)
Chrome/33.0.1750.152 Safari/537.36'}

We can print the content of the list status1 and also its length.

410

```
print(status1)

print(len(status1))
```

```
['200', '301', '200', '404', '200', '301', '301', '200',
'200', '200', '200', '200', '200', '200', '200', '200',
'404', '200', '200', '200', '200']
21
```

Learning Activity 1 : *In the below paragraph, there are typos. The spelling mistakes are in the words: tping, compoonts, programy and binare. Create a dictionary with the key being the incorrect word and the value is the correct word. Then replace the incorrect word with the correct word and print the corrected text.*

myText = '''Python is an interpreted, object-oriented, high-level programming language with dynamic semantics. Its high-level built in data structures, combined with dynamic tping and dynamic binding, make it very attractive for Rapid Application Development, as well as for use as a scripting or glue language to connect existing compoonts together. Python's simple, easy to learn syntax emphasizes readability and therefore reduces the cost of program maintenance. Python supports modules and packages, which encourages programy modularity and code reuse. The Python interpreter and the extensive standard library are available in source or binare form without charge for all major platforms and can be freely distributed.'''

Learning Activity 2: *In the below paragraph, find the number of occurrences of words - of, the and food.*

Coral reefs are some of the most biologically rich and economically valuable ecosystems on Earth. They provide food, jobs, income, and protection to billions of people worldwide. However, coral reefs and the magnificent creatures that call them home are in danger of disappearing if actions are not taken to protect them. They are threatened by an increasing range of impacts including pollution, invasive species, diseases, bleaching, and global climate change. The rapid decline and loss of these valuable, ancient, and complex ecosystems have significant social, economic, and environmental consequences in the United States and around the world.

Introduction

In Python, collections module
[https://docs.python.org/3/library/collections.html] implements specialized
high-performance container datatypes that can be used in addition to built-in
data types such as lists, dictionaries, sets and tuples.

Some of the datatypes available in the collection modules are:

1. Counter

2. Named Tuple

3. Default Dictionary

4. Ordered Dictionary

5. Deque or Double Ended Queue (pronunciation: deck)

Counter

A Counter container keeps track of number of times an element appears in an
iterable object such as list, tuple, string, another Counter etc. It is a subclass
of a Python dictionary where the key is an element and the value is the count.
Since it is a dictionary type, the elements of the collection must be of
immutable type.

We will begin by creating a Counter from a string, which are a collection of
immutable characters. The output demonstrates that the key is the character
in the string and the value is the frequency or count of the character
including space. The keys are ordered is descending order of occurrence.

```
import collections
c = collections.Counter("Python is cool")
print(c) # Prints the individual letter and also its
frequency
```

```
Counter({'o': 3, ' ': 2, 'c': 1, 'i': 1, 'h': 1, 'l': 1,
'n': 1, 'P': 1, 's': 1, 't': 1, 'y': 1})
```

If we are interested only in few of the values in the Counter, then we can use the most_common() method to obtain a list of tuples that contain the key-value pair. In the example below, we are requesting only the top 3 values from the collection. If no arguments are supplied to the most_common() method, then all key-value pairs will be returned.

```
print(c.most_common(3))
```

```
[('o', 3), (' ', 2), ('s', 1)]
```

We can reset the value of a certain key using by indexing to a specific key. The print function clearly indicates that the value of the key 'o' has changed from 3 to 1.

```
# Resetting the value of 'o' to 1
c['o'] = 1
print(c)
```

```
Counter({' ': 2, 'c': 1, 'i': 1, 'h': 1, 'l': 1, 'o': 1,
'n': 1, 'P': 1, 's': 1, 't': 1, 'y': 1})
```

Since it is a dictionary subclass, we can obtain the values of the Counter
using the values() method and also can iterate over the keys and values using
items() method.

```
print(c.values()) # This will return all the values
for k,v in c.items(): # You can iterate through a
counter like dictionary
    print(k, v)
```

```
[2, 1, 1, 1, 1, 1, 1, 1, 1, 1, 1]
  2
c 1
i 1
h 1
l 1
o 1
n 1
P 1
s 1
t 1
y 1
```

Just like in case of sets, we can perform several operations on a counter such as addition, subtraction, intersection and union. Below, we show some examples.

```
c1 = collections.Counter(['s', 'a', 'n', 'j', 'o', 's', 'e'])
c2 = collections.Counter('santaclara')
print(c1)
print(c2)
print(c1+c2) # Addition combines the values in the two containers
```

```
Counter({'s': 2, 'a': 1, 'e': 1, 'j': 1, 'o': 1, 'n': 1})
Counter({'a': 4, 'c': 1, 'l': 1, 'n': 1, 's': 1, 'r': 1, 't': 1})
Counter({'a': 5, 's': 3, 'n': 2, 'c': 1, 'e': 1, 'j': 1, 'l': 1, 'o': 1, 'r': 1, 't': 1})
```

Subtraction removes the value from c1 that is present in c2. If the difference between the count for a particular element is negative then that key is ignored. Below, note that c1 has one 'a' and c2 has four 'a's. When we subtract c2 from c1, 'a' will not be in the result. However, when we subtract c1 from c2, the result will have 'a' with count 3.

```python
print("c1-c2: ", c1-c2)
print("c2-c1:", c2-c1)
```

```
c1-c2: Counter({'s': 1, 'j': 1, 'e': 1, 'o': 1})
c2-c1: Counter({'a': 3, 'c': 1, 'r': 1, 'l': 1, 't': 1})
```

Intersection of two counters will result in elements that are common in both counters with minimum value.

```python
print(c1 & c2) # Intersection finds the positive minimum value
```

```
Counter({'a': 1, 's': 1, 'n': 1})
```

Union of two counters will result in all the elements in both the counters with highest value.

```python
print(c1 | c2)
```

```
Counter({'a': 4, 's': 2, 'c': 1, 'e': 1, 'j': 1, 'l': 1, 'o': 1, 'n': 1, 'r': 1, 't': 1})
```

Named tuples

Classes encapsulate multiple related variable under one umbrella. In many cases, a class is created to encapsulate multiple variables and its associated methods. However, in some cases, a class may be used only for storing values with no associated methods. In such cases, one can use namedtuple and avoid typing the boiler plate code seen in a class.

One such example is shown below. The Person class contains two variables name and age. The values for the variable is assigned in the initializer. The __str__ method is used to pretty print the content of the class.

```
class Person(object):
    def __init__(self, name, age):
        self.name = name
        self.age = age
    def __str__(self):
        return "The person's name: %s and age: %d"%(self.name, self.age)
p = Person('Leo', 74)
print(p)
print("The person's name: %s and age: %d"%(p.name, p.age))
```

```
The person's name: Leo and age: 74
The person's name: Leo and age: 74
```

The six lines of the class definition code is mostly boiler plate. The amount of code can be reduced by using namedtuple as shown below. The 2nd line defines a namedtuple with two values name and age. This is similar to the class definition. An instance of the namedtuple is then created with value of name='Leo' and age=74. Thus, nine lines of code above is reduced to five.

418

```
import collections
Person = collections.namedtuple('Person', 'name age')
p = Person(name='Leo', age=74)
print(p)
print("The person's name: %s and age: %d"%(p.name,
p.age))
```

```
Person(name='Leo', age=74)
The person's name: Leo and age: 74
```

However, there is one shortcoming. The class definition allows overloading the initializer, so that variable number of arguments can be supplied. However, in the case of namedtuple, all values need to be supplied for successful initialization. Hence the code below will fail.

```
p = Person(name="Leo") # This will throw an error
```

```
------------------------------------------------------------
--------------
TypeError                                 Traceback (most
recent call last)

<ipython-input-17-ef5d93d79e66> in <module>()
----> 1 p = Person(name="Leo") # This will throw an
error
```

```
TypeError: __new__() takes exactly 3 arguments (2 given)
```

Since the variables in the Person namedtuple is defined as a string, it allows creation of new definitions on the fly. For example, a list of variable names can be read from a file and a new namedtuple definition can be created.

Another common use case for namedtuples is to use them as a substitute for regular tuples. This provides the ability to access fields by name instead of position index. In the code below, the variable basictuple is a tuple whose elements can only be accessed by index.

```
basictuple = ('Newton', 84, 'Scientist')
print(basictuple[0]) # To index, we need to use a number
```

```
Newton
```

Below we define a named tuple called FamousPeople. Inside the parentheses we provide the name, in this case it is same as the name of the variable. However, we can choose any other name. We also pass the field names such as name, age and occupation for the elements inside the tuple. We create two instances of FamousPeople f1 and f2. In f1, we use field names that we defined to pass values. In f2, we pass the values without field names. We print f1 and f2. Note that in the output for both f1 and f2, the namedtuple along with the field names is returned. We also print f1.name and f2.name.

```python
import collections
FamousPeople =
collections.namedtuple('FamousPeople','name age
occupation')
f1 = FamousPeople(name="Newton", age=84,
occupation="Scientist")
f2 = FamousPeople("New", 4, "Zoologist")
print(f1)
print(f2)
print(f1.name)
print(f2.name)
```

```
FamousPeople(name='Newton', age=84,
occupation='Scientist')
FamousPeople(name='New', age=4, occupation='Zoologist')
Newton
New
```

Deque

Deque or Double Ended Queue (pronunciation: deck) is a container with fast
appends and pops on either end that is memory efficient and thread safe.

Below we create an empty deque. We use Python's truthiness property to
check whether d is empty or not. Since d is empty and corresponds to a
trivial value, the boolean of d is False and so, the else clause is executed.

```
import collections
d = collections.deque() # Creates an empty deque
if d: # You can perform truthiness
    print("Deque not empty")
else:
    print("Deque is empty")
```

```
Deque is empty
```

If instead, we supply an iterable object, a deque with elements from the iterable object will be created. In the example below, we define a deque and supply a string 'Python is cool'. The print function outputs the individual elements in the deque d.

```
d = collections.deque('Python is cool')
print(d)
```

```
deque(['P', 'y', 't', 'h', 'o', 'n', ' ', 'i', 's', ' ',
'c', 'o', 'o', 'l'])
```

The deque behaves like a list and hence the list operations such as slicing, len etc. can be applied to. In the code below, we print the first and last values in d and also the length of d.

```
print(d[0]) # Accessing first element
print(d[-1]) # Accessing the last element
print(len(d)) # Length of deque
```

P
1
14

We can also iterate through elements of a deque using the for-loop.

```
for items in d:
    print(items, end=" ")
```

P y t h o n   i s   c o o l

Append method in deque is similar to the one in lists. Append will add the item to the end of the deque as shown below.

```
d.append('Yes it is')
print(d
```

```
deque(['P', 'y', 't', 'h', 'o', 'n', ' ', 'i', 's', ' ',
'c', 'o', 'o', 'l', 'Yes it is'])
```

However, if we want to append the individual elements in an iterable object, then we need to use extend similar to the one in lists. In the example below, we use extend method to append elements from the string 'Yes it is'. Since 'Yes it is' is a string that is iterable, the extend method appends each character from the iterable to the deque as can be seen in the output.

```
d = collections.deque('Python is cool')
d.extend('Yes it is') # Extend behaves like it works on
list
print(d)
```

```
deque(['P', 'y', 't', 'h', 'o', 'n', ' ', 'i', 's', ' ',
'c', 'o', 'o', 'l', 'Y', 'e', 's', ' ', 'i', 't', ' ',
'i', 's'])
```

Since deques are mutable like lists, we can assign new values to them.

```
d[0] = 'CP' # Change the content of first index to CP
print(d)
```

```
deque(['CP', 'y', 't', 'h', 'o', 'n', ' ', 'i', 's', '
', 'c', 'o', 'o', 'l', 'Y', 'e', 's', ' ', 'i', 't', '
', 'i', 's'])
```

The difference between deque and list is in the process of append or extend. In lists, values can be appended or extended only to the right. In the case of deque, append and extend can be performed on both left and right. The append to the left of a deque can be done using appendleft method and the extend to the left of a deque can be done using extendleft.

Below we define a deque and then use extend and extendleft methods. For extendleft, notice the order in which the items get extended. First '!' will be extended then 'w' followed by 'o' and at last 'W'.

```python
d = collections.deque('Python is cool')
d.extend('Yes it is')
print(d)

d.extendleft('!woW')
print(d)
```

```
deque(['P', 'y', 't', 'h', 'o', 'n', ' ', 'i', 's', ' ',
'c', 'o', 'o', 'l', 'Y', 'e', 's', ' ', 'i', 't', ' ',
'i', 's'])
deque(['W', 'o', 'w', '!', 'P', 'y', 't', 'h', 'o', 'n',
' ', 'i', 's', ' ', 'c', 'o', 'o', 'l', 'Y', 'e', 's', '
', 'i', 't', ' ', 'i', 's'])
```

Learning Activity 1: If d1 = ['d'], a deque. Add 'c' then 'b' and then 'a' to the left of d.
Add 'e' then 'f' and then 'g' to the right of 'd'. Print the new deque. Then remove 'a' and 'g' from the deque.

Learning Activity 2: Create a class named Student. Then pass attributes:

425

name, age, city and field. Create an instance of the class and print the values. Then create a namedtuple called StudentTuple with the same attributes. Compare the number of lines of code written for the 2 cases..

Default dictionary

Default dictionary is a dictionary where value for missing keys can be defaulted to a specific value. **In a Python dictionary, a KeyError is raised if a value is requested for a missing key. However, in a defaultdict, the key is entered in to the dictionary with the default value.**

Below, we define people as a defaultdict with integer default value of zero. We assign values to two keys. **Later,** we access the value for the key 'Bohr'. Since **the variable people does no**t have a key 'Bohr' and since we defined people as a defaultdict, instead of raising KeyError exception, the default value will be assigned to Bohr. Note that when we print people **again**, the key Bohr is now included in the dictionary.

```
from collections import defaultdict
people = defaultdict(int) # default value for int = 0
people['Euler'] = 76
people['Newton'] = 84
print(people)
print(people['Bohr'])
print(people)
```

```
defaultdict(<type 'int'>, {'Newton': 84, 'Euler': 76})
0
```

426

```
defaultdict(<class 'int'>, {'Euler': 76, 'Newton': 84,
'Bohr': 0})
```

The default value is specified as a function. In this case, we used int which defaults to 0. Instead if we would like to supply a different integer value, we need to supply a default function as in the example below. The lambda function does not take any input but returns the int 60 as output. One can instead create a function and pass the function object as input as well.

```
people = defaultdict(lambda : 60)
people['Euler'] = 76
people['Newton'] = 84
print(people)
print(people['Bohr'])
print(people)
```

```
defaultdict(<type 'int'>, {'Newton': 84, 'Euler': 76})
0
defaultdict(<class 'int'>, {'Euler': 76, 'Newton': 84,
'Bohr': 60})
```

You can learn more about collections module from
https://docs.python.org/3/library/collections.html and
http://pymotw.com/3/collections/

Introduction

We have seen many data structures such as lists, tuples, dictionaries and sets. We referred to them generically as iterable objects as they can be iterated using for-loop for example.

In addition to the built in iterable objects, Python provides functionality to create custom iterable objects generally called as iterators. In this chapter, we will discuss generators which are created using function and also iterators which are created using classes.

Why iterators and generators?

Iterators are memory efficient cousin of traditional collections such as list, tuple etc. There are two ways of creating a custom iterator. The first method uses the yield keyword that was introduced in Python 2.3. The function that uses yield keyword is also called a generator. The second method implements __iter__ and next method for Python 2 and __iter__ and __next__ method for Python 3. The change was made to keep the signature consistent between all the magic methods [https://www.python.org/dev/peps/pep-3114/]. As you can imagine, the change from next to __next__ is a breaking change in Python 3 and programmers who need to run their code in both versions need to be cognizant.

We will begin with an example that does not contain iterator/generator and then convert it to iterator/generator. The function squared_list takes a list of numbers and returns a new list that contains squares of every item using list comprehension. The amount of memory needed is a sum of memory occupied by the input list, output list and at various time the individual elements (such as items and sq) in the list. For a large list, the memory occupied by the individual elements will be considerably smaller than the list itself. For example, for a list with 100 items where each item takes 4 bytes, then the total memory needed is 400 bytes while the memory occupied by one item is 4 bytes, a mere 1%. The actual memory used by a Python list is considerably different but the argument still stays the same. So, the amount of memory used by a list is considerably larger than the individual item and hence for this memory analysis we will only consider the memory occupied by the list.

If the original list length is 100 and 400 bytes in total, then the output list will also occupy 400 bytes. We will analyze the memory usage of a generator that performs the same functionality as the example below.

```python
def squared_list(listofnumbers):
    return [items*items for items in listofnumbers]
for sq in squared_list([5, 6, 7, 8]):
    print(sq)
```

```
25
36
49
64
```

Generator

The example below shows a generator. The generator is called squared_generator, which squares every item in the list. In the for-loop outside the function, the squared_generator function is called.

Before we begin our discussion on generators, we will discuss the yield keyword. The word yield is similar to return. When yield is executed, the state of the generator (function or method) is frozen and the control is handed back to the caller. When the control is returned back to the generator, the state of the function is restored and Python continues to execute the next possible statement.

In the first function call, the listofnumbers variable is assigned the value from the list [5, 6, 7, 8]. In the first iteration of the for-loop, items will be assigned a value of 5 and the function will return to the caller with a value 5*5. This value will be assigned to the variable 'sq'. Since the call exited with a yield statement, in the second iteration of the for-loop outside the function, the call will return to the yield statement again and the values such as listofnumbers, items inside the function will be restored. The next possible statement namely the 2nd iteration of the loop will be executed and the 2nd value will be yielded. The loop inside the function will continue to run until all the elements in listofnumbers are visited. We thus produced the same effect as our first example with minimal code change.

In the example, when the code inside the function is being run, the variables in memory are listofnumbers and items and the generator object.

If the original list length is 100 and 400 bytes in total, in the generator we are generating only one item at a time. Thus, the amount of memory needed is the sum of memory occupied by the list and memory to hold one item that the generator returns. The former takes 400 bytes and the latter takes 4 bytes whereas the list version of the function takes 800 bytes, resulting in approximately 50% savings. As the list size grows larger, the percentage savings might still be the same but the actual memory usage will be significantly smaller.

```python
def squared_generator(listofnumbers):
    for items in listofnumbers:
        yield items*items


for sq in squared_generator([5, 6, 7, 8]):
    print(sq)
```

```
25
36
49
64
```

Iterator

Custom iterable objects created using classes are called iterators. They can be created in Python by implementing two methods __iter__ and __next__. In Python 2, __next__ method is called next.

The __iter__ method generally returns an iterable object. Since in many cases the iterator that we are creating is an iterable object, __iter__ typically returns self.

The __next__ method has functionality to determine the next item in the sequence. When all the elements are exhausted, the iterator stops by raising the StopIteration exception.

In the example below, we create an iterator called SquaredIterator that takes a list as input. The __iter__ method returns the iterator itself by using the self word. The __next__ method checks if the current value of idx is less than the length of the list. If so, store the value at that index, increment idx and return the square of the value. When the index reaches a value of 4, then the else clause will be executed and the StopIteration exception will be raised. The for-loop will handle the exception and exit the loop.

```python
class SquaredIterator:
    def __init__(self, lst):
        self.lst = lst
        self.idx = 0
    def __iter__(self):
        return self
    def __next__(self):
        if self.idx < len(self.lst):
            v = self.lst[self.idx]
            self.idx += 1
            return v*v
        else:
            raise StopIteration
sqo = SquaredIterator([5, 6, 7, 8])
for sq in sqo:
    print(sq)
```

25

36

49

64

In a generator / iterator, the value needs to be computed on demand and hence its computational cost is a little higher compared to list based functions. Yet, it is still efficient to create generator / iterator as it results in considerable memory saving.

NOTE: An important observation that we can make from the behavior of an iterator / generator is that they support 'lazy evaluation'. This is a process where until the time the object is needed for further processing, it will be created or loaded. In the case of generator example above, we can see that the square is only calculated on call of the for-loop outside the function and not pre-created.

Introduction

Databases are one of the most common tools used for storing and retrieving data. They can be found in almost all computing devices such as desktops, laptops and even small devices like RaspberryPi. In this chapter, we will concern ourselves with one form of databases called the Relational database management system (RDBMS). These systems store data in one or more tables that have rows and columns and a relationship may exist between them. A general analogy for such as system is a spreadsheet with one or more columns. The spreadsheet may contain one or more sheets akin to a table in RDBMS. In addition to storing, RDBMS systems, also allow query, update and delete rows, columns and tables.

Most of the popular RDBMS today such as SQLite [https://www.sqlite.org/], MySQL [https://www.mysql.com/], PostgreSQL [https://www.postgresql.org/], Oracle [https://www.oracle.com/] etc., follow a language called SQL [https://en.wikipedia.org/wiki/SQL] which stands for Structured Query Language. Hence these systems are referred as SQL systems.

In this chapter, we will discuss programming the simplest of all SQL system, SQLite. The principles you learn in programming SQLite is similar to programming MySQL and others. We will begin with using SQL to create tables, insert data in to the table and finally query (read) from the table. We will then present a more general solution where you can access any SQL systems using a single code via Object Relational Mapper (ORM). In this

435

chapter, we are assuming that you are familiar with SQL systems. If not, we recommend reading https://www.w3schools.com/sql/.

Accessing SQLite

In the example below, we will begin with a non-ORM method for creating a student table. We set the first column, 'id' to be auto-incrementable. The second column, 'name' is a string of maximum length of 250 and it cannot be set to null. The third column, 'year' is an integer that can be null. As the "CREATE TABLE" command shows, the student table is only created if it does not already exist.

We then insert three rows using the 'INSERT INTO' command. Notice that we only supply the last 2 columns as id is auto incremented and will be automatically populated by sqlite3. Finally, we commit the changes, which writes the insert to the database. At this point, a new file called studentdb_no_orm.sqlite3 will appear in the same folder as this program.

```python
import sqlite3
conn = sqlite3.connect('studentdb_no_orm.sqlite3')


c = conn.cursor()
# autoincrement primary key
c.execute(''' CREATE TABLE IF NOT EXISTS student
                (id INTEGER PRIMARY KEY ASC AUTOINCREMENT,
name varchar(250) NOT NULL, year INTEGER NULL)''')

# input name and year only
```

```
c.execute("INSERT INTO student (name, year)
VALUES('Leo', 2)")
c.execute("INSERT INTO student (name, year)
VALUES('Newton', 0)")
c.execute("INSERT INTO student (name, year)
VALUES('Fourier', NULL)")

conn.commit()
conn.close()
```

If you need to read the content, modify the content, add new table etc., you need to create the appropriate SQL statement and call execute method. You can learn more about SQL commands at https://www.w3schools.com/sql/sql_syntax.asp.

Object Relational Mapper (ORM)

Although SQL is the language followed by SQL systems like SQLite, MySQL, PostgreSQL, Oracle etc., the exact commands and its options may change in some cases. Hence the code written in the previous example might work on SQLite but not in another SQL system. So, if we need to run it on another system, we need to make code change which is impractical in a large code. If we need to run on two different SQL systems, we need to maintain two different versions of code which is also impractical for large code. These issues can be fixed by using an Object Relational Mapper (ORM).

What is an ORM?

ORM as applied to a database is a process of converting a row in a table to an object. So instead of using SQL commands to manipulate the table, one can use OOPS principles.

Let's say we have a student table that has 3 columns: id, name and year. In an ORM, this can be modelled as a Student class that has three attributes id, name and year. To add a new row in the table, we will then create an object of type Student and use the add() method to insert the row. To read one or more rows, we use the query() method.

Python has few general purpose ORM such as SQLAlchemy, SQLObject etc. The web programming module Django has its own ORM. In this chapter, we will concern ourselves with SQLAlchemy. The syntax may be different for other ORMs but the discussions are still valid.

We will convert the above code written for SQLite in to an SQLAlchemy version. We begin by importing all the required modules and its attributes. We will then create a base class called 'Base' from the declarative_base() function. This class is the base class for all the classes that we will be creating.

```
from sqlalchemy import Column, Integer, String,
ForeignKey
from sqlalchemy.ext.declarative import declarative_base
from sqlalchemy import create_engine
from sqlalchemy.orm import sessionmaker
```

```
# Base class for all models
Base = declarative_base()
```

We then inherit this 'Base' class to create a child class called, 'Student'. The student class has the three-column created using the Column function. The id is of type integer and its set to be the primary key, which are by default auto-incremented. The name is a string of maximum length 250 and cannot be null as the nullable argument is set to False. The year is an integer that can be null as the nullable argument is set to True.

```
class Student(Base):
    __tablename__ = 'student'
    # Set the id column to be the primary key
    id = Column(Integer, primary_key=True)
    # The name column will be a string of max length of
250.
    # It also cannot contain null
    name = Column(String(250), nullable=False)
    # The year column is an integer. 1 for freshman, 2
for sophomore
    # 3 for junior and 4 for senior, 0 if the student
graduated
    # and finally null for cases where the student has
not enrolled
    year = Column(Integer, nullable=True)
```

We will create an engine, which is the starting point for executing any SQLAlchemy instruction [http://docs.sqlalchemy.org/en/latest/core/engines.html]. We need to supply a name for the DB. If the DB already exist, it will be loaded. If it does not exist, a new one will be created.

```
engine =
create_engine('sqlite:///studentdb_orm.sqlite3')
# Create all tables
Base.metadata.create_all(engine)
```

We will now create a session [http://docs.sqlalchemy.org/en/latest/orm/session_api.html?highlight=session#module-sqlalchemy.orm.session] using the engine. We will create three instances of Student class called st1, st2 and st3 and add them to the session. The values supplied to the three objects are same as the one we supplied in the previous example. For st3, we do not pass value for year and is automatically populated with NULL. At this point, the three objects have not been written to the database, even though they have been added to the session. A call to commit() method is needed to write to database.

```
DBSession = sessionmaker(bind=engine)
session = DBSession()

# Insert 3 students
st1 = Student(name='Leo', year=2)
session.add(st1)
```

```
st2 = Student(name='Newton', year=0)
session.add(st2)


st3 = Student(name='Fourier')
session.add(st3)


session.commit()
```

At this point, you can open the database from command line or from a
SQLite viewer such as DB Browser for SQLite [http://sqlitebrowser.org/].
Open the DB in DB Browser for SQLite and click the "Database Structure"
tab. You will see an image similar to the one below.

Name	Type	Schema
◢ Tables (1)		
◢ person		CREATE TABLE person (
id	INTEGER	`id` INTEGER NOT NULL
name	VARCHAR(250)	`name` VARCHAR(250) N
year	INTEGER	`year` INTEGER
Indices (0)		
Views (0)		
Triggers (0)		

The table was successfully created with all the supplied parameters. If you click the "Browse Data" tab, you will see an image similar to the one below.

Table: person

	id	name	year
	Filter	Filter	Filter
1	1	Leo	2
2	2	Newton	0
3	3	Fourier	NULL

The table was successfully populated with three rows with all the supplied values.

Why do we need ORM?

This is a simple example yet it is a good example of the power of ORM. In the non-ORM example, we used to AUTOINCREMENT keyword to indicate that the id needs to be auto-incremented. This keyword is different for different databases. For example: MySQL uses AUTO_INCREMENT, Microsoft SQL Server uses IDENTITY etc. You can read more about it at https://www.w3schools.com/sql/sql_autoincrement.asp. Thus, this simple code will only work in SQLite but not in other SQL systems. But the ORM code will work in all SQL systems. This is because the ORM converts all instructions to SQL commands. In the process, it prepares the commands depending on the SQL system and hence it is more general purpose. In addition, the ORM code is more Pythonic compared to the non-ORM code.

Foreign key

Foreign key in a database is a field in SQL table that uniquely identifies a row in another SQL table. We will demonstrate this with 2 tables. The two tables 'student' and 'address' are connected by a foreign key.

We first create an address table with an auto-incremented primary key called id, a non-nullable street address of type string with a maximum length of 250, a non-nullable city of type string with a maximum length of 50 and a non-nullable state of type string with a maximum length of 2. The student table is similar to the previous example with one change, the addition of foreign key relationship to the address table.

Finally, we enter the value for one student and the corresponding address. Note that when we add the foreign key value in student table, we supply a value of 1, the id number in the address table.

```
import sqlite3

conn =
sqlite3.connect('studentdb_no_orm_address.sqlite3')


c = conn.cursor()


c.execute(''' CREATE TABLE IF NOT EXISTS address
              (id INTEGER PRIMARY KEY ASC AUTOINCREMENT,
streetaddress varchar(250) NOT NULL,
              city varchar(50) NOT NULL, state
varchar(2) NOT NULL)''')
```

```python
# We added a foreign key to the address table
c.execute(''' CREATE TABLE IF NOT EXISTS student
                (id INTEGER PRIMARY KEY ASC AUTOINCREMENT,
name varchar(250) NOT NULL, year INTEGER NULL,
                address_id INTEGER NOT NULL, FOREIGN
KEY(address_id) REFERENCES address(id))''')

c.execute("INSERT INTO address (streetaddress, city,
state) VALUES('123 Python Street', 'Santa Clara',
'CA')")
# Here we manually added the foreign key
c.execute("INSERT INTO student (name, year, address_id)
VALUES('Leo', 2, 1)")

conn.commit()
conn.close()
```

The code below is the corresponding ORM code. We begin by importing all the necessary functions from the sqlalchemy module and create a base class from which all models are derived.

```python
from sqlalchemy import Column, Integer, String,
ForeignKey
from sqlalchemy.ext.declarative import declarative_base
from sqlalchemy import create_engine
from sqlalchemy.orm import sessionmaker
from sqlalchemy.orm import relationship
```

```
Base = declarative_base()
```

The Address class has 4 attributes: id, streetaddress, city and state whose
properties are integer, a non-nullable string with a maximum length of 250, a
non-nullable string with a maximum length of 50 and a non-nullable string
with a maximum length of 2.

The Student class is same as the previous one, except for the new
ForeignKey attribute address_id.

```python
class Address(Base):
    __tablename__ = 'address'
    # Here we define columns for the table address.
    # Notice that each column is also a normal Python
instance attribute.
    id = Column(Integer, primary_key=True)
    streetaddress = Column(String(250), nullable=False)
    city = Column(String(50), nullable=False)
    state = Column(String(2), nullable=False)

class Student(Base):
    __tablename__ = 'student'
    # Set the id column to be the primary key
    id = Column(Integer, primary_key=True)
    # The name column will be a string of max length of
250.
    # It also cannot contain null
```

```
    name = Column(String(250), nullable=False)
    # The year column is an integer. 1 for freshman, 2
for sophomore
    # 3 for junior and 4 for senior, 0 if the student
graduated
    # and finally null for cases where the student has
not enrolled
    year = Column(Integer, nullable=True)
    address_id = Column(Integer,
ForeignKey('address.id'))
    address = relationship(Address)
```

We create an engine, so that a session can be subsequently created.

```
engine =
create_engine('sqlite:///studentdb_orm_address.sqlite3')
# Create all tables
Base.metadata.create_all(engine)
```

One instance of the Address class is created and is supplied as a foreign key to the Student instance, st1. Note that we pass the foreign key address as an object and not as an integer as in the previous example. SQLAlchemy then figures out the id for that address and populates the database with the correct id. As a programmer, we worked only on objects but SQLAlchemy handled the SQL transactions for us.

```
DBSession = sessionmaker(bind=engine)
session = DBSession()

address1 = Address(streetaddress='123 Python Street',
city='Santa Clara', state='CA')
session.add(address1)

st1 = Student(name='Leo', year=2, address=address1)
session.add(st1)

session.commit()
```

Read SQL table

Finally, we will see an example where we read the content of the database. We open an engine followed by a session object. To query the database (SELECT in SQL), we use the query() method in SQLAlchemy. The all() method indicates that SQLALchmey must fetch all the rows and columns in that table. This is equivalent to the SQL command, 'SELECT * from student'. As the print statement shows, the all() method returns a list of Student objects. Here SQLAlchemy fetched the response from SQL which contains int, float and string and converted them in to Python objects.

We then iterate through each of these objects and print its content. The first print function call prints the name of the student and the year. The second print function uses the foreign key relationship between student and address. To obtain the street address for a given student, we can use the dot (.)

operator. The first part student.address fetches the address object for a given student. The streetaddress can then be obtained using student.address.streetaddress.

```
engine =
create_engine('sqlite:///studentdb_orm_address.sqlite3')
Base.metadata.bind = engine
DBSession = sessionmaker()
DBSession.bind = engine
session = DBSession()
allstudents = session.query(Student).all()
print('A list of all students is', allstudents)
for students in allstudents:
    # Note that the year is an integer and so we are
using %d for formatting
    print("The students name is %s and is in year
%d"%(students.name, students.year))
    print("The address is: %s, %s,
%s"%(students.address.streetaddress,
students.address.city, students.address.state))
```

```
A list of all students is [<__main__.Student object at
0x000000000720EBE0>]
The students name is Leo and is in year 2
The address is: 123 Python Street, Santa Clara, CA
```

We discussed only a limited aspect of SQLAlchemy. If you are developing a large application that needs to connect to a SQL system, it is highly recommended to write your database calls using an ORM like SQLAlchemy. You can learn more about SQLAlchemy from https://www.sqlalchemy.org/. You can learn more about SQLObject at http://sqlobject.org.

22. Logging

Introduction

Logging is a record of the user's actions on a software and it helps the developers understand issues and bugs and it helps product owners determine the usage pattern of the software. Logging is an important part of applications irrespective of its size.

Python provides logging via the logging module. The logging module can write the log information to a file, socket, database etc. It also rotates the log file, a process of creating a new file to log when the previous file reaches a certain size or certain age etc. Most of the popular modules support logging with minimal configuration. So, if you enable logging on your application, then those modules will also write log files.

To check whether you have the logging module [http://docs.python-guide.org/en/latest/writing/logging/] installed, open the Python interpreter and type 'import logging'. If you receive an import error, then install logging module by typing 'pip install logging' in the OS command prompt.

In this chapter, we will discuss the different ways of configuring a logger and then discuss the logging process itself.

Logging is hard. Do I really need it? Can't I just use print?

One of the questions we are asked often is, "Do I really need logging? Can't I just use print?" The answer depends on what you want to achieve.

The print function is convenient. You pass in a Python object and it automatically appears on the command window. The logging on the other hand requires configuring. However, once it is configured, it provides rich information that cannot be obtained from a simple print statement. Here are some of its features.

1. Logs can be written to command line, file, email, socket etc. while print only sends the value to command line.

2. Unlike print function output which disappear on the close of the command line, a log is a permanent record of an event as it can be stored to a file, database etc.

3. Logs have different categories like critical, errors, warning etc. and hence convenient for discerning the difference in the criticality of messages. The print function does not distinguish between an exception which is an error and printing of information, while logs can.

Logging is generally considered to be part of a large software development especially the ones that involve large number of people. However, this is far from truth. It can be used for projects of all sizes. For example, a quality engineer performing automated tests can store results of the test to a log file. A system administrator managing 1000s of nodes can use logs to store the status of the machines and revisit them to understand the history of machine status.

There are two steps to enable logging.

1. Configure the logger
    a. code based configuration
    b. ini based configuration
    c. dictionary based configuration
2. Call the appropriate method and write to logger

Code based configuration

As the name indicates, the configuration is specified in the Python code as shown in the example below. We begin by importing the logging module. Once imported, we obtain a logger using getLogger() function. There can only be one instance of logger in an application. Multiple calls to getLogger() will only return one version. We then create a file handle and supply a file name. When the logger is called to store log lines, it will be written to the specified log file. We then specify the formatting of the log line. In the example below, the first column in a log line will contain the date and time when the log line was written, the second column will contain the log level and finally the last column will be the message specified in the log line. We finally set the log level to INFO. The exact purpose of setting the log level will be discussed soon.

Now that the configuration is complete, we can write error logs using logger.error() method or info logs using logger.info() method.

The configured logger is used in the code below. First, the value of a and b are set to 10 and 0. We then write an info message to the logger that the values are set. Inside the try block, an info message that the division of a over b is being conducted is written followed by the actual division. Since the denominator b is zero, we will receive the ZeroDivisionError which the except block catches. It sets the value of c to a and writes the error message from the exception. Since the exc_info is set to True, the details of the exception are added to the log.

```
import logging
```

```
# Configure the Logger
logger = logging.getLogger('mylogger')
hdlr = logging.FileHandler('myapp.log') # Create a log
file called myapp.log
formatter = logging.Formatter('%(asctime)s %(levelname)s
%(message)s')
hdlr.setFormatter(formatter)
logger.addHandler(hdlr)
logger.setLevel(logging.INFO)

# Write to Logger
a = 10
b = 0
logger.info('The values of a and b are set.')
try:
    logger.info('Dividing a over b....')
    c = a/b
except ZeroDivisionError as e:
    c = a # Since denominator is zero, we will reset c
to something else
    logger.error('Failed to divide as the denominator is
zero', exc_info=True)
```

After running this code, open the file 'myapp.log' in the same directory as the given Python file using a text editor and notice that there are lines similar to the one below.

```
2017-02-10 13:18:22,325 INFO The values of a and b are
set. 2017-02-10 13:18:22,326 INFO Dividing a over b....
2017-02-10 13:18:22,336 ERROR Failed to divide as the
denominator is zero. integer division or modulo by zero
Traceback (most recent call last): File "", line 17, in
c = a/b ZeroDivisionError: integer division or modulo by
zero
```

In the above example, we use info and error method that are part of the logger object. The former is used to log information that is relevant to the working of the code while the latter is used to log any error message such as exceptions. There are few other log levels that we will discuss in a later section.

This configuration method is suitable for small programs and is not viable for large applications where a more centralized configuration would be suitable.

INI based configuration

In this method for configuration, we define an INI file, a format used for defining configuration file [https://en.wikipedia.org/wiki/INI_file]. An INI file consists of one or more sections. A section in an INI file begins with a name enclosed inside []. The content of the section is specified below similar in syntax to the assignment operator in Python. The code below is the content of the logconfig.ini. The configuration file contains value that are same as the example before but in INI format.

The file handler is declared in the handlers section and then defined in the handler_file_handler section. The file handler is configured to store logs in mylog.log and the log level is indicated as INFO. The formatter_formatter section defines the format for storing the log lines in a format that we discussed in the previous example.

```ini
# The file name is Logconfig.ini
[loggers]
keys=root

[handlers]
keys=file_handler

[formatters]
keys=formatter

[logger_root]
level=INFO
handlers=file_handler

[handler_file_handler]
class=FileHandler
filename='client.log'
level=INFO
formatter=formatter
args=('mylog.log', )

[formatter_formatter]
format=%(asctime)s %(levelname)s %(message)s
```

We then create a new Python file called fileconfig.py that will contain the code below. The fileConfig() function from logging module is given the logconfig.ini file. The fileConfig reads the INI file and configures the logger accordingly. We then call the getLogger() to get that single instance of the logger. We then use that logger to write error and info log message in the try-except block using an example similar to the previous. After saving all the file, when you run it, you will see two entries in the log file.

```python
import logging
from logging.config import fileConfig

fileConfig('logconfig.ini')
logger = logging.getLogger()
# Write to Logger
a = 10
b = 0
logger.info('The values of a and b are set.')
try:
    logger.info('Dividing a over b....')
    c = a/b
except ZeroDivisionError as e:
    c = a # Since denominator is zero, we will reset c
to something else
    logger.error('Failed to divide as the denominator is
zero.', exc_info=True)
```

```
2017-02-10 13:18:22,325 INFO The values of a and b are
set. 2017-02-10 13:18:22,326 INFO Dividing a over b....
2017-02-10 13:18:22,336 ERROR Failed to divide as the
denominator is zero. integer division or modulo by zero
Traceback (most recent call last): File "", line 17, in
c = a/b ZeroDivisionError: integer division or modulo by
zero
```

The main advantage of using INI instead of code-based logger is the ability to separate configuration from code.

Dictionary based configuration

The most common method for configuring a logger for large application is using a dictionary-based configuration. As the name indicates, in this method, the logger configuration is specified as a dictionary. The configuration includes specification of a formatter, handler and a root that combines the two. The handler in this example is a console and a file. Using the former, the output will be written to command line and using the latter, the output will be written to a file. It is possible to other handlers such as socket, database etc. as well. All the handler will write the same log. Once the dictionary has been configured, it is passed to the dictConfig function to complete the logger configuration.

In every file that needs to be configured, an instance of the logger can be obtained by using the getLogger() function. The rest of the code is same as the previous example.

```python
# configuring with dictionary.
import logging
from logging.config import dictConfig

logging_config = dict(
    version = 1,
    formatters = {
        'f': {'format':
              '%(asctime)s %(name)-12s %(levelname)-8s
%(message)s'}
    },
    handlers = {
        'console': {
                    'class': 'logging.StreamHandler',
                    'formatter': 'f',
                    'level': logging.DEBUG
            },
        'file': {
                    'class':
'logging.handlers.RotatingFileHandler',
                    'level': 'INFO',
                    'formatter': 'f',
                    'filename': 'myapp1.log',
                    'mode': 'a',
                    'maxBytes': 10485760,
                    'backupCount': 5
            },
```

```python
        },
    root = {
        'handlers': ['console','file'],
        'level': logging.DEBUG,
        },
)
# Once the logger is configured, it becomes part of the
Python process.
dictConfig(logging_config)

# Put the lines below in to the file where logging needs
to be done
logger = logging.getLogger()
# Write to logger
a = 10
b = 0
logger.info('The values of a and b are set.')
try:
    logger.info('Dividing a over b....')
    c = a/b
except ZeroDivisionError as e:
    c = a # Since denominator is zero, we will reset c
to something else
    logger.error('Failed to divide as the denominator is
zero.', exc_info=True)
```

After running this code, open the file 'myapp1.log' in the same directory as the given Python file using a text editor and notice that there are lines similar to the one below.

```
2017-02-12 17:54:16,610 root          INFO      The values
of a and b are set.
2017-02-12 17:54:16,612 root          INFO      Dividing a
over b....
/Users/chityala/Library/Enthought/Canopy_64bit/User/lib/
python2.7/site-packages/ipykernel/__main__.py:47:
DeprecationWarning: BaseException.message has been
deprecated as of Python 2.6
2017-02-12 17:54:16,614 root          ERROR     Failed to
divide as the denominator is zero.
integer division or modulo by zero
Traceback (most recent call last):
  File "<ipython-input-9-c74fed72c6cc>", line 44, in
<module>
    c = a/b
ZeroDivisionError: integer division or modulo by zero
```

You can learn more about the various options available in Python logger from [https://docs.python.org/3/library/logging.html, https://pymotw.com/3/logging/]

Log levels

Not all log lines are equal. There are some log lines to record errors and some log lines are meant only for debugging by a software or service

460

engineer. When writing to log, it is important to understand the severity of an event, so that you can choose the appropriate log level.

There are several levels of logging. They are

1. Critical

2. Error

3. Warning

4. Info

5. Debug

6. Not set

The critical log line, written using logger.critical() method, are for catastrophic error such as loss of data or potential safety issues. For example, if you have an application that treats patients and if the application crashes in the middle of the treatment, it should be logged under critical.

The error log line, written using logger.error() method, are for errors that do affect the software but are not catastrophic. An example of error log will be a case where a file could not be found while opening for read or write. Another case would be a user unable to access a web page due to server error. The cause of the error can be recorded using the error log line.

The warning log line, written using logger.warning() method, are used for cases, where the software engineer needs to be informed that there could be issues that need to be looked in to.

The info log line, written using logger.info() method , are used for recording information about any event. For example, when a user signs up to a service, the info log line can be used to record the id of the user, so that it can be used to determine the number of users and also the user's activity history.

The debug log line, written using logger.debug() method, are for software engineers, to record system information, that will assist in debugging.

Log level choice

In any code with logging, there will be one or more of log lines in various log levels. However, in deployment, we do not want to record logs with debug log level. In the logging configuration process, we can indicate a log level. Only messages whose log level is above the configured log level will be output to the log file. The determination of order of log level is based on the list critical, error, warning, info, and debug. Critical is a higher order log level than error which in turn is a higher log level than warning etc.

For example, if you set log level to warning and if the message is of type error, then it will be in the log file.

If you set log level to warning and if the message is of type debug, then it not will be in the log file.

Typically, during the development process, the log level is set to debug, so that the software engineer can obtain all the logs. When the application is deployed the log level is generally set to info.

23. Unit Testing

Introduction

Unit testing is a software testing process in which individual units of code are tested. The general unit of code is a function or a class. In other words, we test if a given function works by passing a known input for which there is a known output. The testing of the function can be manual or automated. It is usually automated and is run as a part of continuous integration [https://en.wikipedia.org/wiki/Continuous_integration].

Do I need to write unit test?

The question that is always asked is: Do I need to write unit test? The common complaint is that a unit test takes time to write and maintain. So why spend time writing a unit test that could be spent adding features to your code? The answer is if you need to set a solid foundation to your code, then you need to write unit test. If you are working with multiple programmers, writing unit test is recommended. If you are working on an enterprise application, writing unit test must be mandated.

Manual testing

We will begin the discussion of unit testing by demonstrating a mechanism for testing functions manually. In the cell below, we have 2 functions: multby2() and iseven(). The former as the name indicates, multiplies a given number by 2 and returns it while the latter takes a number x and checks if it is even.

464

```
def multby2(x):
    return x*2


# Return True if x is even, otherwise return False
def iseven(x):
    return x%2==0
```

The code below can be used to test the two functions that we defined above. We begin with calling the multby2() function with an input of 4. Since the expected output is 8, we check using an if-statement. The aim of this testing is to run the code below every-time a change is made to the multby2() or iseven() function. If the function was changed that causes the test to return False, then the programmer can determine whether the cause of the test failing is due to the function being incorrect or if the test needs to be refactored.

These tests are called manual tests. The programmer has to curate a list of tests and run it every-time they make the code change. Automated unit test on the other hand can curate a list of tests and run them automatically and report back with a list of passed and failed tests.

```
if(multby2(4) == 8):
    print("Success! multby2 is working.")
else:
    print("Failure! multby2 not working.")


if(iseven(4)):
```

```
    print("Success! Number is even.")
else:
    print("Failure! Number is odd.")
```

```
Success! multby2 is working.
Success! Number is even.
```

This approach is cumbersome and requires code to be written to check if the function failed or succeeded. A better approach is automated testing using unit test.

Automated testing using pytest

In Python, there are many automated testing modules such as doctest, unittest, pytest etc. In this chapter, we will discuss pytest [http://pytest.org]. Even though there are many such testing modules, they are similar and this chapter will provide enough background material and you can learn other modules.

We will begin by first storing the code below in a file called myfunc.py.

```
# Store this in to a file: myfunc.py
def multby2(x):
    return x*2


# Return True if x is even, otherwise return False
def iseven(x):
    return x%2==0
```

We will then write unit test to test these two functions using pytest. This can be done in two ways either using functions or classes. We will discuss both methods.

Function based pytest

We will begin by storing the code below in a file named test_myfunc.py. The file name must either start with test_ or end with _test. Ensure that both files are in the same directory.

```python
# copy the content of this cell to test_myfunc.py
import myfunc
# The function name has to start with test_
# So one can have more methods that do not start
# with test_ as support functions
def test_multby2():
    assert myfunc.multby2(4) == 8
def test_iseven():
    assert myfunc.iseven(4) == True
    assert myfunc.iseven(5) == False
```

In test_myfunc.py file, we import the myfunc module. In the first function test_multby2, we call the myfunc's multby2 function and pass a value of 4. We then assert if the value returned is 8. In the second function test_isEven, we call myfunc's iseven function with value of 4 and assert if it is True and also with a value of 5 and assert if it is False. The functions that need to be run by pytest must be prefixed with 'test_'.

You can run this code from the OS command line. Change directory to the folder where the files are and then type

pytest -v

The -v flag provides a verbose output similar to the one below. This will produce the following output which has been truncated to show only the relevant information.

```
collected 2 items
test_myfunc.py::test_multby2 PASSED
test_myfunc.py::test_isEven PASSED
=================== 2 passed in 0.01 seconds
======================
```

When the code is run, all the test functions are discovered and executed. The two functions that start with test_ namely, test_iseven and test_multby2 are run. Since the tests ran successfully, the word "PASSED" is printed next to their name.

Class based pytest

In the class based pytest, we create one or more classes that will contain methods to be discovered and executed by pytest. It is important to follow the following rules

1. The file name must either start with test_ or end with _test.

2. The class name must begin with 'Test'.

3. The methods that need to be run by pytest must be prefixed with 'test_'

4. The test class cannot contain __init__ method.

5. The class can contain methods that will not be executed by pytest.

We will begin my storing the code below in a file name test_class_myfunc.py.

```python
import myfunc
# The class name must start with Test
class Test_MyFunc:
    def test_multby2test(self):
        assert myfunc.multby2(4) == 8
    def test_checkeven(self):
        assert myfunc.iseven(4) == True
        assert myfunc.iseven(5) == False
    def nontestfunction(self):
        print("This print statement will never be called")
```

The class Test_MyFunc consists of three methods in which two methods start with test_ and hence are discoverable by pytest. In the first test method, test_multby2test we are testing the multby2 function. We call the multby2() function with an input of 4 and then assert whether its output is equal to 8.

In the second test method, test_checkeven, we are performing two different assertions. The first assert statement checks whether the iseven function is returning True for an input which is even while the second assert checks whether the iseven function is returning False for an input which is odd. The first assert call will succeed as iseven returns True and the assert calls is testing for True. The second assert statement will also succeed as iseven returns False while the assert checks for False.

We also added one non-test function named, "nontestfunction". This function will not be automatically run as it does not start with test_.

You can run this code from the OS command line. Change directory to the folder where the files are and then type

pytest -v

The -v flag provides a verbose output similar to the one below. This will produce the following output which has been truncated to show only the relevant information.

```
collected 2 items
test_class_myfunc.py::Test_MyFunc::test_multby2test
PASSED
test_class_myfunc.py::Test_MyFunc::test_checkeven PASSED

=================== 2 passed in 0.02 seconds
===============
```

When the code is run, all the test methods in the class are discovered and executed. The two methods that start with test_ namely, test_checkeven and test_multby2test are run. Since the tests ran successfully, the word "PASSED" is printed next to their name.

If we change the second assert call in test_checkeven method from 5 to 6, the test will fail with an output similar to one below. The point at which the error occurred is clearly identified.

```
collected 2 items
test_class_myfunc.py::Test_MyFunc::test_multby2test
PASSED
test_class_myfunc.py::Test_MyFunc::test_checkeven FAILED

==================== FAILURES ======================
_____ Test_MyFunc.test_checkeven

_____

self = <test_class_myfunc.Test_MyFunc instance at
0x10757c5a8>
    def test_checkeven(self):
        assert myfunc.iseven(4) == True
>       assert myfunc.iseven(6) == False
E       assert True == False
E        +  where True = <function iseven at
0x1076aa398>(6)
E        +    where <function iseven at 0x1076aa398> =
myfunc.iseven

test_class_myfunc.py:17: AssertionError
================= 1 failed, 1 passed in 0.06 seconds
===================
```

NOTE: Things to remember while writing unit test are:

1. You can use more than one-unit test method or function to test a given function.

2. Name the unit test methods appropriately, so that is easier to read the test report.

3. When testing a function, write unit test(s) that test for both positive and negative cases.

Pytest has become popular due to an ecosystem of plugins that have created around it. For example:

a) pytest-html [https://pypi.org/project/pytest-html/] allows creation of HTML reports from the tests.

b) Pytest-cov [https://github.com/pytest-dev/pytest-cov] determines code coverage.

c) Pytest-xdist [https://github.com/pytest-dev/pytest-xdist] allows distributed testing across machines and across cores.

Introduction to The Zen of Python

Tim Peters, a long time Pythonista has created a list of 19 aphorisms that explains the working of Python. In this chapter, we will discuss some of these aphorisms with Python examples and in the process discuss good programming habits.

The aphorisms can be viewed from Python command prompt by importing the module, "this" as shown below

```
import this
```

```
Beautiful is better than ugly.
Explicit is better than implicit.
Simple is better than complex.
Complex is better than complicated.
Flat is better than nested.
Sparse is better than dense.
Readability counts.
Special cases aren't special enough to break the rules.
Although practicality beats purity.
Errors should never pass silently.
Unless explicitly silenced.
In the face of ambiguity, refuse the temptation to guess.
There should be one-- and preferably only one --obvious
```

way to do it.

Although that way may not be obvious at first unless you're Dutch.

Now is better than never.

Although never is often better than *right* now.

If the implementation is hard to explain, it's a bad idea.

If the implementation is easy to explain, it may be a good idea.

Namespaces are one honking great idea -- let's do more of those!

We will discuss a few of these aphorisms in the context of writing better Python code.

Beautiful is better than ugly

Python uses code indentation as the mechanism to define blocks of code. Hence, any code written is well structured. However, code indentation is not the only mechanism to keep the code looking beautiful. Here are some examples of ugly code and the corresponding beautiful one.

The function, ugly_func shown below has the function signature and the body of the code in the same line. This function calculates the square of the input, stores in to the variable sqrval and then returns it. The statements in the function are separated by semi-colons.

```python
def ugly_func(val): sqrval = val*val; return(sqrval)
print(ugly_func(10))
```

100

The function, "beautiful_func" shown below is readable compared to the previous function. The signature is in a separate line and is clearly distinguishable from the body of the function. It performs the same operation as the ugly_func but it is readable.

```python
def beautiful_func(val):
    sqrval = val*val;
    return(sqrval)
print(beautiful_func(10))
```

100

If the function needs to be a one liner and to still satisfy the, "Beautiful is better than ugly" aphorism, a lambda function could be used. In the function, "lambda_func", the input is in the right of the : (colon) and the output of the function is to the right of the : (colon).

```python
lambda_func = lambda val: val*val
print(lambda_func(10))
```

100

Simple is better than complex

Python's guiding philosophy is simplicity. If there are many ways to arrive at a solution, it is recommended to choose the simplest, obvious and most readable one.

In some cases, using the power of data structures and its associated functions allow for simplicity in code.

For example, in the code below, a list, "ml" is checked to see if it only contains unique element. The code works as follows.

- Set a boolean unique to True.
- Iterate through every element in the list.
- For every element, visit every other element to its right.
- If there is at least one match, set the boolean unique to False and break from the inner loop.

This process will take O(n^2) operations to check if the list only contains unique elements as for every item in the list, the algorithm visits all other values in the list. Moreover, excluding the if-else statement and the initialization, the program requires 7 lines of code.

```python
# Complex way to find if all items are unique.  There is
not only too much code but also needs O(n^2) operations.
ml = [1, 2, 3, 1, 4]

unique = True
len_ml = len(ml)
for i, vi in enumerate(ml):
```

```
    for j in range(i+1, len_ml-1):
        if(vi == ml[j]):
            unique = False
            break
if unique:
    print("All unique by complex way")
else:
    print("Some duplicates by complex way")
```

Some duplicates by complex way

The code above can be improved based on the observation that if a list contains all unique elements, then the length of the list and the length of a set created from that list will have the same value.

The list, 'ml' is converted into a Python set, 'ml_uniq'. The length of this set is compared with the length of the original list. The outcome is stored in the variable unique. Excluding the if-else statement and the initialization, the program requires only 2 lines of code, a saving of 5 lines of code, 2.5x savings in lines of code. Fewer code written is fewer bugs. It also needs only O(n) operation for converting the list to a set and hence considerably faster for large values of n.

```
ml = [1, 2, 3, 4]


ml_uniq = set(ml)
unique = len(ml_uniq) == len(ml) # Store the boolean
```

```
if unique:
    print("All unique by simple way")
else:
    print("Some duplicates by simple way")
```

```
Some duplicates by simple way
```

Readability counts

Python is one of the few languages where the code written is readable because of the language design. However, due to the scope of the language, it is possible to create unreadable code. In the next few examples, two sets of code, one readable and one unreadable is discussed.

In the first example, the value a is compared with 50. If it is True, the value of b is set to 1 otherwise b is set to 0. Excluding the initialization and print function call, the code requires 4 lines.

```
a = 54
if a  > 50:
    b = 1
else:
    b = 0
print('Value of b using if is {0}'.format(b))
```

Value of b using if is 1

The code below is more concise. Excluding the initialization and print function call, the code runs for 4 lines.

The code is more concise and it works as follows:

- The second [ ] contains the expression a>50. This will return either a True or False, whose decimal equivalent is 1 or 0 respectively. The 1 or 0 can be used as index.

- The first [ ] is a list with value 0 and 1. The second [ ] provides a mechanism to index to a particular position in the first [ ].

- If the expression a>50 is True, then the corresponding decimal value is 1 and hence the expression b = [0, 1][a > 50] will reduce to b = [0, 1][1], which will result in b = 1.

- If the expression a>50 is False, then the corresponding decimal value is 0 and hence the expression b = [0, 1][a > 50] will reduce to b = [0, 1][0], which will result in b = 0.

However, this code is unreadable. It is easier for a well-trained individual but not for a new programmer. In such cases, aim for readability and not line count.

```python
a = 54
b = [0, 1][a > 50]
print('Value of b using lists is {0}'.format(b))
```

Value of b using lists is 1

Performing arithmetic on truthiness

Python allows performing arithmetic on truthiness. In the following code, a boolean c is created by checking if a > 50. In this case c is True. However in the line, 'cplusplus = (a > 50)+1', Python implicitly converts the boolean True to the integer value of 1 as it needs to add a boolean to an int. Similar argument can be made for the case where the value of (a > 50) is False, then (a > 50) would have been converted to 0.

If the boolean (a > 50) is not hardcoded but instead returned at run time from a function call, such implicit conversion can lead to intractable errors. Thus, care must be placed for such conversion. One way to make the intent clear is to explicitly convert the boolean (a > 50) to an int by typecasting as shown in the case where we calculate cplusplusint.

```
a = 100
c = a > 50
print('The value of c is {0} of type {1}'.format(c,
type(c)))


cplusplus = (a > 50)+1
print('The value of cplusplus is {0} of type
{1}'.format(cplusplus, type(cplusplus)))


cplusplusint = int(a > 50)+1
```

```
print('The value of cplusplusint is {0} of type
{1}'.format(cplusplusint, type(cplusplusint)))
```

```
The value of c is True of type <type 'bool'>
The value of cplusplus is 2 of type <type 'int'>
The value of cplusplusint is 2 of type <type 'int'>
```

Errors should never pass silently

Exception handling are the mechanism through which the software can handle any error generated without causing crash which could result in anything from minor inconvenience to major breakdowns depending on the complexity of the software. We discussed it in detail in an earlier chapter.

Python's exception is powerful, simple and extensible. The aim of exception is to inform all the callers that an error occurred in the software, so that corrective action may be taken. The best practice is to write the details of the exception to a log file using the Python's logging module which was discussed previously. Also, appropriate changes to variables and other state may be needed.

There are a few guidelines that needs to be followed while handling exceptions.

- Never use a catch-all exception. Always specify the exception being caught.
- If the exception occurs in a function or class method handle it in that function. In some cases, it is preferable to inform the caller by raising the exception again and not just silenced by the callee.

Never use a catch-all exception. Always specify the exception being caught

In the example below, the input, "val" is inversed and returned. The function will work fine if the value of val is non-zero. However, if val = 0, Python will raise the ZeroDivisionError exception. Since we did not specify the exception in the except clause, Python will catch this exception and print the error message, "Zero division error in the callee." The function then returns a reassigned value of 1.0 as the inverse.

```python
def findinverse(val):
    try:
        return(1.0/val)
    except: # Catch all exception is even worse
        print('Zero division error in the callee')
        return(1.0)

print('The inverse is {0}'.format(findinverse(0)))
```

```
Zero division error in the callee
The inverse is 1.0
```

However, the above approach of using catch-all exception will catch errors that the developer never imagined and hence the handling of the error might not be complete.

The function below is same as the one above except in the calculation of the inverse, the variable in the denominator is val1 instead of val. This is a programming error. This will raise a NameError, as Python cannot find the

482

name, 'val1.' Since we catch all exception using one method, we will see the error message printed as being ZeroDivisionError. This will create difficulties in debugging the error.

```python
def findinverse(val):
    try:
        return(1.0/val1) # The variable was incorrectly
named as val1 instead of val
    except:
        print('Zero division error in the callee')
        return(1.0)

print('The inverse is {0}'.format(findinverse(0)))
```

```
Zero division error in the callee
The inverse is 1.0
```

The correct approach to this problem is shown below. Both the exceptions, ZeroDivisionError and NameError are caught and handled individually and the printed error messages are appropriate to the exception.

```python
def findinverse(val):
    try:
        return(1.0/val1) # The variable was incorrectly
named as val1 instead of val
    except ZeroDivisionError:
        print('Zero division error in the callee')
```

```
        return(1.0)
    except NameError:
        print('Name error. Cannot find val1')
        return(1.0)


print('The inverse is {0}'.format(findinverse(0)))
```

```
Zero division error in the callee
The inverse is 1.0
```

Handling the exception and re-throwing

In the various example seen so far, the function that raises the exception, handles it. The caller of the function is not aware of any error(s) in the function.

In some cases, the function must inform the caller that an exception occurred in the callee. This is useful in cases where a function in a library will handle the error(s) and in case if additional work needs to be performed must inform the caller. One mechanism would be return an error code to the caller and the caller will look up the error code and handle the error appropriately.

A more reasonable scenario would be for the function to raise (also called as throw) the exception again after the exception is first handled as in the example below.

The function, findinverse determines inverse of the input value as in previous examples. The one difference with the other example is the use of the 'raise' keyword to throw the exception again in the except block, so that the caller is informed.

Since the function could potentially return with an exception, in the call to the findinverse function, a try-except block is used.

```
# Callee
def findinverse(val):
    try:
        return 1.0/val
    except ZeroDivisionError as ze:
        print('Zero division error in the callee')
        # Log to file if needed
        raise ZeroDivisionError
        # If you just say raise, it will raise the error too

# Caller
invval = 0.0
try:
    invval = findinverse(0)
except ZeroDivisionError as ze:
    print('Zero division error in the caller')
else:
    print('The inverse is {0}'.format(invval))
```

```
Zero division error in the callee
Zero division error in the caller
```

25. Miscellaneous

Introduction

This chapter is a catch-all chapter where we will discuss aspects of Python that otherwise could not be placed in other chapters.

Running your code on various versions of Python

A Python code might be written for a specific version such as 3.5. However, it might be executed on older or newer versions including version 2+. In such cases, the code needs to be written in such a way that it can be run on multiple versions.

There are several Python idioms that have been developed for such cases. One such idiom is for importing module specific to a version.

We have already discussed pickle in an earlier chapter for serializing of Python objects, so that they can be stored or transmitted.

Before Python 2.x, programmers used pickle module. Subsequently cPickle [https://docs.python.org/2/library/pickle.html, https://pymotw.com/2/pickle/#module-cPickle] module was introduced that allowed faster serialization and deserialization. The pickle module in Python 2.x is slower than the cPickle module as the former is implemented in Python while the latter is implemented in C. Python 3 has the pickle module which is the cPickle under the hood. What if you need to write a code that could be run on any version of Python and might use Python 2 version of pickle or cPickle or might use the Python 3 verison of pickle? How would you write a code that can handle all scenarios? Before we discuss the solution, we will do a refresh of pickle and cPickle with code.

In the code below, the pickle module is imported and a file, somefile.pickle is opened for writing. The value in ml is then dumped (written) to the file. Since the context manager is used, the file will be automatically closed on the exit of the with block. The code below runs on all versions of Python. However, it is preferable to use the faster cPickle module available in Python 2+.

```python
import pickle

ml = [1, 2, 3]
with open('somefile.pickle', 'wb') as fo:
    pickle.dump(ml, fo)
```

In the example below, the module being imported is changed to cPickle to take advantage of its speed. Since the name of the module is changed, the function call dump() is changed from pickle.dump() to cPickle.dump(). Otherwise the code is identical to the one above.

This code will only work for version 2+. It does not work in version 3.0+ as it does not have cPickle module import but only pickle module import [https://docs.python.org/3/library/pickle.html]

```python
import cPickle

ml = [1, 2, 3]
with open('somefile.pickle', 'wb') as fo:
    cPickle.dump(ml, fo)
```

The two versions of the code can be combined using the following idiom. The code below will work with all versions of Python and also for both pickle and cPickle. The try block imports cPickle module and aliases it to pickle. If the code is run in Python version lower than 2.0, this import will fail with ImportError exception. In such case, the except block's, 'import pickle' will be executed.

In case of Python 3+, where cPickle does not exist, the try block will fail and hence the except block's, 'import pickle' will be executed.

Since the cPickle module is aliased to pickle, the code for the function call dump() can remain the same making it a very clever trick that keeps the code reusable across various versions.

```python
try:
    import cPickle as pickle
except ImportError:
    import pickle


ml = [1, 2, 3]
with open('somefile.pickle', 'wb') as fo:
    pickle.dump(ml, fo)
```

Some cool things about pickle and cPickle

The modules pickle and cPickle are normally used to store objects. In Python everything is an object. So int, float, string etc. are objects. Even functions and classes are also objects. So, one can store a class definition in a pickle file, retrieve it and then create objects from it. Here is an example that accomplishes it.

The example below demonstrates a class called Person that contains one instance variable name. The class definition is then stored in the pickle file, 'file.pickle'.

```
try:
    import cPickle as pickle
except:
    import pickle

class Person(object):
    def __init__(self, name):
        self.name = name

# You can also store a class definition in a pickle
file.
with open('file.pickle', 'wb') as pkfo:
    pickle.dump(Person, pkfo)
```

The code below reads the pickle file and retrieves the class definition. The new class definition is called, 'NewPerson' to distinguish it from the previous class name.

An instance of the NewPerson class is created with the name, 'Tom'. The print function call indicates that the Person class was recreated successfully and that an instance was created.

```
with open('file.pickle', 'rb') as pkfo:
    NewPerson = pickle.load(pkfo)

print(NewPerson)
np = NewPerson('Tom')
print(np)
```

```
<class '__main__.Person'>
<__main__.Person object at 0x103b75fd0>
```

Ignoring values during assignment

One of the obscure features of Python is the ability to ignore values during assignment. In the example below the three values in tuple t are assigned to the variables a, b and c.

```
t = (4, 5, 6,)
a, b, c = t
print(a)
print(b)
print(c)
```

```
4
5
6
```

If the value corresponding to c does not have to be assigned, then one approach would be the following. The tuple t is indexed and the first value is assigned to a, and the second value is assigned to b. This requires the use of extra syntax for indexing which is not as concise as the previous code.

```python
t = (4, 5, 6,)
a = t[0]
b = t[1]
print(a)
print(b)
```

```
4
5
```

A better solution is to use an _ (underscore) to identify values that are not assigned. The values of a and b are assigned and the third variable is marked with an underscore.

```python
t = (4, 5, 6,)
a, b, __ = t
print(a)
print(b)
```

```
4
5
```

In-place value swapping

Value swapping is the process of exchanging the values in two variables and can be achieved by the following code. This method uses a temporary variable for swapping.

```
a = 5
b = 4
temp = b
b = a
a = temp
print(a, b)
```

4 5

A more elegant approach is shown below. Unlike the previous example, a temporary variable is not needed, the coded is readable and Pythonic.

```
a = 5
b = 4
b, a = a, b
print(a, b)
```

4 5

Programming models

There are four different programming models available in Python.

1. Procedural

2. Declarative

3. Object oriented and

4. Functional

Certain languages such as SQL are purely declarative languages. Python does not enforce a particular type of programming. In fact, it is possible to mix the different programming model in a given Python file. For example, a for-loop can be used to process a list in procedural paradigm in which another list can be created using declarative paradigm which in turn can be passed to a class created using object-oriented paradigm.

Procedural programming

It is a programming paradigm where procedures or functions or subroutines are used to define a series of computation that need to be performed.

Procedural programming is achieved by writing steps of instruction that the computer needs to execute in order to achieve a certain outcome. Hence, the programmer thinks in terms of instruction to computer and not necessarily as humans view the problem.

In the example below, the function, "calceven" creates a new list which contain only even numbers from the input list, "ml." A boolean flag, "checkforeven" is set to True prior to the call to the function. It is important to note that the boolean is not passed as an argument to the function. Instead it is a global variable accessible inside the function.

The function performs the following steps. An empty list, "even_ml" is created. Every item in the list, "ml" is visited and if the boolean checkforeven is set to True, then the item is checked if it is even. If the item is even, it is added to the other list, "even_ml".

Few things to notice in this procedure are:

1. The programmer determines the exact step that the computer must perform. In essence, the programmer thinks like a computer and programs accordingly.

2. The change in value of "checkforeven" outside the function will cause the function to return a different value. For example, if checkforeven is False, the function will return an empty list, even if the input list contains even numbers. This is called a side-effect, as the main input (ml) is not the only variable that determines the output but an extra variable can produce side effect. In a large application, such side-effects can make debugging difficult.

```
checkforeven = True
ml = [1, 2, 3, 5, 6, 8, 11]

# checkforeven is a global variable here
def calceven(ml):
    even_ml = []
    for items in ml:
        if checkforeven and items%2==0:
            even_ml.append(items)
    return(even_ml)
```

```
print(calceven(ml))
```

```
[2, 6, 8]
```

Declarative programming

In declarative programming, the programmer declares their intent and it is the responsibility of the interpreter to compute based on the intent.

One of the most popular albeit specialized declarative programming language is Structured Query Language (SQL) used by most of the popular database systems.

In Python, list comprehension or generator comprehension are good examples of declarative programming. In the function below, a list of even numbers is obtained by indicating the intent "Get all items from every item in the list ml provided checkeven and mod of item with 2 are True." This intent is expressed using list comprehension. Due to Python's expressive nature and simplicity, the intent can be easily converted in to a list comprehension.

This function still suffers from the side effect problem where change in value of "checkforeven" outside the function will cause the function to return a different value. For example, if checkforeven is False, the function will return an empty list, even if the input list has any even numbers.

```
checkforeven = True
ml = [1, 2, 3, 5, 6, 8, 11]
```

```
# checkforeven is a global variable here
def calceven(ml):
    even_ml = [items for items in ml if checkforeven and
items%2==0]
    return(even_ml)


print(calceven(ml))
```

[2, 6, 8]

The advantage of the declarative programming is in its ability to express the output needed and not necessarily think like a computer.

Functional programming

Functional programming is a paradigm that treats all computation like a mathematical function. This methodology does not have side effect like procedural programming and hence it is easier to debug.

In the example below, we pass value of the variable checkforeven as an argument to the calceven function in addition to the list ml that we passed in the previous code. Since the checkforeven is passed, at the time of calling the function calceven, there is no side effect. If checkforeven is True, we get a list that contains even numbers only and if we passed checkforeven as False, we get an empty list.

In functional programming, do not store values in variables unnecessarily. Since the values are not stored, there is less chance that the values will become stale and cause side-effect.

496

```
checkforeven = True
ml = [1, 2, 3, 5, 6, 8, 11]

# checkforeven_ip is an argument and is different from
checkforeven
def calceven(ml, checkforeven_ip):
    even_ml = [items for items in ml if checkforeven_ip
and items%2==0]
    return(even_ml)


print(calceven(ml, checkforeven))
```

```
[2, 6, 8]
```

Object oriented programming

We have discussed object-oriented programming in great details. Hence, the code below should be familiar. The example below performs the same calculation as the last three programs but with classes and objects.

We create a class called, CheckEvenClass. This class has a __init__ method that takes the list, ml and checkforeven as inputs. The method stores ml and checkforeven in instance variables self.ml and self.checkforeven. Another instance variable, self.even_ml is also created to store the output list. The calceven method calculates the even_ml list using list comprehension.

We then create an instance of the CheckEvenClass by passing the list, ml and checkforeven. We then call the calceven() method for that instance and finally print the value of even_ml in that instance.

```python
class CheckEvenClass(object):
    def __init__(self, ml, checkforeven):
        self.ml = ml
        self.checkforeven = checkforeven
        # We are setting it to None, so that if somebody
        requests the value
        # and it is not yet initialized, we will know.
        self.even_ml = None

    def calceven(self):
        self.even_ml = [items for items in self.ml if
        self.checkforeven and items%2==0]

checkforeven = True
ml = [1, 2, 3, 5, 6, 8, 11]
ce = CheckEvenClass(ml, checkforeven)
ce.calceven()
print(ce.even_ml)
```

```
[2, 6, 8]
```

It is important to notice that classes remember everything while functional programming remembers nothing.

Made in the USA
Las Vegas, NV
17 June 2024

91162179R00291